I0803216

IMAGES
*of America*

# GREENVILLE TEXTILES

**On the Cover: Warping Room.** Operatives work on transferring many yarns from the creel of single packages to a warp beam. The yarns will form a parallel sheet of yarn wound onto the beam. The yarns of the warp beam are then coated in a chemical mixture called size for protection in a process called slashing. The beam may contain several thousand ends of yarn that will be used on a loom for weaving. (Courtesy of the Coxe Collection, Greenville County Historical Society.)

IMAGES
*of America*

# GREENVILLE TEXTILES

Kelly L. Odom

ARCADIA
PUBLISHING

ISBN 978-1-4671-1474-5

Published by Arcadia Publishing
Charleston, South Carolina

Printed in the United States of America

Library of Congress Control Number: 2015937129

For all general information, please contact Arcadia Publishing:
Telephone 843-853-2070
Fax 843-853-0044
E-mail sales@arcadiapublishing.com
For customer service and orders:
Toll-Free 1-888-313-2665

Visit us on the Internet at www.arcadiapublishing.com

# Contents

# Acknowledgments

With much gratitude, I thank Sidney Thompson and Lucy Quinn of the Greenville County Historical Society, along with Susan Boyd and Rebecca Kilby of the Greenville County Library System-South Carolina Room. Without their vast resources and knowledge, none of this would be possible. I would also like to thank fellow commissioners Penny Forester, Dot Bishop, Anne Peden, and Rick Owens and Greenville County Historical Society board members Max Cochran and Don Koonce for the expertise in the history of the region. William Brigham, Carroll L. Stone, James Bowen, Ben Team, and James Thomas were a great help in understanding the mechanics of textile machinery. I would also like to thank Tom Finley, Col. Frank Foster, Joyce Moody Johnson of the Union Bleachery Historical Society, Karen Cleveland of the Slater Hall Citizens' Committee, Marion Cruell, Martha Duncan of the Monaghan Historical Society, Kay Bayne of the Poinsett Mills Historical Society, John Hall, Becky Kingery of the Poe Historical Group, Don Roper of the Piedmont Historical Collection, Jean Gilstrap of the Camperdown Historical Society, Gladys Richardson of Palmetto Loom Reed, Jim Terry with Hollingsworth Funds, the Louis P. Batson Company, the family of Mack P. Niven Sr., and Don Harkin of the Greenville Textile Heritage Society.

I have drawn upon a number of published sources. The most notable of these are Judith Bainbridge, *Greenville County Community* series; Ray Belcher, *Greenville County, South Carolina: From Cotton Fields to Textile Center of the World*; Choice McCoin, *Greenville County a Pictorial History*; A.V. Huff, *Greenville*; Jeff Willis, *Remembering Greenville*; Bob A. Nestor, *Baseball in Greenville and Spartanburg*; John R. Hall, *Woodside Story*; Clemson University textile archives; Society for American Baseball Research; South Carolina Department of Archives and History; and Gary Nock, *Textile Titans*.

# Introduction

Prior to the Civil War, Greenville County had three mills, all relatively small and built with little capital. After the war, the area desperately needed an economic shot in the arm, and textiles became that antidote. By 1882, Greenville had seven mills and was quickly moving to the forefront of the New South. Out-of-state investors followed suit and migrated to the area, bringing large amounts of capital resulting in massive mills with high output. Most of these new mills were situated around the Southern Railroad line on the western side of Greenville, creating what came to be known as the "Textile Crescent."

The villages associated with the mills were becoming larger as well. No longer were villages consisting of a couple of dozen homes at best; now they were numbering in the hundreds. Seeing this flourishing industry with its secure income and ability to support living in a community, families left the isolated rural areas, along with the economic uncertainties of farming, and flocked to the mills for employment.

In 1915, Greenville had its first Southern Textile Exposition at the Piedmont and Northern Railroad warehouse, with an estimate 40,000 attending. By 1917, the second exposition was held at the state-of-the-art facility specifically built for the event. This led to Greenville being named the "Textile Center of the South" and, later, "the World."

Supporting companies began to move to the area to meet the industry's, as well as the employees', needs. Machine manufacturers, supply houses, restaurants, and stores alike all moved or opened shop in the area to cash in on the boom. With this growing population and industry in the area that had become West Greenville came the need for infrastructure, education, fire, and safety.

Post–World War II years saw the dissolution of the mill-owned villages, as the homes were sold to its millworker tenants or village outsiders who continued to rent out the homes. As a result, the entire mill way of life was forever altered. This change was also coupled with social issues, labor practices, unions, and modernization. Even with all of these aspects, the local textile industry continued to flourish in the 1950s and1960s. It was not until 1970 that the industry had a new adversary to face: the influx of foreign imports. US textiles as a whole could not compete with cheap labor and lower-priced goods, and many century-old companies were forced to shut their doors.

As the mills have closed and businesses moved overseas, new life has sprung up in these mammoth buildings. New communities have formed, and individuals have taken residence in the once-commercial spaces. Although the industry has not completely dissolved in the area, it has become a memory of what once was.

# *One*

# The Mills

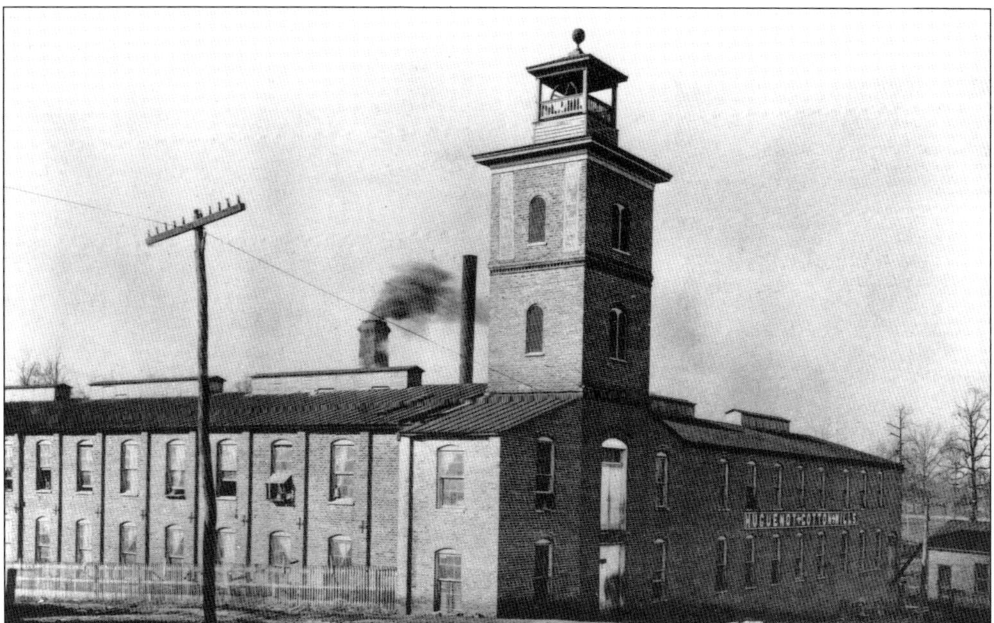


**Huguenot Cotton Mill.** Built in 1889 on the banks near Reedy River Falls, the mill was organized by Charles E. Graham and Charles H. Lanneau with a capital of $150,000. Lanneau had already served as treasurer of Reed River Mill at Conestee. The mill was a two-story brick structure that incorporated the latest in fireproof techniques. Although the mill was situated on the Reedy, its 200 looms were powered by an 80-horsepower engine. It originally employed 120 operatives and was the first mill in South Carolina to produce plaids. In 1908, the mill went into receivership, and by 1913, Huguenot had reemerged as Nuckaseegee Manufacturing. (Courtesy of the Coxe Collection, Greenville County Historical Society.)

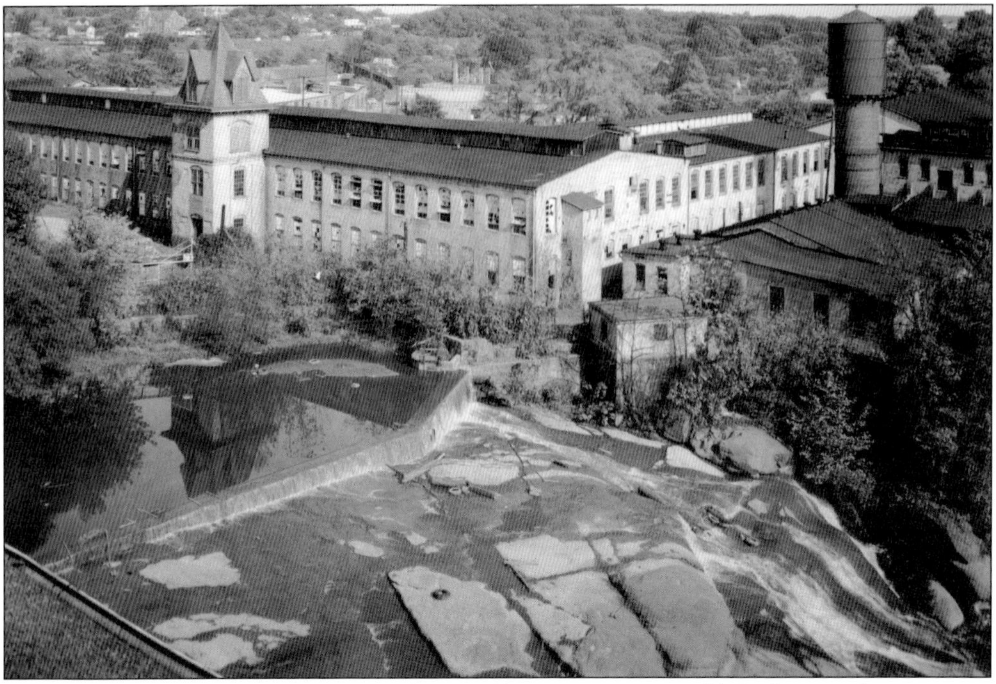

**Camperdown Mills Company.** Camperdown Mills Company was established in 1874 by Bostonian businessmen Oscar H. Sampson and George F. Hall on land located at Reedy River Falls leased from Alexander and Vardry McBee. The 1876 board consisted of noted businessmen Oscar Sampson (president), Hamlin Beattie (vice president), George Hall (treasurer), Alexander McBee (secretary), Thomas M. Cox, H.C. Markley, and George Putnam. Henry Hammett later served as president before starting Piedmont Mill. (Courtesy of the Coxe Collection, Greenville County Historical Society.)

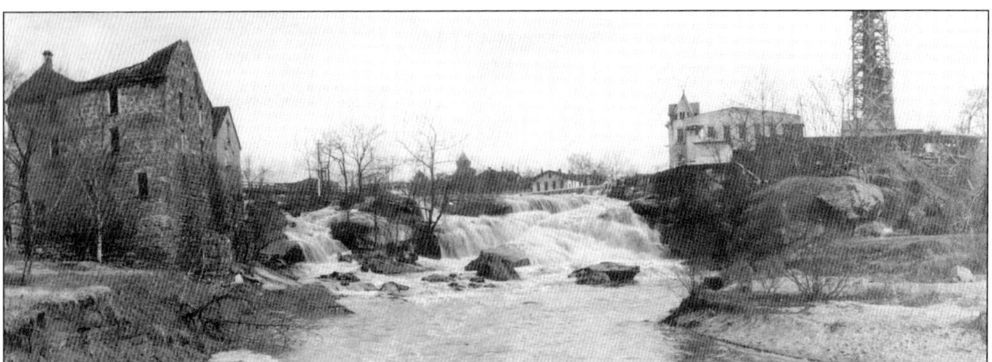

**Camperdown Mills Company.** Camperdown Mill No. 1 began production of cotton yarns in June 1874 and was located in the old Vardry Mill on the south side of Reedy River Falls. Mill No. 2 was located on the north side and began production in January 1875. In 1911, the company built a cotton warehouse on Main Street in what is known today as Falls Place. Camperdown No. 1 burned in November 1943, and No. 2 closed in 1956 due to growing competition. The No. 2 mill was deconstructed in 1960. (Courtesy of the Coxe Collection, Greenville County Historical Society.)

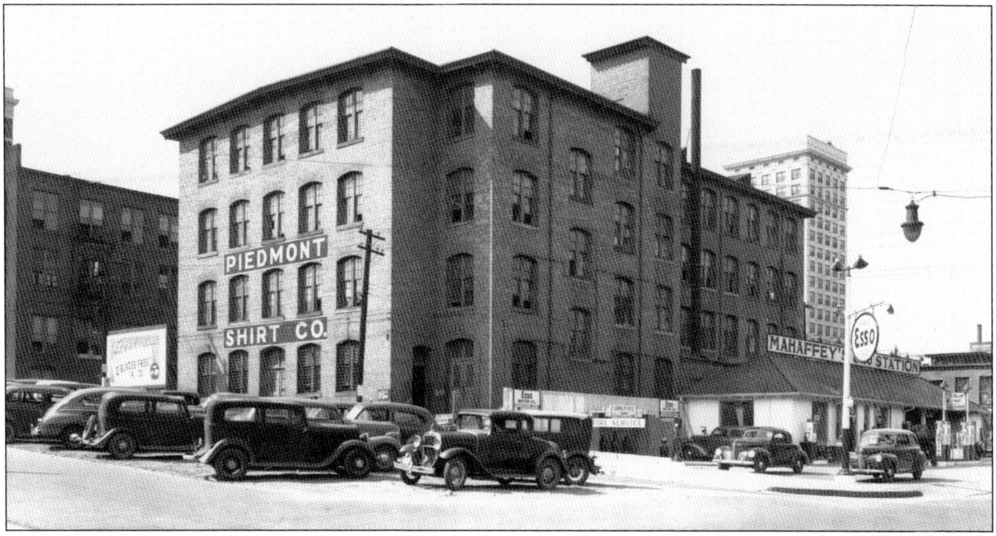


**PIEDMONT SHIRT COMPANY.** Located at the corner of East Court and Falls Streets, the building was first home to the American Cigar Company. It was constructed by the firm Ebaugh and Ebaugh and built with funds raised by the Greenville Board of Trade in 1903. The building was later occupied in the early 1930s by the Piedmont Shirt Company, owned by Shepard Saltzman. In 1942, Eugene E. Stone relocated the Stone Manufacturing Company from its plant on River Street to the then-vacant building. As Stone Manufacturing continued to grow to become the largest manufacturer of undergarments in the world, it moved to its modern Cherrydale Plant on Buncombe Road in 1951. (Courtesy of the Coxe Collection, Greenville County Historical Society.)

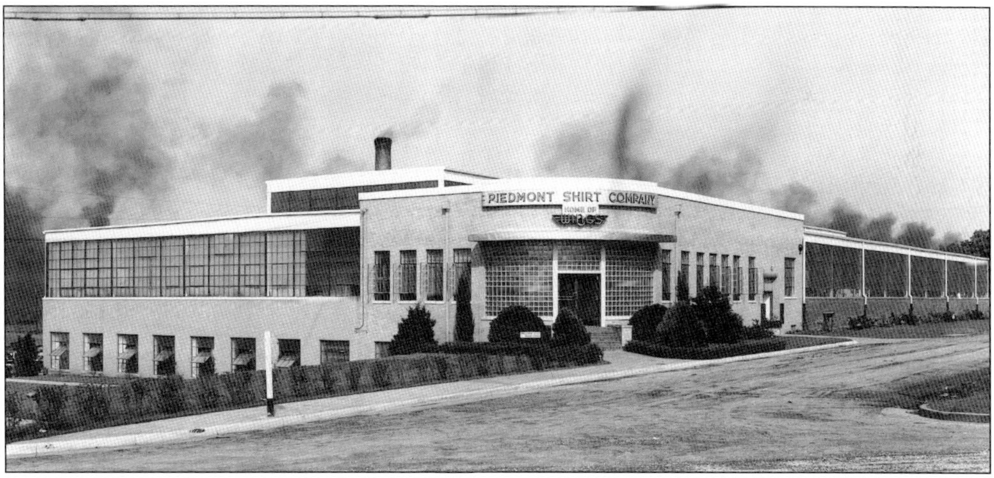


**PIEDMONT SHIRT COMPANY.** Piedmont relocated to its modern plant at the corner of Hammett Street and Poinsett Highway in 1942. In 1937, Austrian Max Heller met Greenville native Mary Mills in Vienna. When the Nazis occupied Austria, the 19-year-old Heller wrote Mills asking for help. She contacted Piedmont Shirt owner Shepard Saltzman to help, which he did. He was able to get the Heller family into the United States and gave Max a job as a shipping clerk. Heller rose the ranks at Piedmont, becoming manager of the company. Heller left Piedmont Shirt in 1948 to start his own business: Maxon Shirt Company. The company began with 16 employees and grew to 700 when he sold the company. After a few years, Max Heller began his political career, serving on the Greenville City Council and then as mayor from 1971 to 1979. (Courtesy of the Coxe Collection, Greenville County Historical Society.)

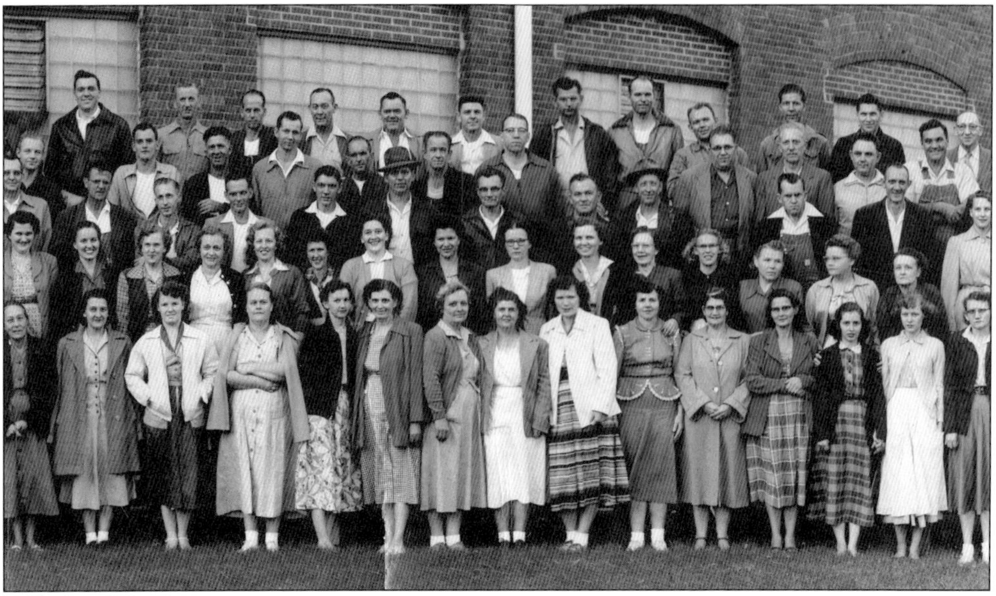

**Poinsett Mill.** Originally named Carolina Mill, the mill was organized in 1900 by J.I. Westervelt. In 1928, the mill along with three others Brandon Mill plants officially formed the Brandon Corporation. All of Brandon was purchased by Abney Mills of Greenwood in 1946. The mill remained in operation until 1981 and is now owned and occupied by the Reynolds Company, an adhesive manufacturer. Seen here is the third shift on October 19, 1954. (Courtesy of the Poinsett Mills Historical Society Collection, Greenville County Library System.)

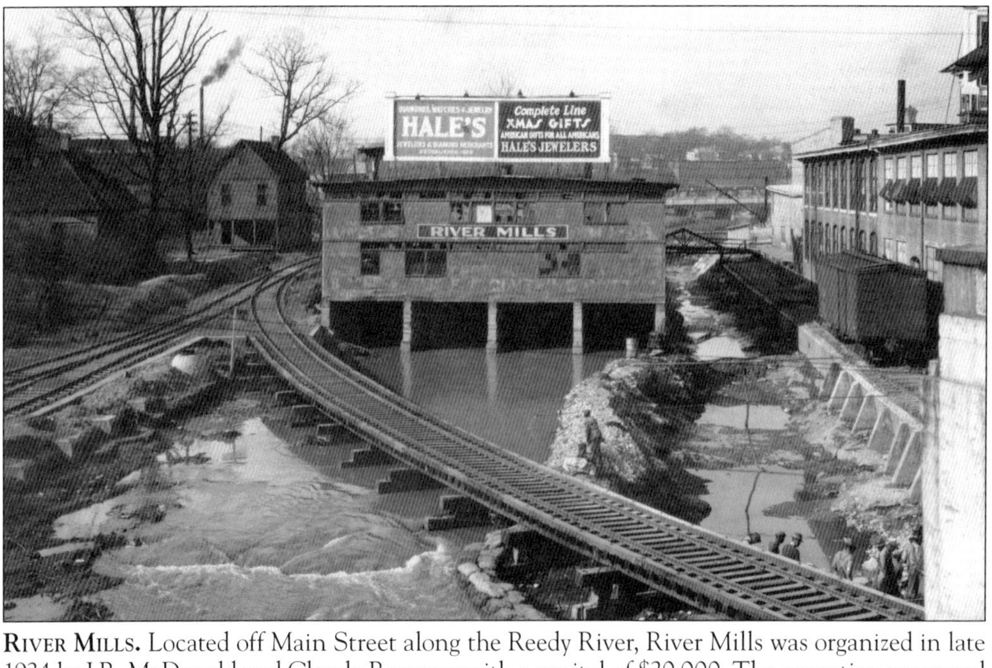


**River Mills.** Located off Main Street along the Reedy River, River Mills was organized in late 1924 by J.R. McDonald and Claude Ramseur with a capital of $20,000. The operation processed clean work waste of all fibers procured from various mills and advertised custom willowing. The building burned on March 31, 1941. (Courtesy of the Coxe Collection, Greenville County Historical Society.)

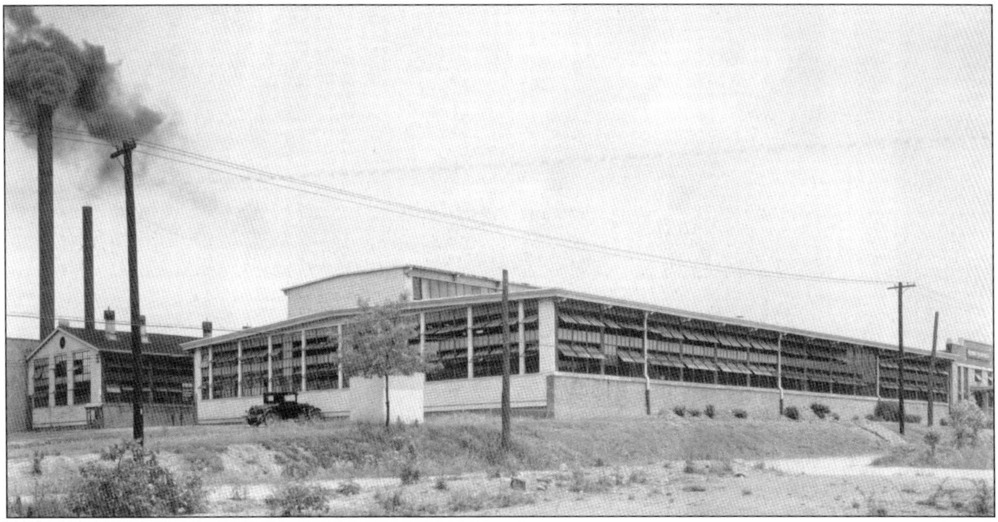

**Piedmont Plush Mills.** Piedmont Plush was founded by Frederick W. Symmes and Clifton Corley in September 1925 on Easley Bridge Road near the Judson Community. It was touted as the first mill in the South to produce velvet upholstery and drapery fabrics. The 12,000-square-foot building was unique with its almost floor-to-ceiling louvered windows. (Courtesy of the Coxe Collection, Greenville County Historical Society.)

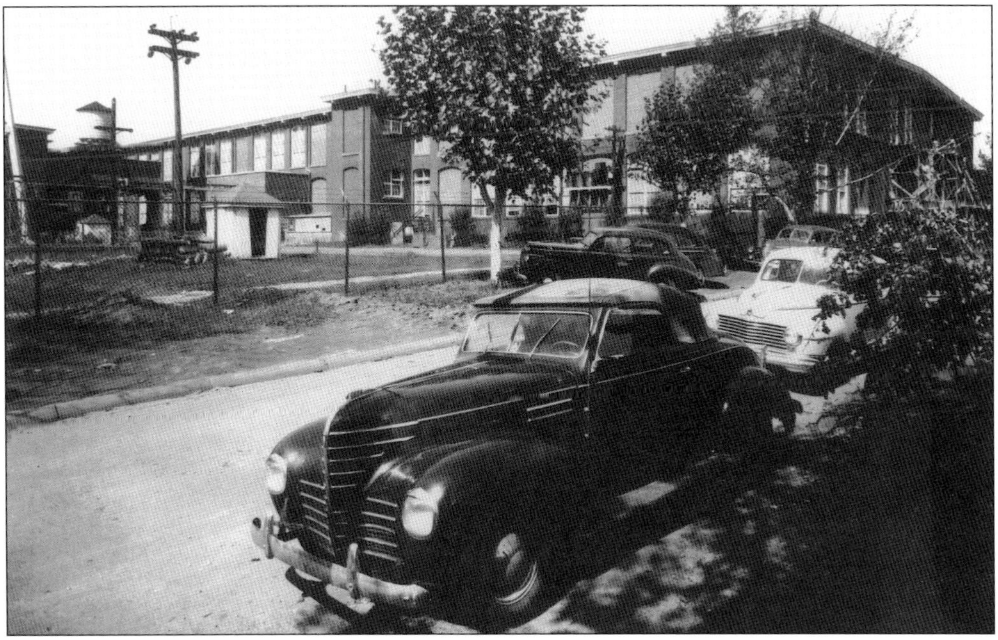

**Judson Mill.** Originally named Westervelt Mill, The Judson Mill began operations in March 1912. The mill was organized by J. Irving Westervelt and Northern textile machinery backers Potter and Johnson (carding), Falles and Jenks (spinning), and Crompton and Knowles (looms). By this time, Westervelt had already served as president of both Brandon and Pelham Mills. Judson is situated on 300 acres of land between Easley Bridge and Anderson Roads and was purchased from B.W. Cely and George B. Thurston. Lockwood, Greene, and Company designed the mill and the village, and Gallivan Construction was the contractor. (Courtesy of the Coxe Collection, Greenville County Historical Society.)

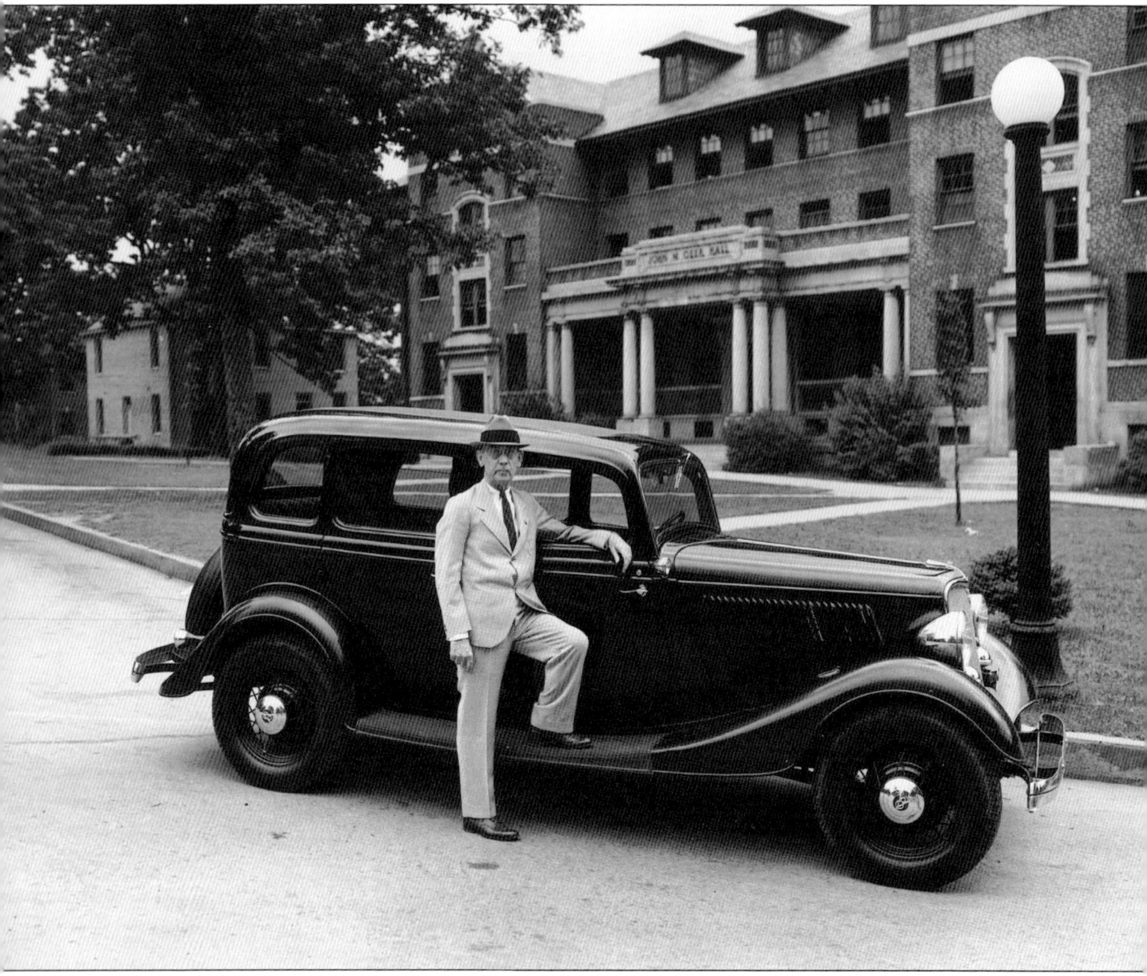

**BENNETTE E. GEER.** The mill opened with 56,000 spindles and 1,200 looms. J. Irving Westervelt was dismissed as president just one year after opening. As his successor, investors chose People's Bank president Frank Hammond, but he died only a few months after being named. After his death, Furman English professor Bennette E. Geer was made president. His first item of business was to change the mill's name to Judson in honor of his mentor, Charles Judson, Furman's treasurer who died in 1907. On November 5, 1915, with the threat of the mill unionizing, Geer closed the plant. One week later, workers petitioned for the mill to reopen, and Geer agreed. He later became president of Furman from 1933 to 1938. This image taken by Bill Coxe was used in a promotional series by Ford Motor Company. (Courtesy of the Coxe Collection, Greenville County Historical Society.)

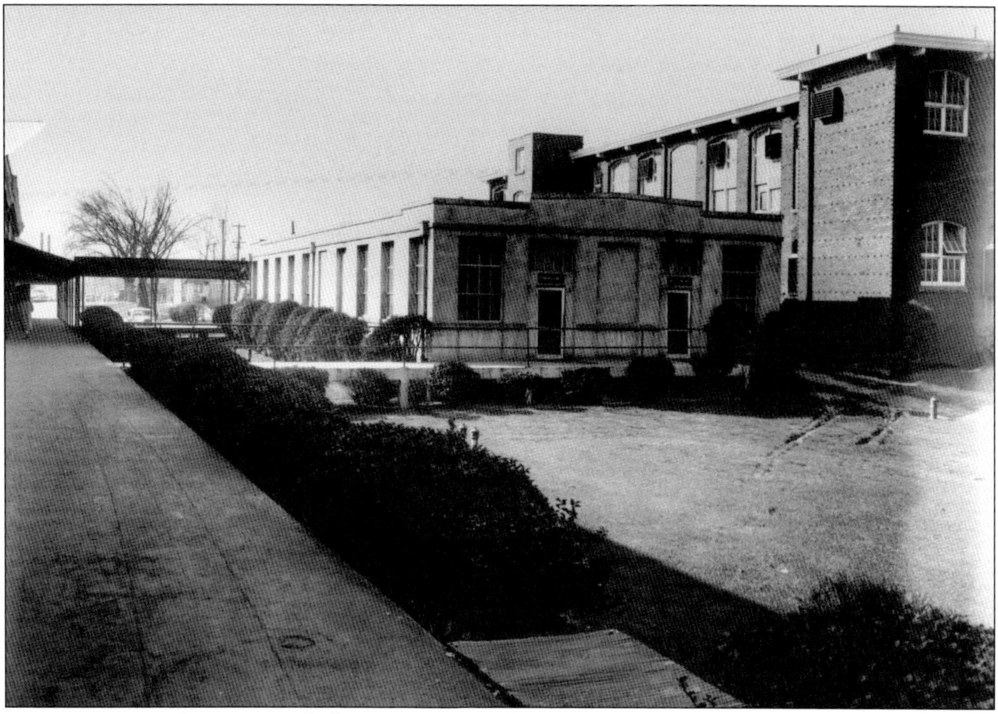

**Judson Mill.** The New York firm Deering-Milliken acted as the mill's selling agent. Gerrish Milliken began to purchase Judson stock, and by 1927, the mill was owned by Deering-Milliken. Geer remained president until 1933, when he left to become the sixth president of Furman University. (Courtesy of the Coxe Collection, Greenville County Historical Society.)

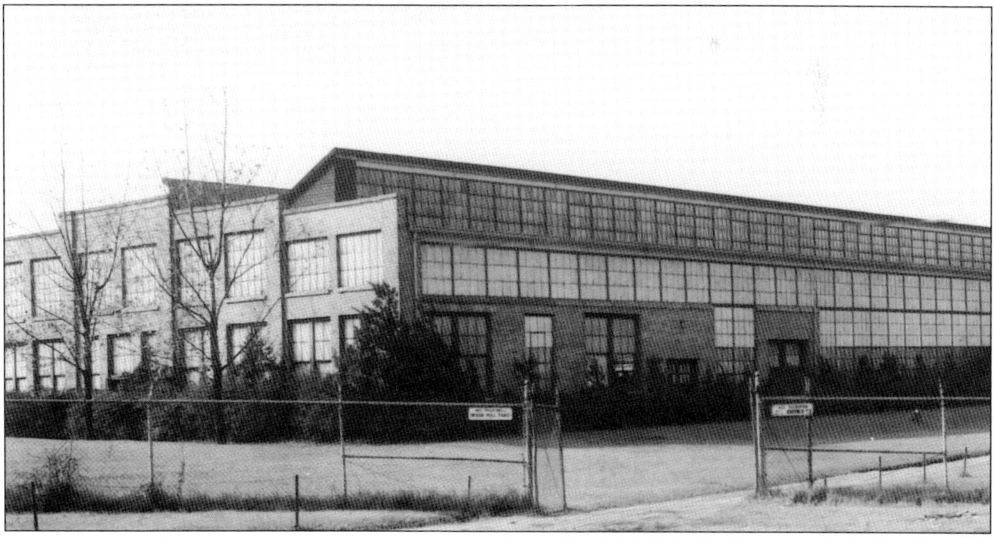

**Judson Mill No. 2.** In the late 1910s, Judson began to blend cotton with Japanese silk, and demand for the product grew rapidly. In 1923, Dupont introduced its new experimental rayon to the South at Judson. One year later, with demand rising for both silk and rayon, the company expanded with addition of a second mill. The Judson Silk Mill was located between East Florida and Virginia Streets and had a small village and school. (Courtesy of the Coxe Collection, Greenville County Historical Society.)

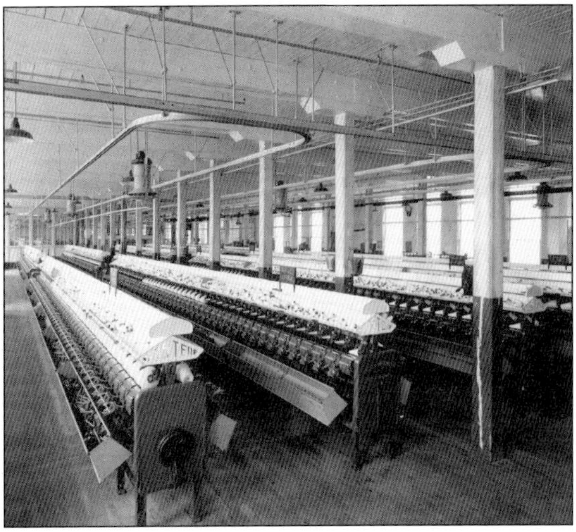

**Judson Mill Terrell Machines.** In 1948, Deering-Milliken purchased all outstanding stock in Judson, and the mill became a division of Cotwool Manufacturing Company. Then, in 1960, it became a division of Milliken and Company and, in 1988, a member of the company's industrial division. In 2015, Milliken announced it would begin closing the plant with a complete shutdown by fall of that year. The Terrell machines in the photograph here were manufactured by Foster Machine Company of Westfield, Massachusetts. (Courtesy of the Coxe Collection, Greenville County Historical Society.)

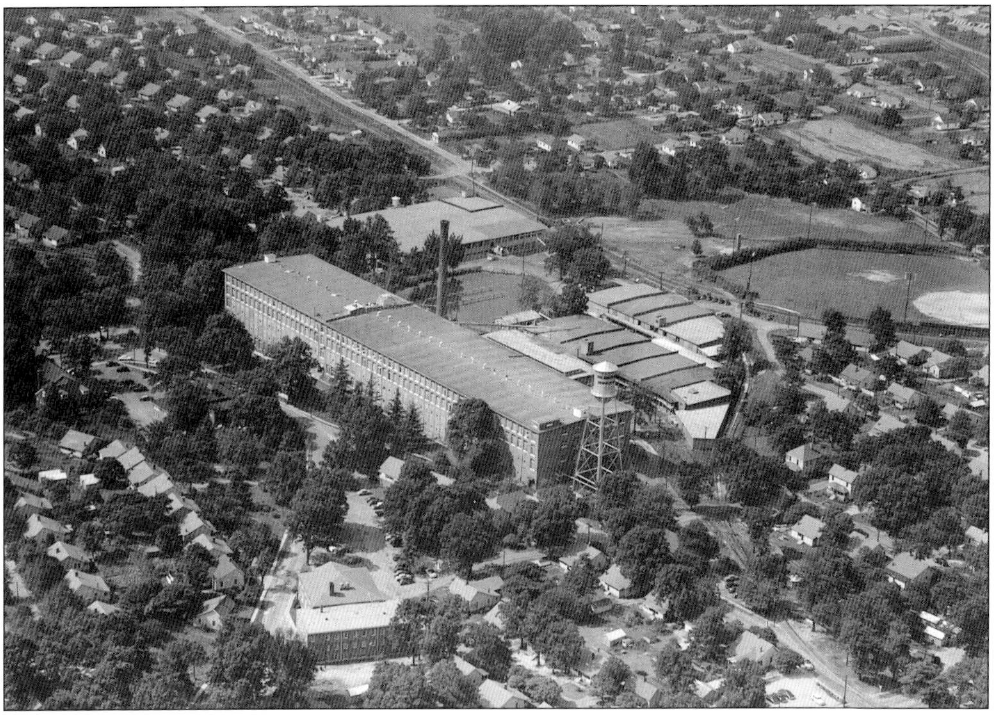

**Brandon Mill.** Organized in February 1900 by J. Irving Westervelt, he originally named his newly founded mill Quentin. Directors of the mill included noted Greenville businessmen William E. Beattie, T.Q. Donaldson, Frank Hammond, and Capt. Ellison Smyth. It was Captain Smyth who convinced Westervelt to change the name to Brandon, after a town near Belfast, Ireland, Smyth's ancestral home and a place where textile manufacturing was prevalent. Similar to other mills in the area, Brandon was designed by the then–New England firm of Lockwood, Greene, and Company and built by local contractor Jacob Cagle. The mill had 400 looms and 10,000 spindles and was described by the *Mountaineer* as "one of the prettiest cotton mill settlements in the state." (Courtesy of the Coxe Collection, Greenville County Historical Society.)

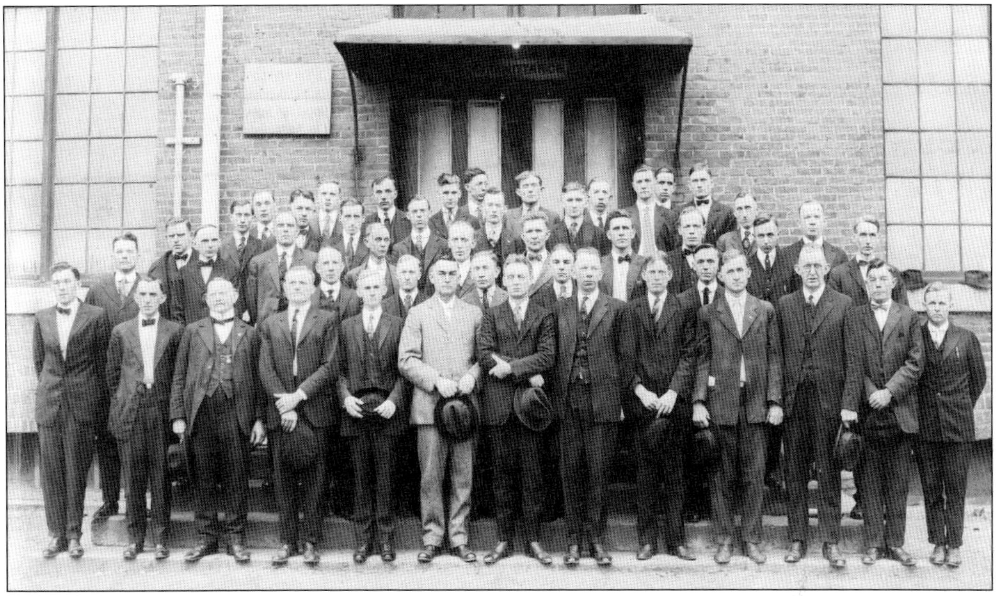

**Brandon Mill Supervisors.** In 1913, Brandon went into receivership, and Aug W. Smith became president; in 1919, its New York selling agent, Woodward and Baldwin, bought controlling stock in the mill. Brandon then shifted production from fine sheeting and print cloth to producing duck fabric. In the 1920s, after the purchase of nearby Poinsett Mill and the completion of Renfrew Bleachery in Travelers Rest, Woodward and Baldwin formed the Brandon Corporation. (Courtesy of the Brandon Mill Historical Society, Greenville County Library System.)

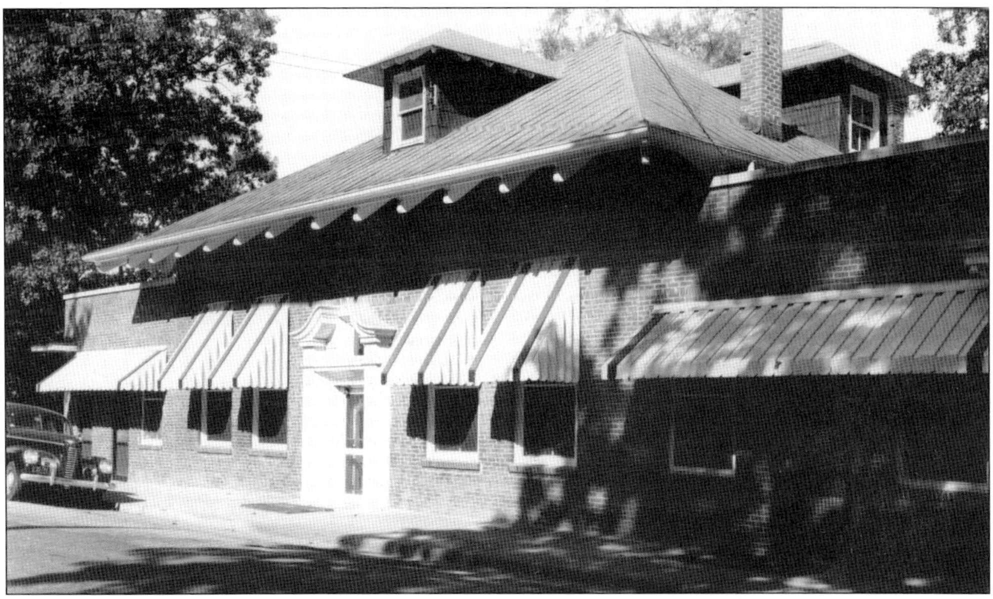

**Brandon Mill Office.** During the years of the Great Depression, mill president Aug W. Smith continued to raise capital to keep the mill running by proclaiming to investors, "I will resign as president of Brandon Corporation before I shut down a mill. Thousands are depending on these mills for a living, and I will not allow any one of them to suffer while I am president." Their equal loyalty to Smith was demonstrated by the entire mill bucking the General Textile Strike of 1934. (Courtesy of the Coxe Collection, Greenville County Historical Society.)

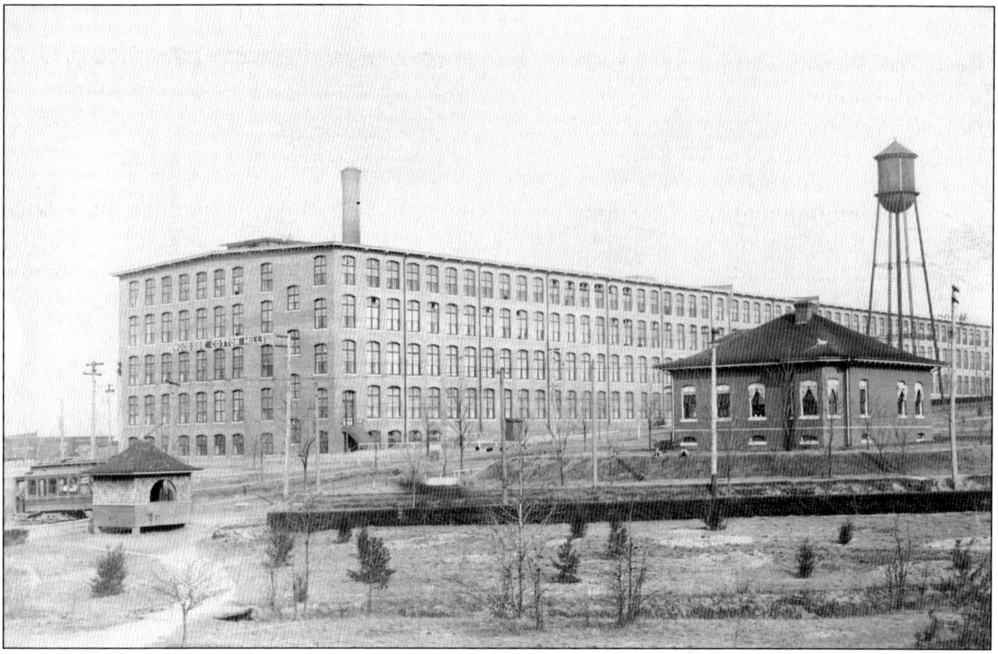

**Woodside Cotton Mill.** Located between Monaghan and Brandon Mills in the Textile Crescent, Woodside Cotton began operations in the fall of 1902. The mill's original capacity was 11,000 spindles and 300 looms, but it increased two years later to 33,000 spindles. Pres. John T. Woodside hired M.O. Alexander as superintendent of the mill. (Courtesy of the John Hall Collection, Greenville County Library System.)

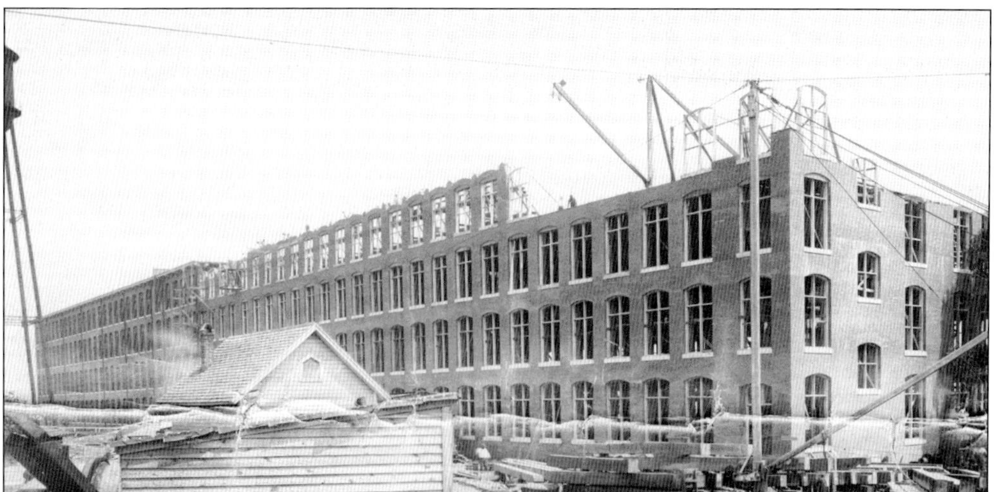

**Woodside Cotton Mill Addition.** In September 1912, Woodside announced it would again expand its Greenville mill to 112,000 spindles and 4,700 looms. The *Greenville Daily News* reported that the expansion made it the largest complete cotton mill in the United States under one roof. The Woodside Cotton Mills Company changed hands after the Stock Market Crash of 1929 to William Iselin and Company. In 1956, the company was sold to Danville, Virginia–based Dan River Mills. Dan River closed the mill in 1984 and sold the company to Alchem Capital in 1986. (Courtesy of the James E. Woodside Collection, Greenville County Library System.)

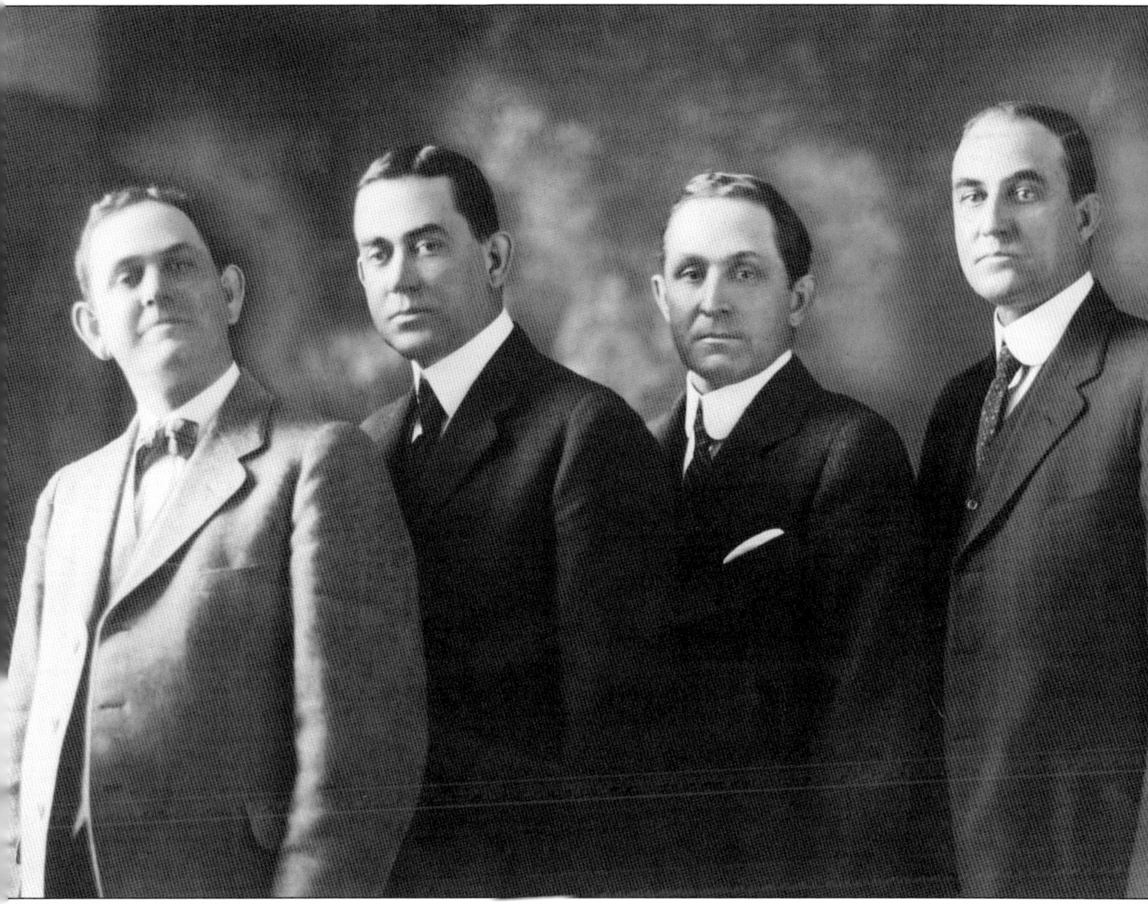

**WOODSIDE BROTHERS.** Known as the "Big Four," Edward F., Robert I., J. David, and John T. Woodside were all born and raised along with nine other siblings in the Woodville community of southern Greenville County. Individually, as well as collectively, these brothers were extraordinary businessmen that left an indelible mark on Greenville's history. The eldest, John T., began his textile career working at his uncle Joe Charles's Reedy River Factory (later known as Conestee Mill). After investing and selling a Pelzer mercantile business, a Main Street Greenville grocery, and a Georgia-based cottonseed oil company, John established the Woodside Cotton Mills Company. The company was organized in 1902, with John as president and David as secretary-treasurer. Edward joined in 1908, having worked at Pelzer Mill, to help establish the Simpsonville mill. Robert served as president of the brothers' Woodside National Bank. The Woodsides are also responsible for the Poinsett Hotel and the now-gone Ocean Forest Hotel, situated on 12 miles of oceanfront Myrtle Beach. Unfortunately, the Stock Market Crash of 1929 would cripple their empire, forcing the sale of their assets. (Courtesy of the Greenville County Library System.)

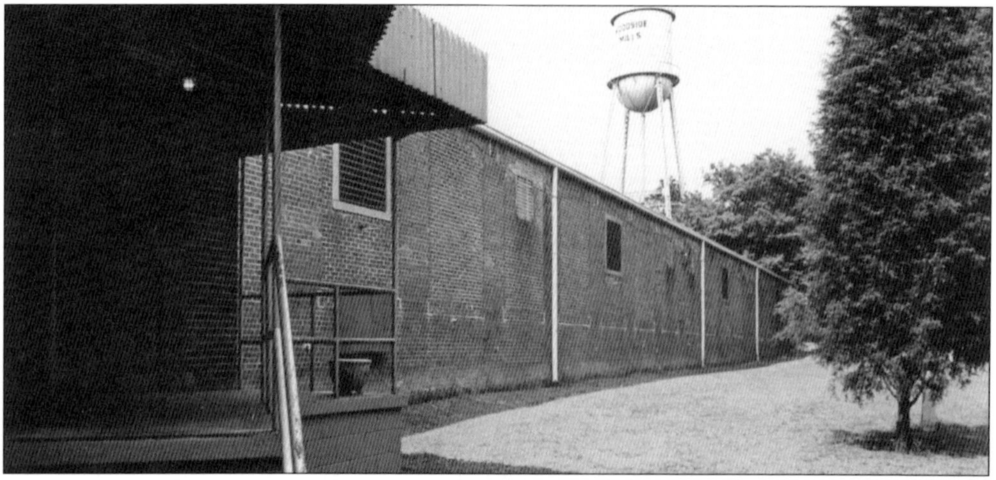

**Fountain Inn Manufacturing Company.** Founded in 1897, the mill was purchased by the Woodside Cotton Mills Company in 1906. At the time, the mill had 10,000 spindles and was immediately increased to 17,000. The mill remained in operation until the mid-1980s and was razed in 2001. (Courtesy of the John Hall Collection, Greenville County Library System.)

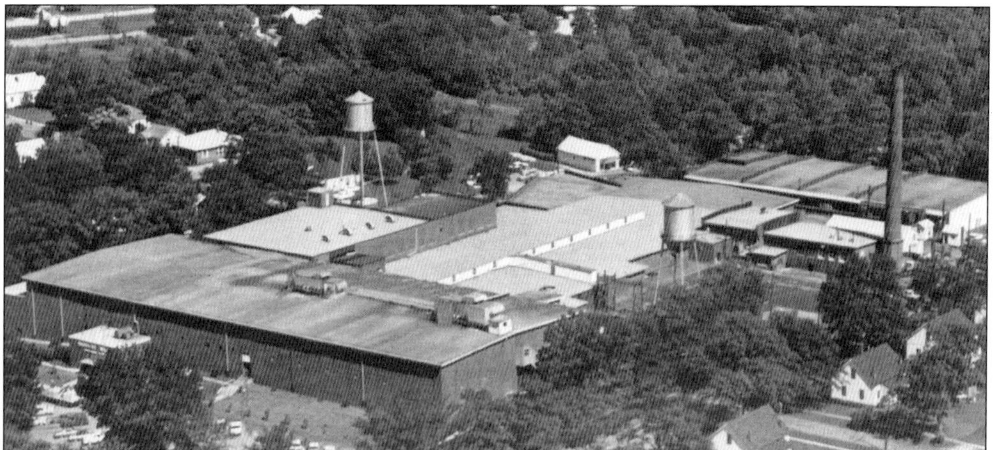

**Woodside Simpsonville.** In 1908, Edward Woodside, who had been working at Pelzer Mill, joined brothers John and David to build the Simpsonville mill. The mill opened with 8,000 spindles, but that number quickly expanded to 25,000. At this time, the Woodside brothers consolidated their three mills into one company, with John as president, Edward as vice president and operations manager, and David as vice president and treasurer. The plant closed in 1989 and has since been converted to residential condominiums. (Courtesy of the John Hall Collection, Greenville County Library System.)

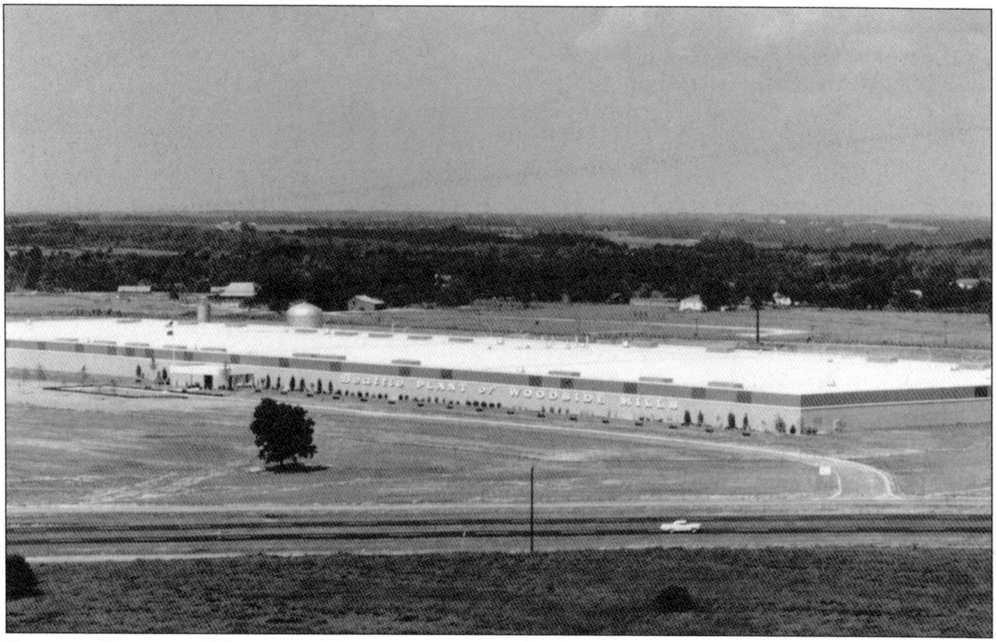

**BEATTIE PLANT OF WOODSIDE MILLS.** In 1962, under the ownership of Danville, Virginia–based Dan River Mills, the Beattie Plant was constructed in Fountain Inn. At a cost of $11 million, the Beattie Plant was the largest funded textile-mill project of the time. In order to remain competitive, the mill underwent a $62-million renovation in 1995. In the wake of Delta Woodside's 2006 Chapter 11 bankruptcy filing, the Beattie Plant was closed. (Courtesy of the Elrod Collection, Greenville County Historical Society.)

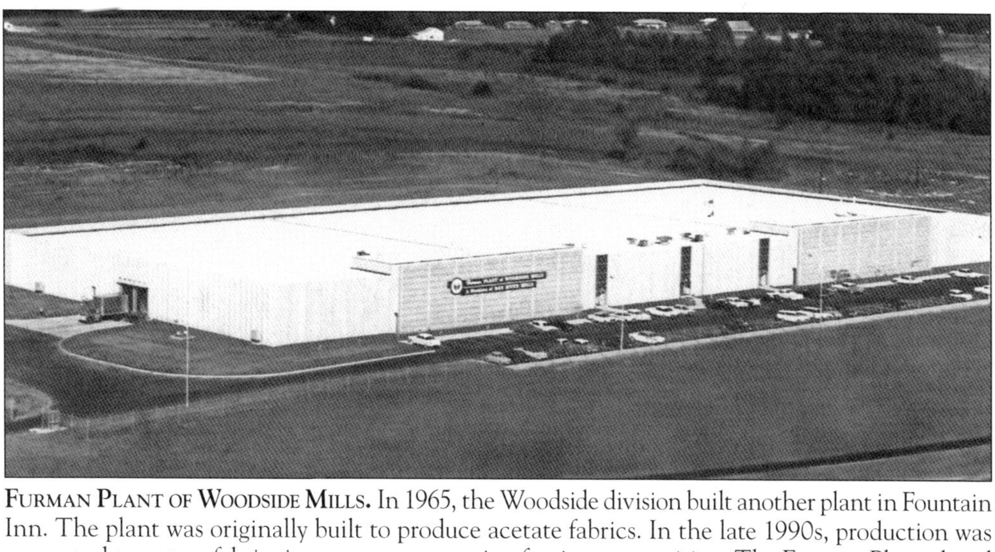

**FURMAN PLANT OF WOODSIDE MILLS.** In 1965, the Woodside division built another plant in Fountain Inn. The plant was originally built to produce acetate fabrics. In the late 1990s, production was converted to cotton fabrics in response to growing foreign competition. The Furman Plant closed in 2001. (Courtesy of the John Hall Collection, Greenville County Library System.)

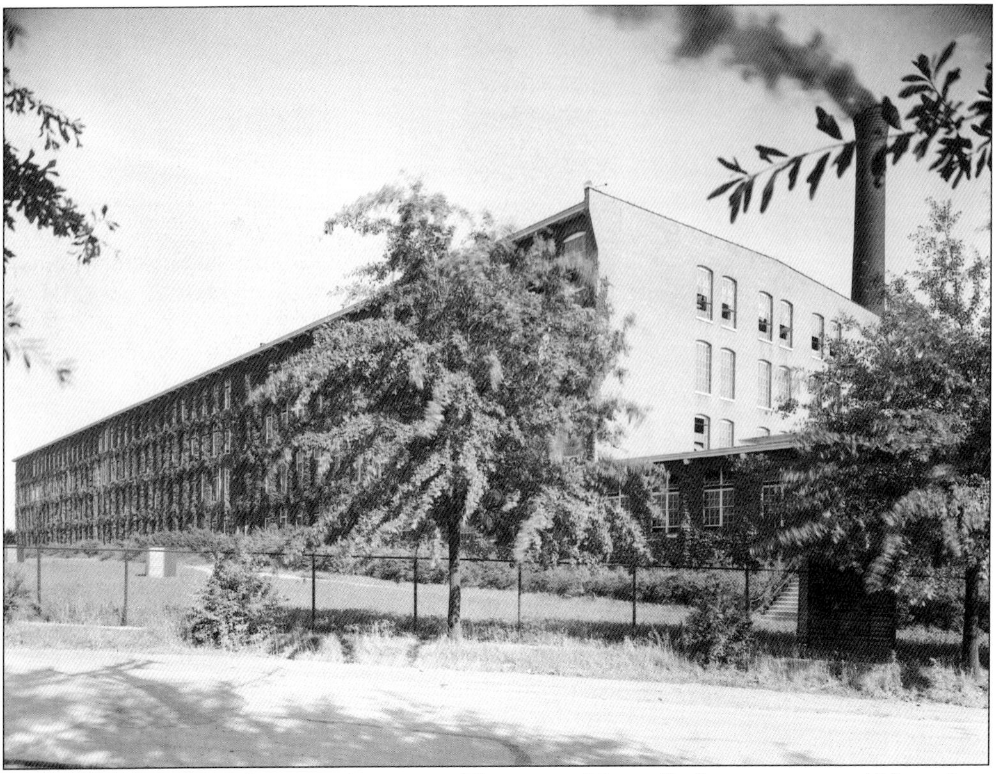

**Monaghan Mill.** In February 1900, cousins Thomas and Lewis Parker incorporated Monaghan Mill through the guidance of Francis W. Poe and the financial help of their grandfather Thomas Fleming. Rhode Island–based Lockwood, Greene, and Company was hired to design the mill and village on 325 acres west of Greenville along the Reedy River. (Courtesy of the Coxe Collection, Greenville County Historical Society.)

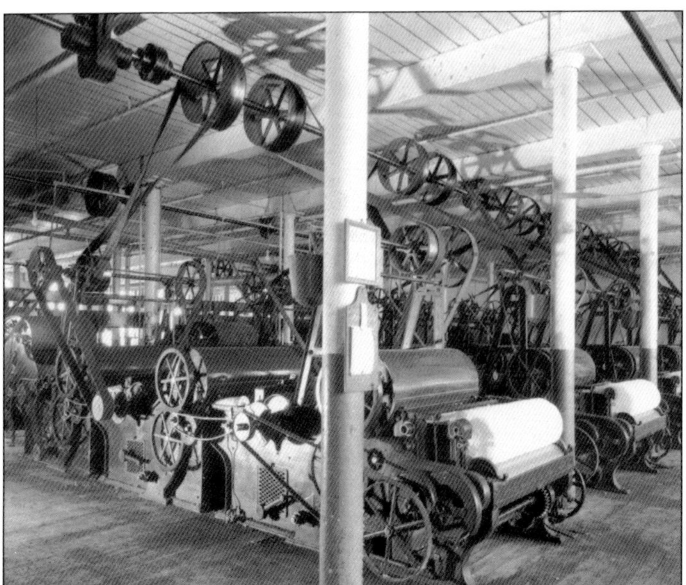

**Monaghan Mill Picking Room.** By 1907, with a capital of $700,000, the mill increased capacity to 60,000 spindles and had 700 operatives. At that time, Monaghan was producing print cloths, shade cloth, fancy goods, and shirting. Seen in this 1911 photograph is the picking room filled with machines from the Kitson Machine Company of Lowell, Massachusetts. (Courtesy of the Coxe Collection, Greenville County Historical Society.)

**Thomas Fleming Parker.** President of Monaghan Cotton Mills and leader of the Parker High School District for which it is named, by adding more mills that were located across South Carolina over the next decade, Parker formed the Parker Cotton Mills Company, consisting of 16 mills. Parker retired as president in 1915 to become a civic leader responsible for the Greenville County Public Library, Phyllis Wheatley Center, and Salvation Army Hospital. (Courtesy of the Greenville County Library System.)

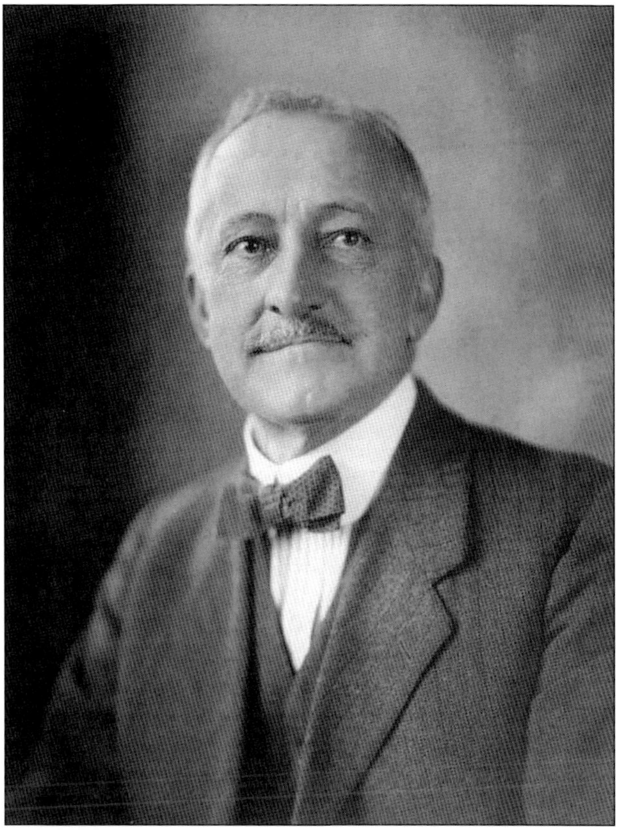

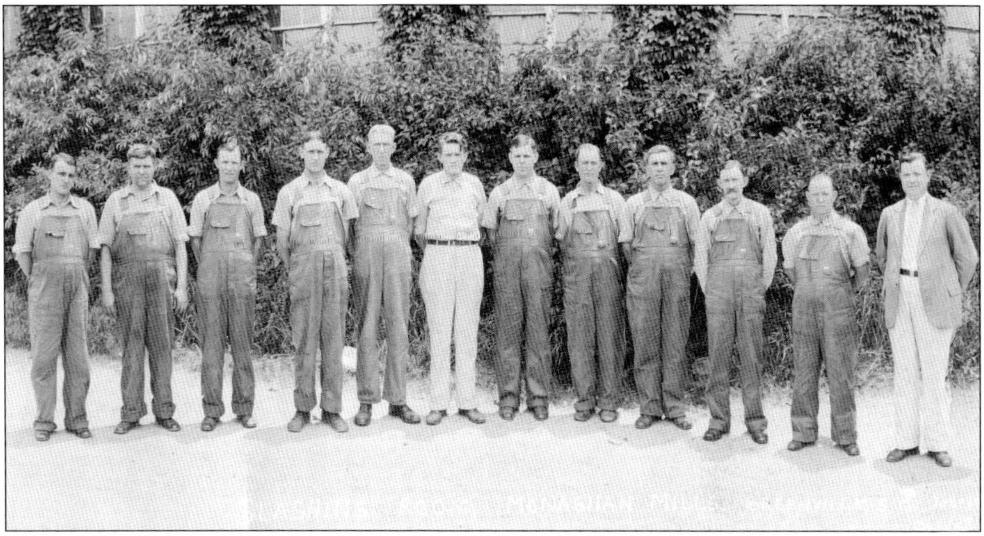

**Monaghan Mill Slashing Room Employees, 1931.** Relations were so strong between management and workers that Monaghan was left uninterrupted by the 1934 General Textile Strike. The mill gate was protected from "flying squadrons," motorcades of union picketers, by the National Guard, who had instructions to fire if they attempted to storm the gate. Upon hearing this order, union activists retreated and left Monaghan alone. (Courtesy of the Monaghan Historical Society Collection, Greenville County Library System.)

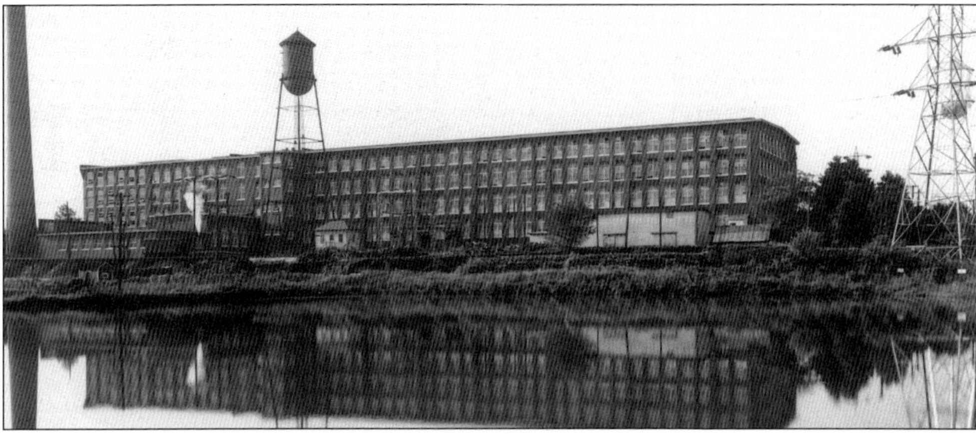

**Monaghan Mill.** Upon the Parker cousins' retirement, the Victor-Monaghan Group was organized in 1917 and continued ownership for the next 30 years until the acquisition by its longtime selling agent, J.P. Stevens and Company. In 1988, portions of J.P. Stevens were sold off in a leveraged buyout, and Monaghan was purchased by JPS Converter and Industrial Group. JPS closed the Monaghan plant in 2001. The mill was placed in the National Register of Historic places in October 2005 as an industrial site with an early-20th-century revival style of architecture. The building reopened in October 2006, as the lofts of Greenville, a residential condominium complex. (Courtesy of the Coxe Collection, Greenville County Historical Society.)

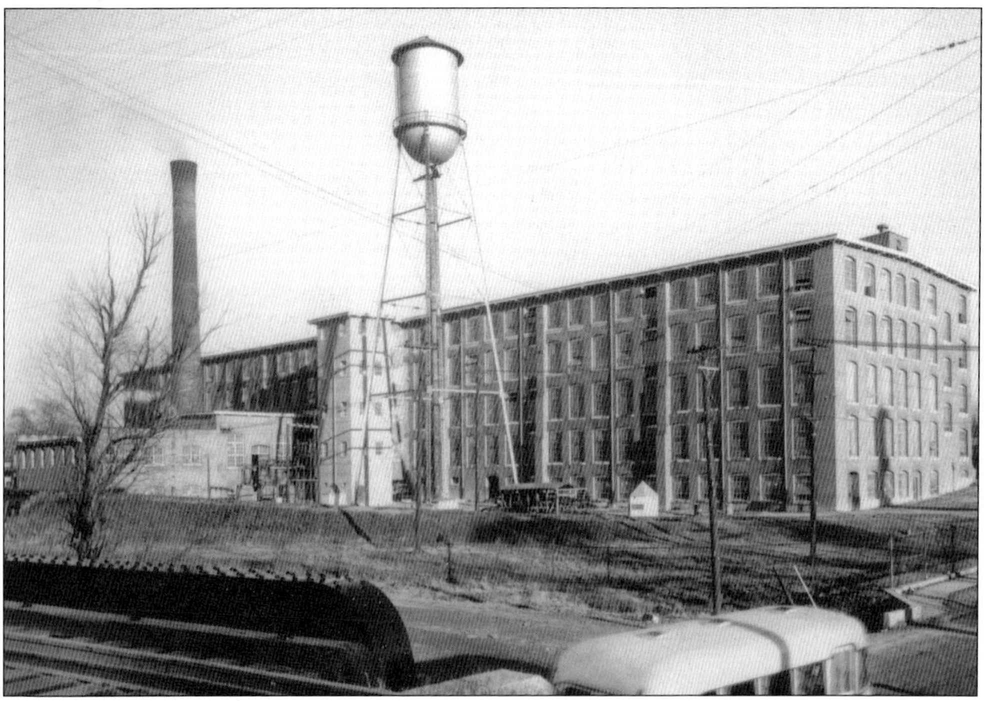

**American Spinning.** In late 1891, Oscar H. Sampson of Sampson, Hall, and Company, a textile selling agent out of Boston, and investor in Camperdown Mill, purchased more than 100 acres of farmland from the estate of Henry P. Hammett. The land extended from Buncombe Road toward the east, past Langston Creek and the Southern Railway. With other investors from Boston, he formed the O.H. Sampson Company and began what was then called the Sampson Mill for this location. (Courtesy of the Coxe Collection, Greenville County Historical Society.)

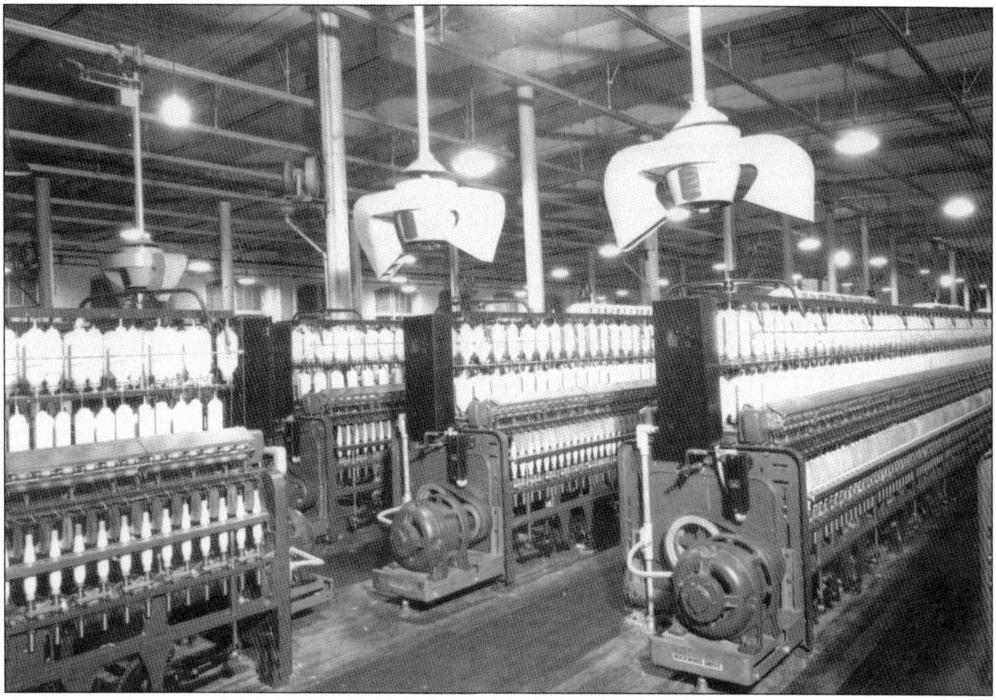

**Spinning Frames in American Spinning.** A budget of $123,000 to construct the mill quickly began to be hard to raise. Sampson turned to local businessmen to invest, such as James Orr, Hammett's executor and head of both the Piedmont and Camperdown Mills, and Orr's brother-in-law James Morgan, who was a successful local merchant. In early 1894, Sampson Mill was announced, and in the summer of 1895, it was incorporated as the American Spinning Company with Sampson, Morgan, Orr, and contractor Jacob Cagle named as officers. (Courtesy of the Coxe Collection, Greenville County Historical Society.)

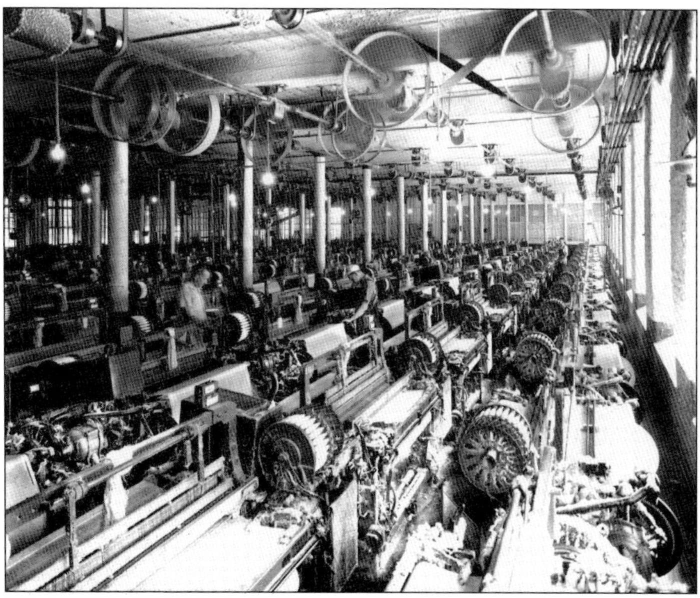

**American Spinning Weave Room.** Production began in September 1895 in a two-story wooden structure that later became known as the "little mill." While under Sampson's leadership, the mill grew, making four additions and adding several warehouses. The town as it is known today was comprised of three villages built at separate times. (Courtesy of the Coxe Collection, Greenville County Historical Society.)

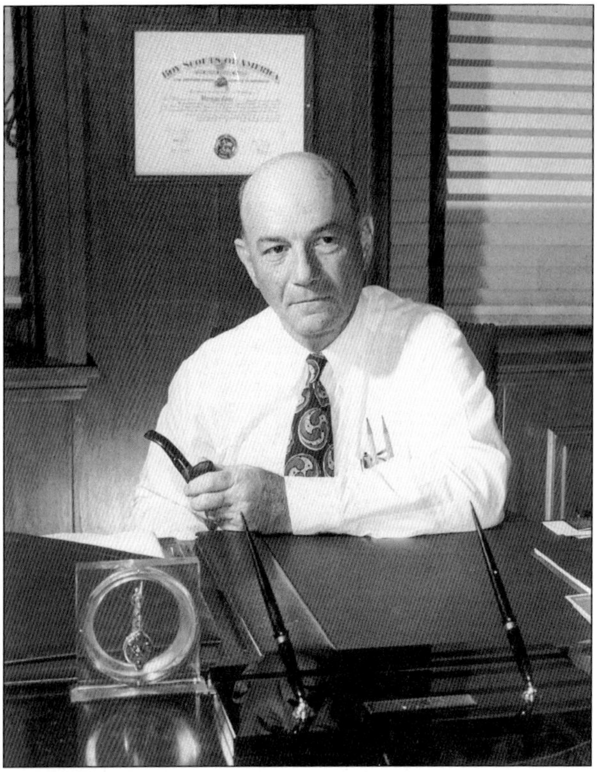

**Herman Cone.** In 1941, Greensboro, North Carolina–based Cone Mills Corporation purchased Florence Mills of Forest City, North Carolina. The acquisition included Florence's subsidiary, American Spinning. Upon purchase, Herman Cone became president American Spinning and remained so until 1955. (Courtesy of the Robert H. Duke Collection, Greenville County Library System.)

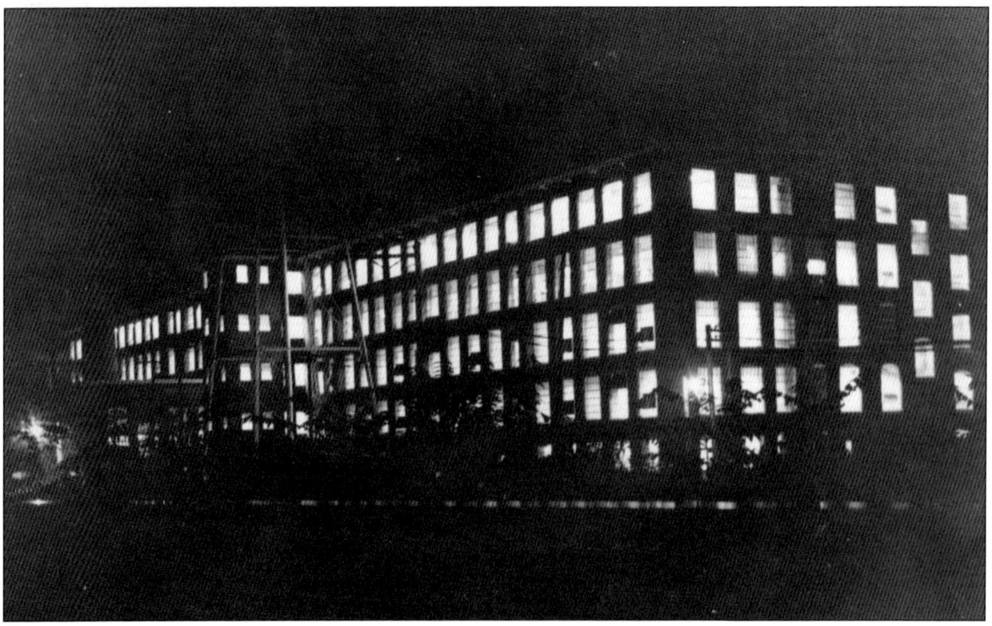

**American Spinning Company.** This night view of the mill prior to having the windows bricked in shows an unobstructed view with all floors in full production. American Spinning operated under different owners, including Cone Mills Corporation. The mill continued to manufacture textiles until it was shuttered at midnight on June 27, 1990. (Courtesy of the Robert H. Duke Collection, Greenville County Library System.)

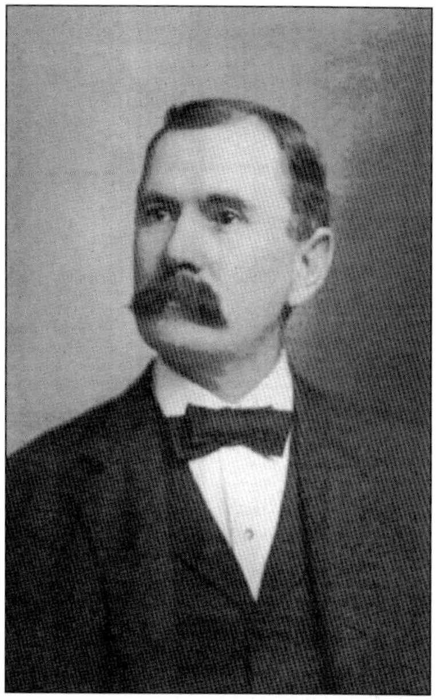

**Francis Winslow Poe.** Poe was the eldest of three brothers, each of which was a Greenville merchant. In 1890, he opened F.W. Poe and Company, a dry-goods store at the corner of McBee and Main Streets. Four years later, with the encouragement and financial backing by friends and associates, he organized F.W. Poe Manufacturing Company. His board consisted of prominent local businessmen such as W.C. Beacham, Frank Hammond, Lewis Parker, N.C. Poe, J.B.E. Sloan, and E.T. Smith. Poe garnered national attention when he refused to allow Northern selling agent Chutt and Peabody to cancel orders in response to the stock market panic of 1907. (Courtesy of the Poe Historical Group Collection, Greenville County Library System.)

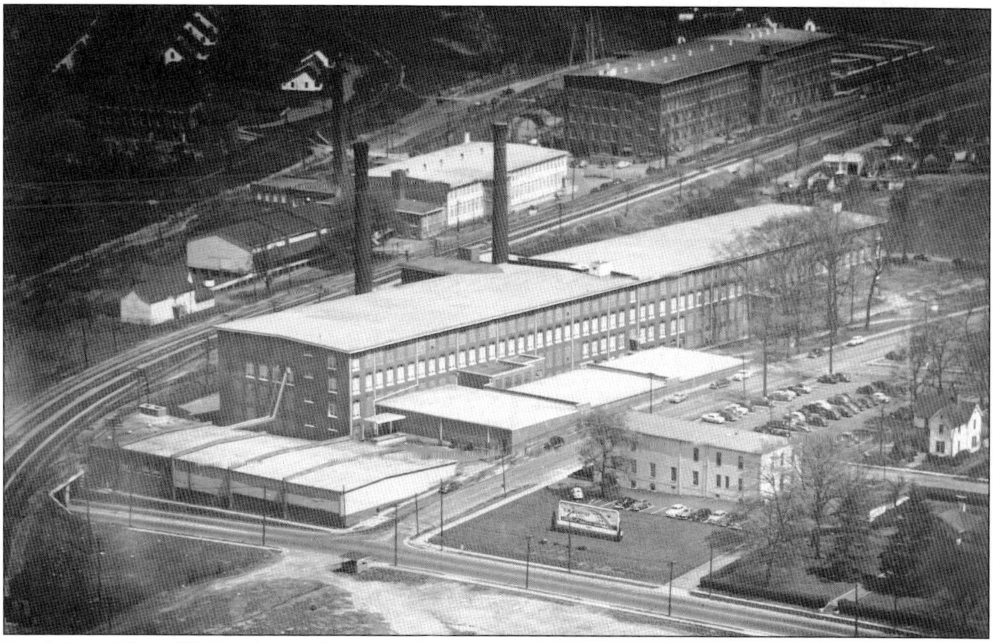

**Poe Mill.** The F.W. Poe Manufacturing Company was organized by Francis Winslow Poe in 1895. Situated on 75 acres, the site was laid out by Joseph E. Sirrine, his first project for Lockwood, Greene, and Company. Poe Mill began operations on New Year's Day 1897, with a paid-in capital of $230,000. The main building, built by Jacob Cagle, was four stories in height and an eighth of a mile long. Equipment included 10,080 spindles and 304 looms. In 10 years, the number of machinery had grown to 61,312 spindles and 1,520 looms. The village was one of the largest in Greenville, with a population of 2,050 in 1930. Poe Mill was first sold to selling agent Ely and Walker Company in 1947 and again in 1954 to Greensboro, North Carolina–based Burlington Industries. The mill closed in May 1977 and was destroyed by fire in 2003. (Courtesy of the Coxe Collection, Greenville County Historical Society.)

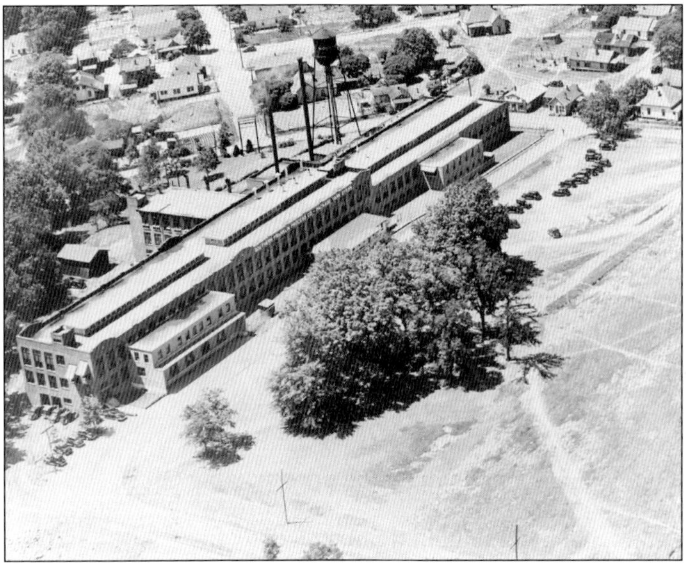

**Southern Franklin Processing Company.** In 1922, Franklin Processing Mill was package dyeing yarns used for weaving and knitting. Located between Dunean and Mills Mill, the mill had a much smaller village than others, consisting of only 20 houses and no school. The mill changed hands during its history, with its final owner being Meridian Industries before closing in 1999. (Courtesy of the Elrod Collection, Greenville County Historical Society.)

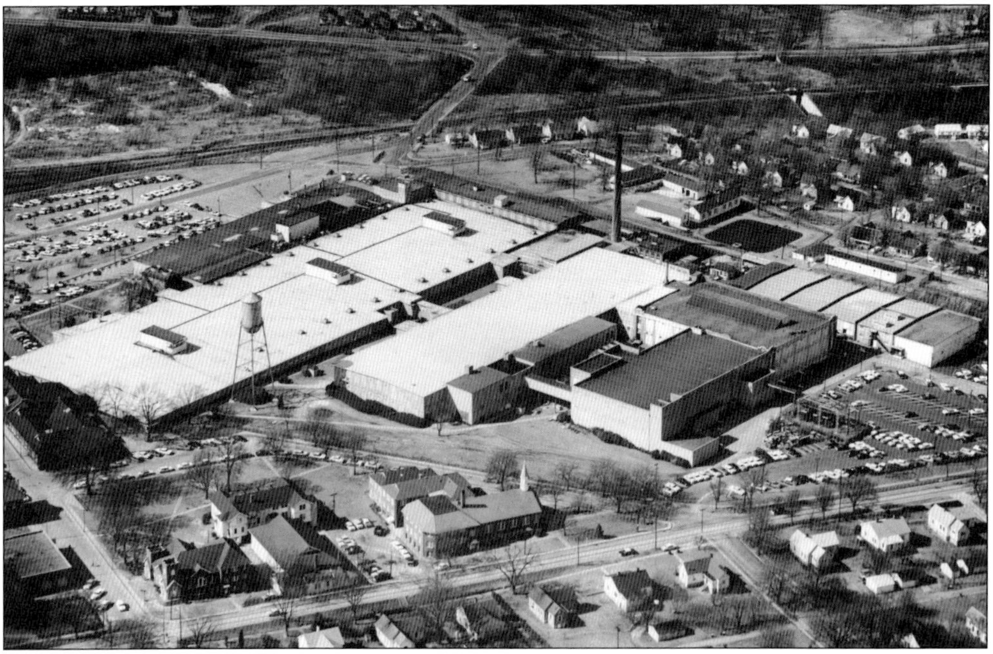

**Dunean Mill.** Rumored to be the costly "Million Dollar Mill," Ellison Adger Smyth proposed a new factory to his Northern backers, who would equally profit from supplying the mill, which included James B. Duke of Southern Utilities Corporation, New York Selling agent J.P. Stevens, Massachusetts loom manufacturer George Whitten, and Providence, Rhode Island–textile machinery manufacturer A.J. Kelly, among others. Dunean was chartered in February 1911 and named in honor of Captain Smyth's great-great-grandfather's linen mill on the Dunean River in Antrim, Ireland. In March, the stockholders met and named the captain's son, J. Adger Smyth, president. Prior to being named president, the younger Smyth had served as treasurer of Watts Mill in Laurens. (Courtesy of the Coxe Collection, Greenville County Historical Society.)

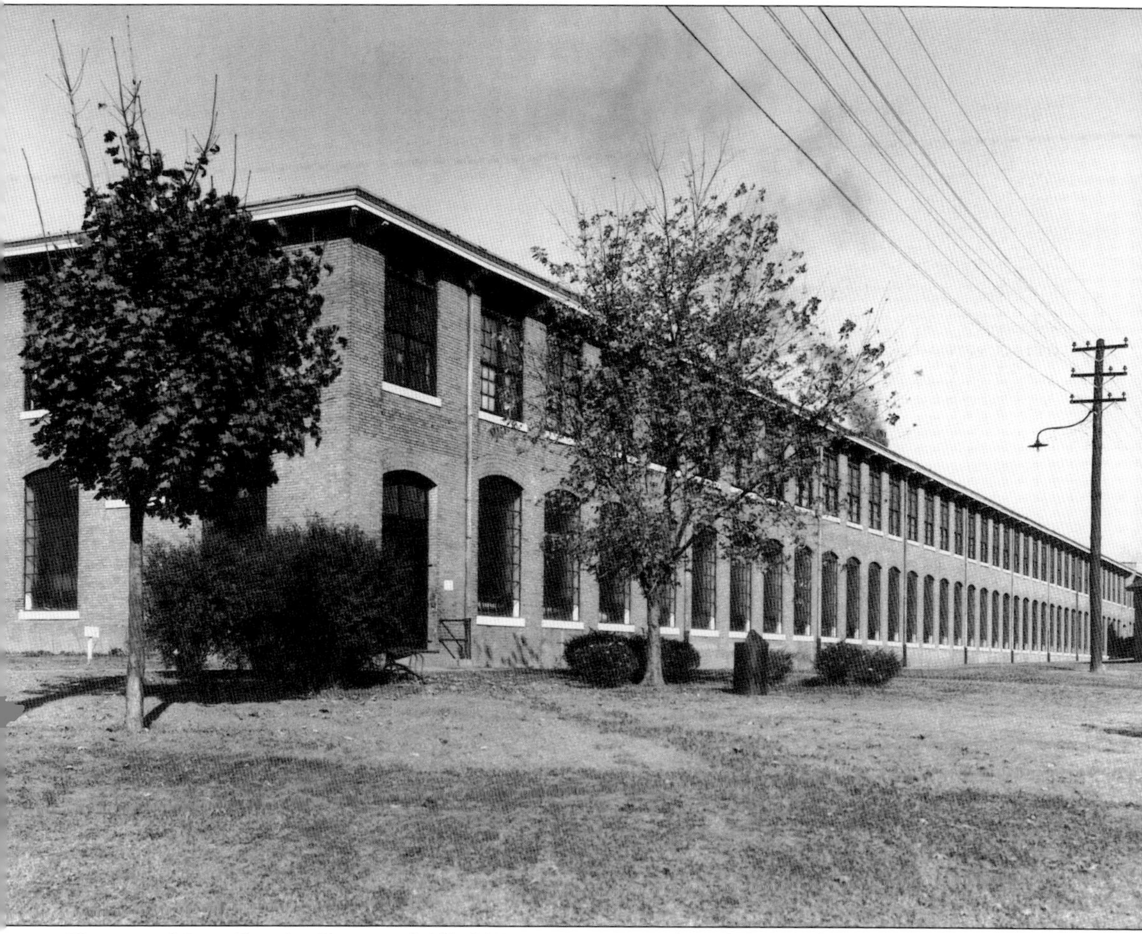

**DUNEAN MILL.** For the Dunean Mill, 237 acres were purchased from Edward Earle, O.P. Mills, Martha Kane, and the Melrose Land Company between Brandon and Mills Mill, and Joseph E. Sirrine was hired to design the plant. In May 1911, construction began on the 50,000-spindle mill built of buff-colored brick and black mortar with concrete flooring and pillars. Each of its machinery had individually driven motors. The first day of operation, April 15, 1912, was the day after the *Titanic* sank, and the *Greenville News* did not cover the opening. (Courtesy of the Coxe Collection, Greenville County Historical Society.)

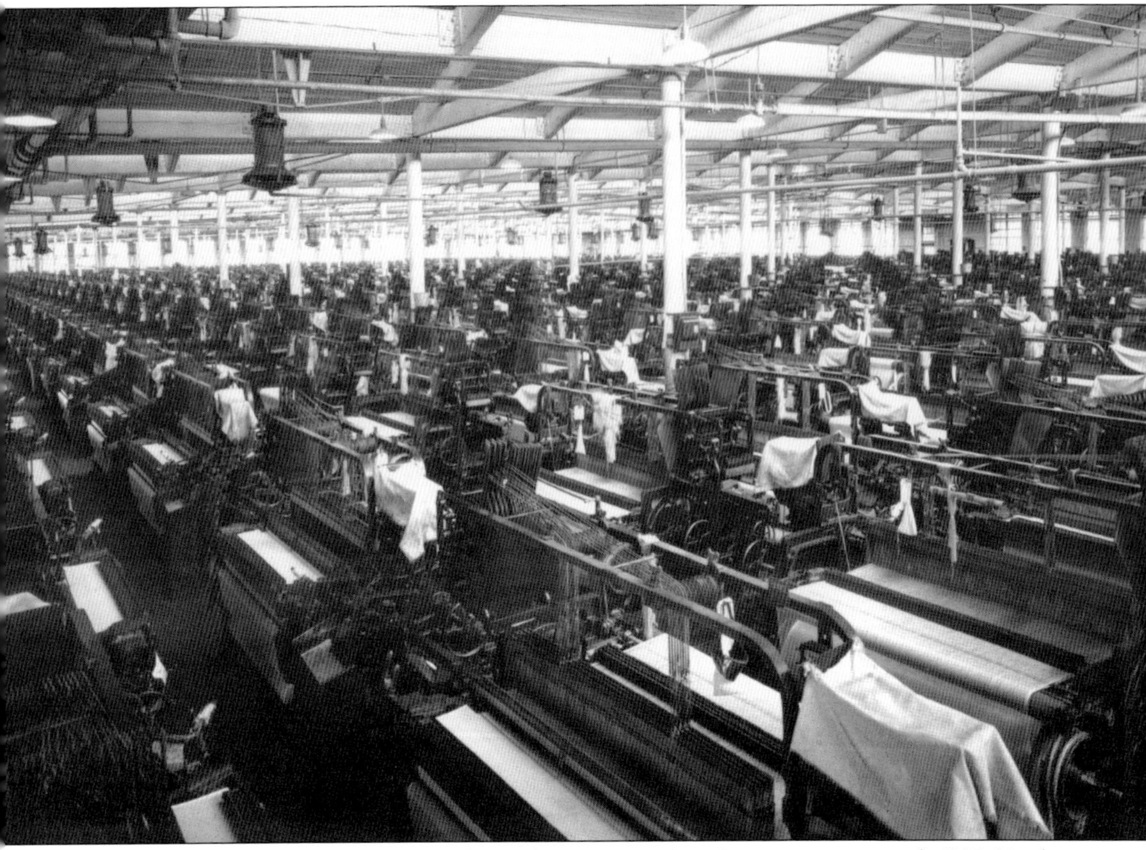

**Dunean Mill Weave Room.** In the early 1930s, workers began a union with O.T. Hopkins serving as president of Greenville local 1684 of the United Textile Workers Union. This came in response to poor working conditions and low wages at the mill. On Labor Day 1934, unionized workers declared a nonviolent strike. Tensions quickly grew as more members of both the National Guard and flying squadrons continued to descend on Dunean. Everything came to a head when John Black, an ex-Dunean employee, was found loitering outside the mill. When approached by a deputy sheriff, he presented a knife and was shot and killed by the deputy. This was the only strike fatality in Greenville, and as a result, for the next three days Dunean only ran a morning shift. On September 9, the *Greenville News* published a letter written by the "Local Workers of Dunean Mill" stating their allegiance to the mill. The strike was over. (Courtesy of the Coxe Collection, Greenville County Historical Society.)

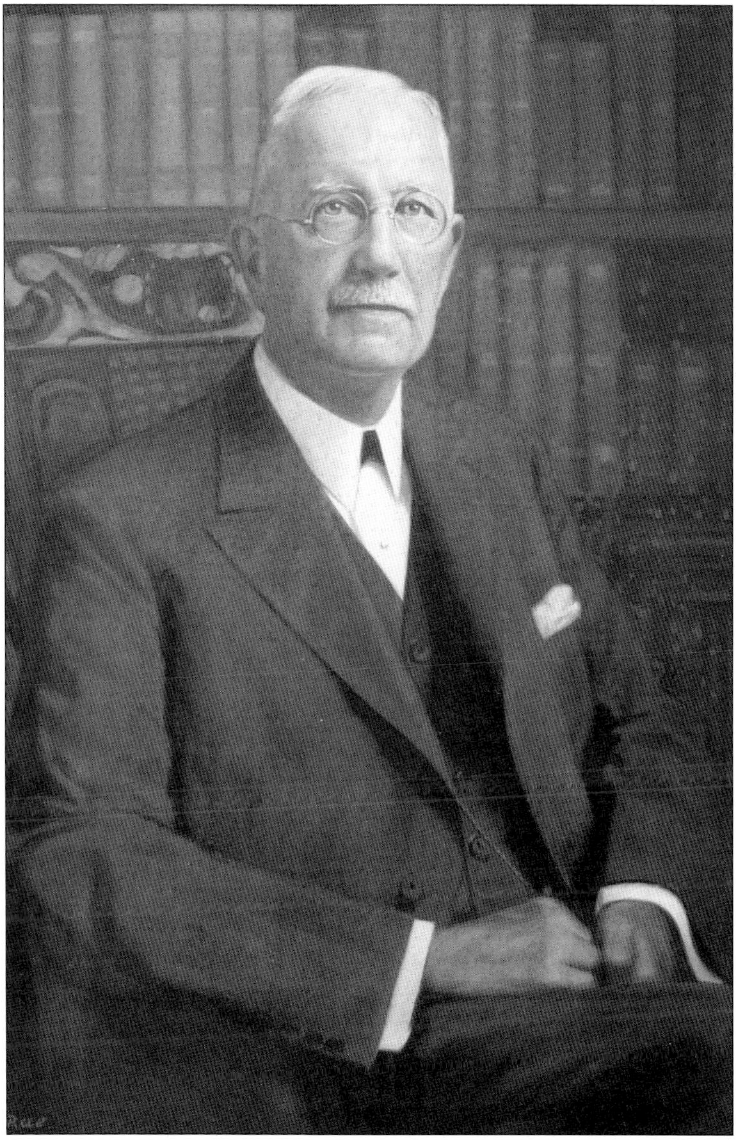

**Ellison Adger Smyth.** Born in Charleston in 1847, the proclaimed pioneer in textiles had many influences that drew him to the industry. Former hometown merchant William Gregg purchased the Graniteville Cotton Mill in 1844 and published materials encouraging people to do the same. Henry Hammett also influenced Smyth with his great success at Piedmont Manufacturing. Smyth entered the industry in 1882 by establishing the first of four mills in Pelzer. Pelzer made him a pioneer by being the first to use incandescent lighting in a mill as well as his constant reinvesting in new equipment. Along with Pelzer, Captain Smyth was involved in many other mills, including Brandon, Conestee, Dunean, Monaghan, Union Bleachery, and Victor Mill. He served as president of the South Carolina Cotton Manufacturers Association for 14 years. Along with H.P. Hammett, D.E. Converse, and John Montgomery, he was a member of the Big Four, referred to as such by virtue of their business and stature. Smyth retired in 1925 and moved to his summer home, Connemara, in Flat Rock, North Carolina. Idle hands did not last long, as he organized Balfour Mills in Henderson County. E.A. Smyth died just short of his 95th birthday, in 1942. (Courtesy of the Greenville County Library System.)

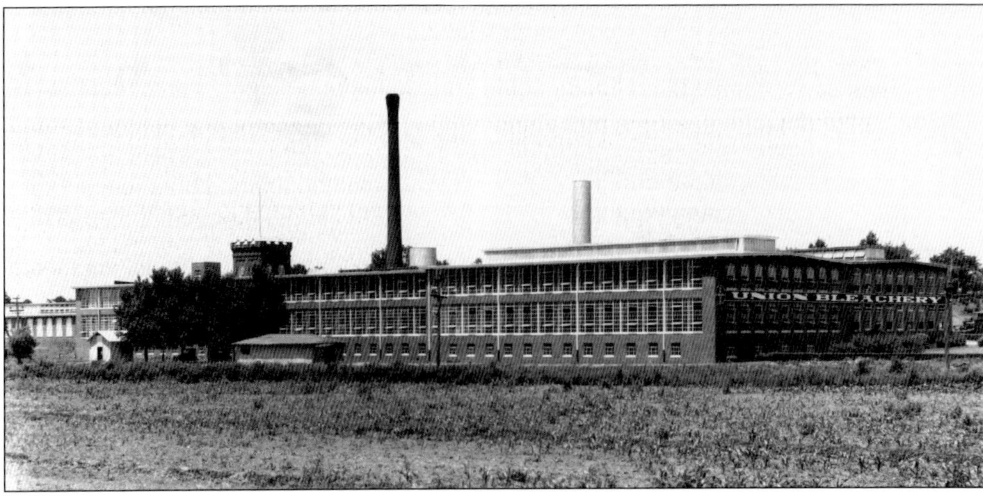


UNION BLEACHERY. Established in 1902 by an all-Northern group of investors, Union Bleachery was the second bleachery established in the South after Clearwater in Aiken. Operations began in 1903, and local textile manufacturers no longer had to ship cloth to the North for finishing. By 1922, the plant had grown exponentially and could process 40 million pounds of fabric a year. The company procured the first license for Sanforization, a process that reduces fabric shrinkage to less than one percent. As a result, the company ran full shifts while other manufacturers cut back drastically. (Courtesy of the Coxe Collection, Greenville County Historical Society.)

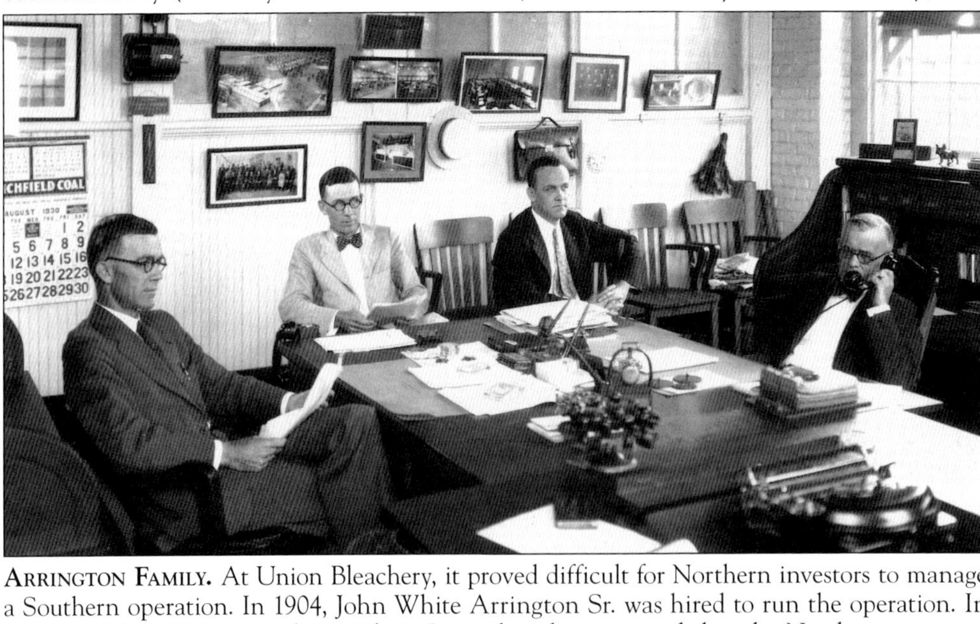

ARRINGTON FAMILY. At Union Bleachery, it proved difficult for Northern investors to manage a Southern operation. In 1904, John White Arrington Sr. was hired to run the operation. In two years' time, he was made president. It was he who suggested that the Northern investors sell their shares to Southern mill owners. Arrington had the foresight to import fast-dye fabrics (only produced in Europe) before the outbreak of World War I. This measure greatly paid off, as other finishing operations struggled to produce. In 1938, John W. Arrington Sr. passed, but little changed in management with sons John Jr., Nelson, and Richard in charge. Just like their father, the three sons saw the importance providing a good village life. Seated from left to right are John Jr., Nelson, Richard, and father John White Arrington Sr. (Courtesy of the Coxe Collection, Greenville County Historical Society.)

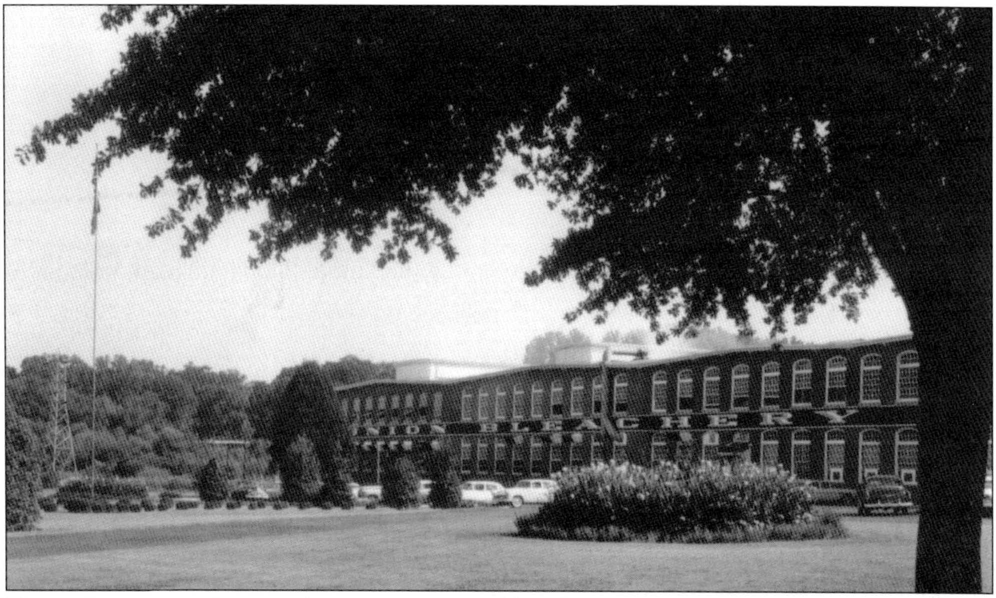

**UNION BLEACHERY.** In 1947, the company was sold to the Aspinook Corporation of Connecticut. Richard Arrington passed away the following year, leaving his three brothers to continue to manage the company. The mill was sold again in April 1952 to Greensboro, North Carolina–based Cone Mills Corporation. In 1984, Cone sold the plant to Spartanburg-based American Fast Print, which renamed the mill US Finishing. The plant continued to operate until it was destroyed by fire in 2003. (Courtesy of the Coxe Collection, Greenville County Historical Society.)

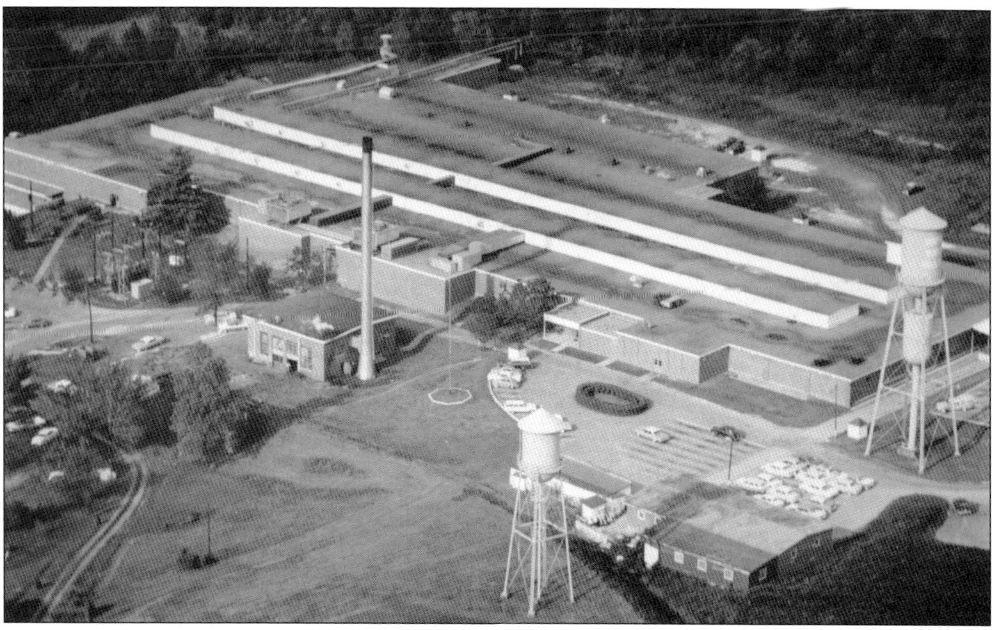

**SOUTHERN WORSTED MILL.** The Southern Worsted Mill was organized in 1923 by Bennette E. Geer as a woolen mill on the former Camp Sevier property off Rutherford Road. The one-story plant was responsible for producing the first woolen garment-quality cloth woven in the South. In order for the plant to run at full capacity, over 100,000 pounds of wool had to be on site at all times. (Courtesy of the Coxe Collection, Greenville County Historical Society.)

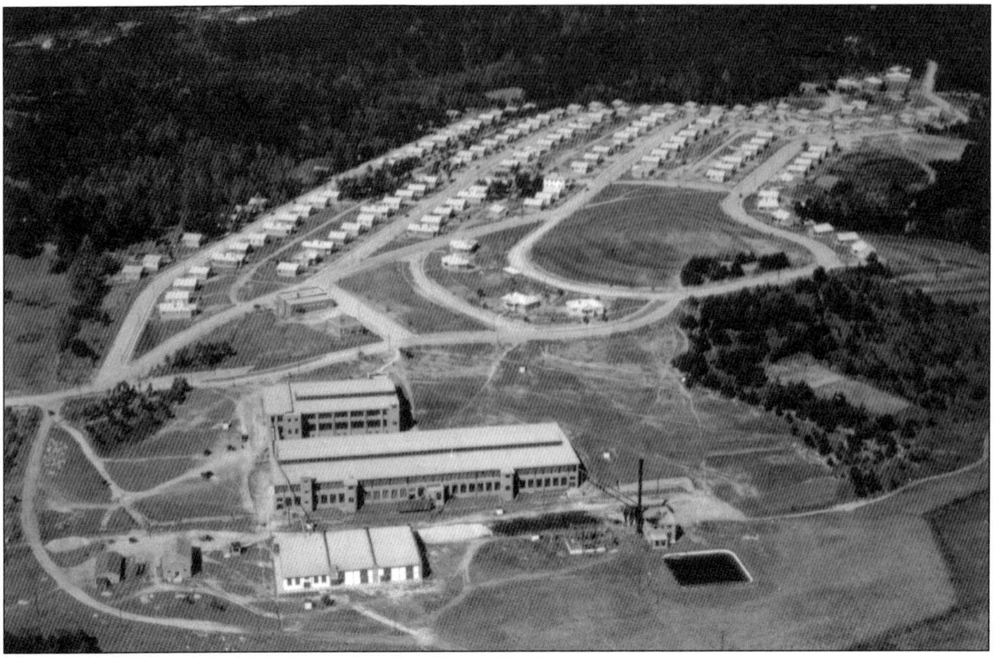

**Slater Mill.** H. Nelson Slater of Pawtucket, Rhode Island, purchased 449 acres in northern Greenville County from Norwood and R. Mayes Cleveland and chartered the Slater Manufacturing Company in Delaware on October 14, 1927. The mill and village was designed by J.E. Sirrine. In this 1920s aerial photograph, one can see the post office, general store, and barbershop in the business district, as well as the absence of the community building. (Courtesy of the Coxe Collection, Greenville County Historical Society.)

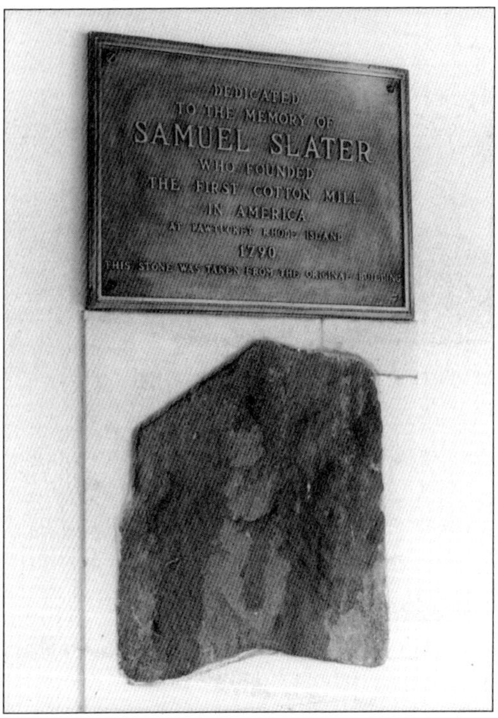


**Slater Stone.** Seen here is a stone from the original Slater Mill in Pawtucket, Rhode Island. The original Slater Mill was the first cotton mill in the United States, founded by Samuel Slater in 1790. The plaque and stone are on display in his honor in Slater, South Carolina. Samuel Slater is often considered the "Father of the American Industrial Revolution." (Courtesy of the Slater Hall Citizens' Committee Collection, Greenville County Library System.)

**Slater Mill Smokestack.** In 1943, a new smokestack replaced the original metal one with "Slater 1790" laid in the brickwork. This further conveyed the mill's ancestry to the first cotton mill in the United States. (Courtesy of the author.)

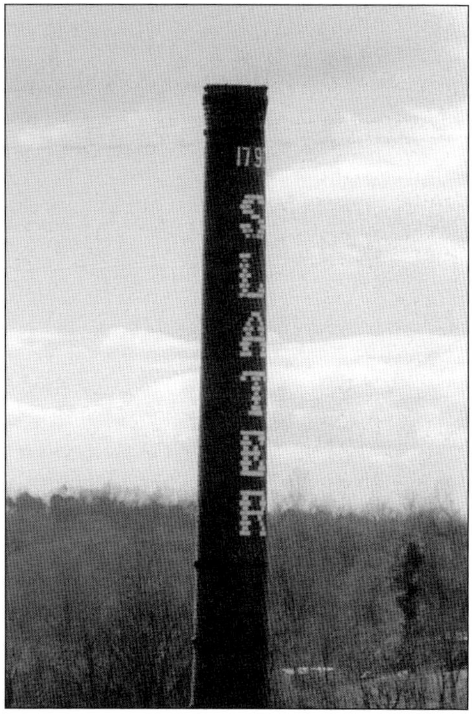


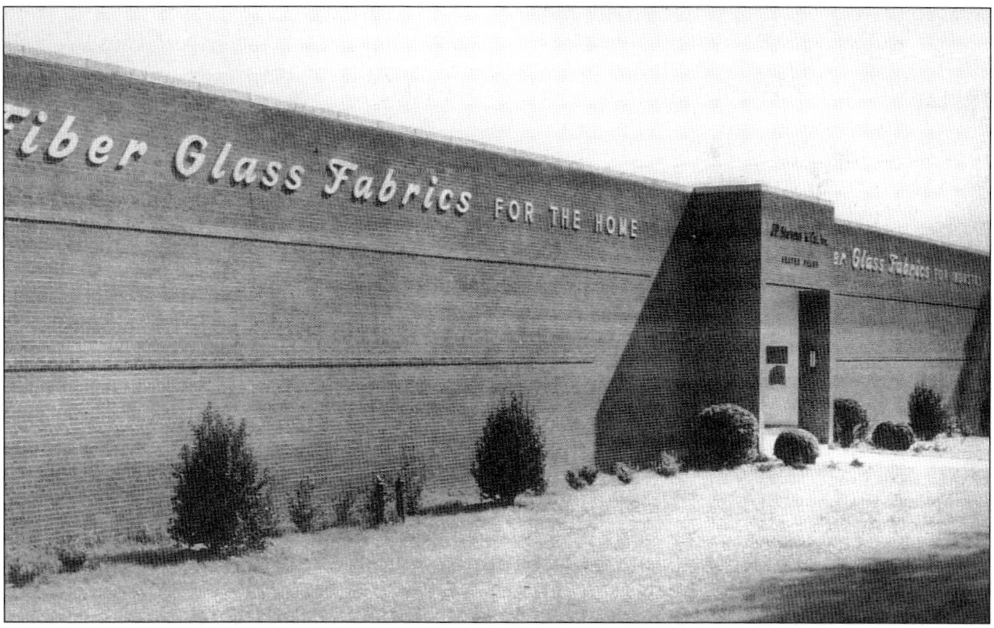


**Slater Mill.** Originally a cotton mill, it later manufactured with rayon, fiberglass, and other synthetics before finally shifting all production to fiberglass in 1951. During World War II, the plant made various fabrics for military use. Slater is also responsible for the fabric used in the Apollo II spacesuits that walked on the moon in 1969. The mill was purchased in 1946 by J.P. Stevens and Company. After the company's leveraged buyout in 1988, the mill became a subsidiary of JPS Textiles and continues to operate today. (Courtesy of the Slater Hall Citizens' Committee Collection, Greenville County Library System.)

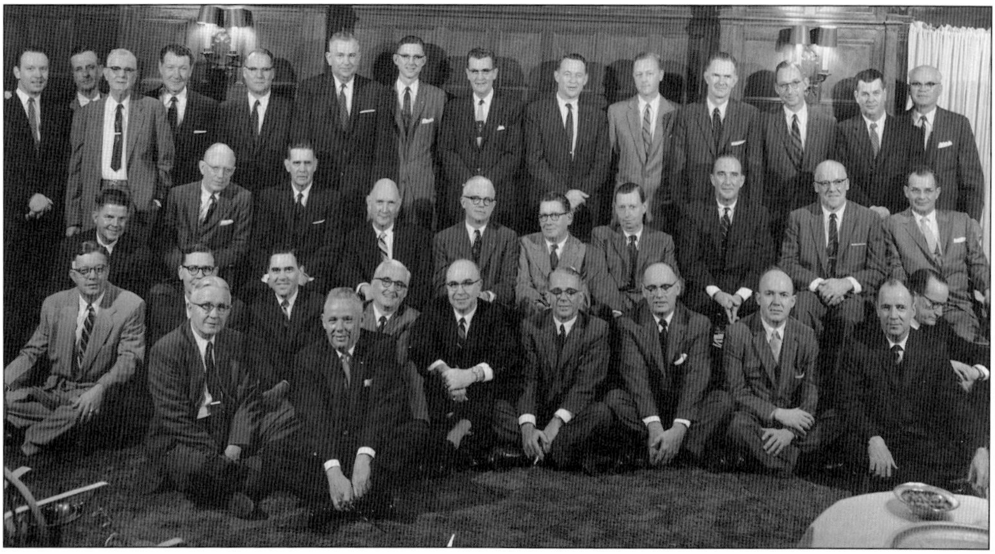

**J.P. Stevens and Company Management.** Seen here are members of the company's manufacturing and advisory committee and plant-management personnel gathered at the Poinsett Hotel on March 25, 1957. In June 1946, New York–based J.P. Stevens and Company announced it would purchase a number of Greenville-based mills, including Dunean, Monaghan, Piedmont, and Slater. (Courtesy of the Coxe Collection, Greenville County Historical Society.)

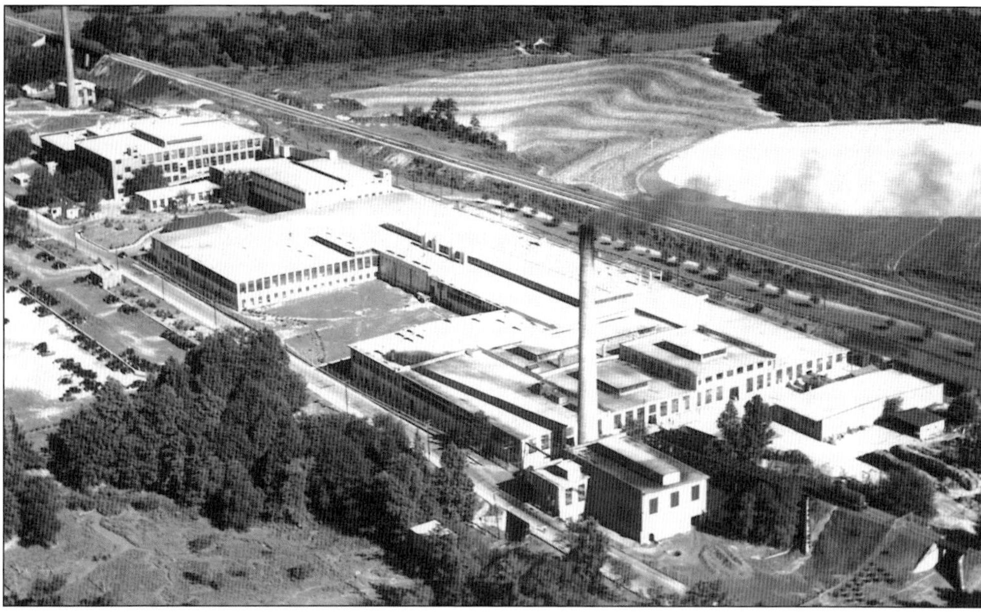

**Southern Bleachery.** Located along the Enoree River in Taylors, Southern Bleachery was built in 1922 on 200 acres that had been quietly assembled by the Alester G. Furman Company for former superintendent of Union Bleachery Harry Roberts Stephenson. Shortly after the mill opened, Stephenson saw the opportunity for a printworks operation. He approached Gerrish Milliken of New England–based Deering Milliken to supply machinery from a shuttered mill in exchange for stock in the new printworks company. Milliken agreed, and in 1928, Piedmont Printworks opened next to the bleachery. In 1936, the two companies merged to become Southern Bleachery and Printworks. (Courtesy of the Coxe Collection, Greenville County Historical Society.)

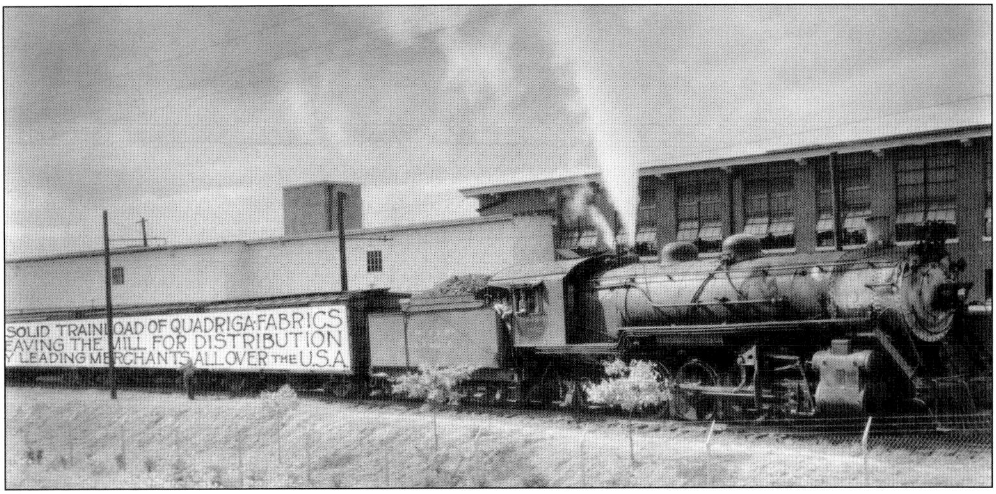


**Southern Bleachery.** In December 1953, mill president Harry Stephenson retired, and his brother and vice president Robert Stephenson passed away. In 1954, the family sold the company to its longtime selling agent Ely and Walker. On January 2, 1965, Ely and Walker sold the plant to Greensboro-based Burlington Industries, which quickly closed the plant in six months. By that September, J.P. Stevens had reopened the plant. Through the buyout of J.P. Stevens in the late 1980s, the mill became part of JPS Automotive until 1994, when it was purchased by Foamex International, which later closed the mill. (Courtesy of the Coxe Collection, Greenville County Historical Society.)

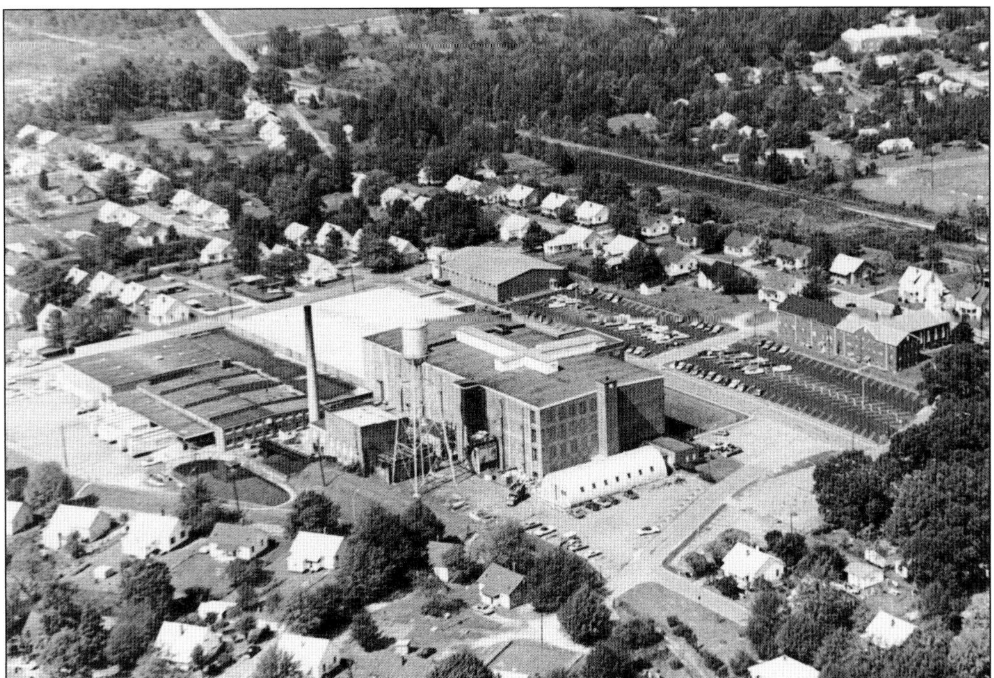

**Greer Manufacturing Company.** Founded in 1908 by John A. Robinson Sr., the plant was often referred to simply as Greer Mill. In 1912, it was sold to Parker Cotton Mills and again later to J.P. Stevens and Company. The mill closed in 1996. (Courtesy of the Greer Heritage Museum Collection, Greenville County Library System.)

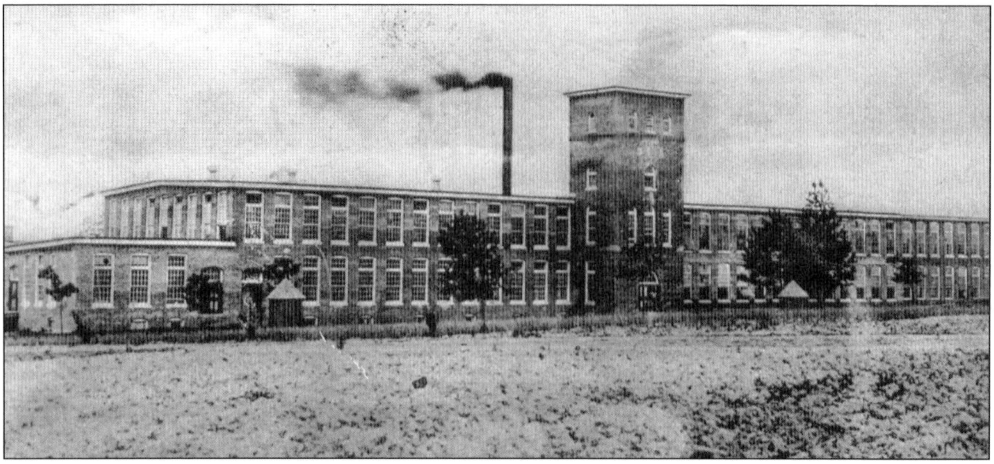

**FRANKLIN MILL.** Organized in 1900 by William W. Burgess, it was the second mill in Greer, just after Victor Manufacturing, on the Spartanburg side. By 1912, J.M. Greer was president and had 200 workers. The mill operated 10,000 spindles and 288 looms and produced sheeting and drills. During the General Textile Strike of 1934, flying squadrons were able to shut down the mill by cutting its power supply. At that time, the mill was already in receivership and barely operating. In 1942, interest in the mill heightened as a result of the wartime economy, and it was sold to Victory Textiles. Victory had military contracts that kept the mill running at full capacity. The mill was reorganized as Greer Manufacturing in the 1950s, until it was sold in 1970 to Heritage Industries. The site is now location of the Greer Commission of Public Works. (Courtesy of the Greer Heritage Museum Collection, Greenville County Library System.)

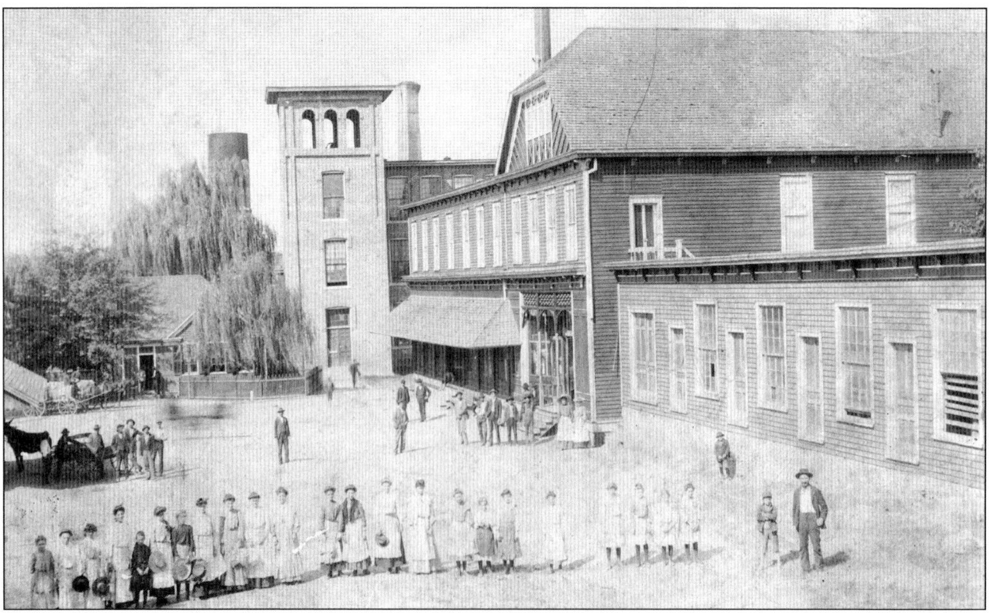

**PELHAM MILL.** The first cotton mill on the site was founded in 1820 as the Hutchings Factory by the Reverend Thomas Hutchings. In 1827, the property was purchased by Philip C. Lester and became known as the Lester Factory. By 1850, the property was known as the Buena Vista Factory and retained that name until 1880, when it was sold to the Pelham Manufacturing Company, that, in 1882, incorporated their property under the name the Pelham Mills. (Courtesy of the Greer Heritage Museum Collection, Greenville County Library System.)

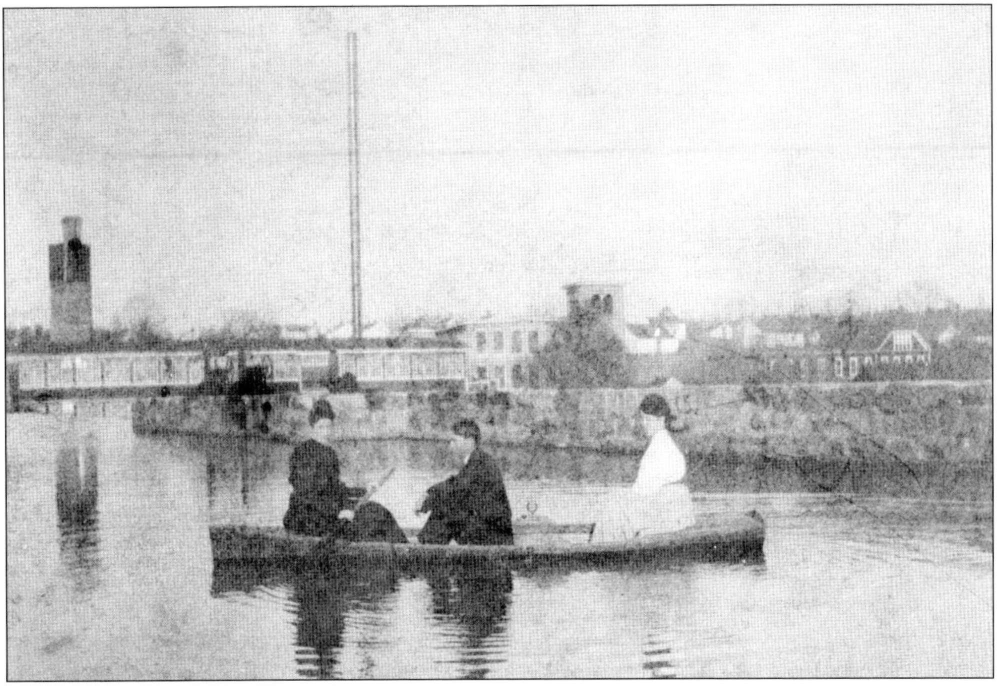

**Pelham Mill Pond.** By 1940, the mill had been vacated, and a fire destroyed the entire complex (as seen in this 1890 photograph) shortly thereafter. (Courtesy of the Greenville County Library System.)

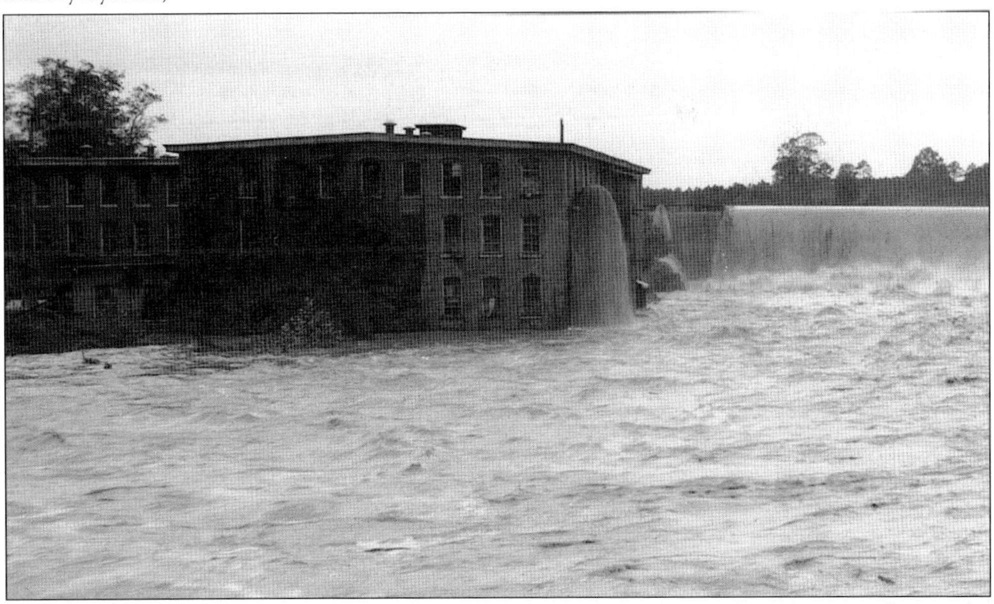

**Conestee Mill.** The Conestee originally dates back to 1837, when "Father of Greenville" Vardry McBee built what became known as the Reedy River Factory. In 1909, the mill was chartered as Conestee Mill. The mill remained in operation until 1939 but later reopened in 1946 under new ownership until finally closing in 1971. The mill, dam, and lake were added to the National Register of Historic Places on March 2, 2014. (Courtesy of the Coxe Collection, Greenville County Historical Society.)

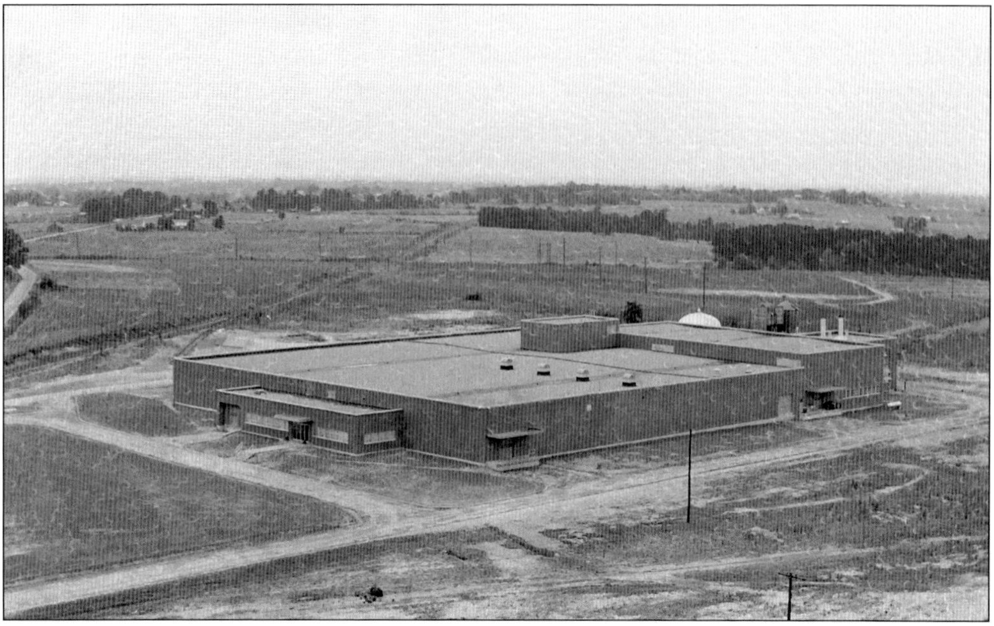

**Fairview Mill.** Located in Fountain Inn, the local Boosters Club raised money and donated the 35 acres for the project. The mill was a tricot knitting, dyeing, and finishing operation, completed in 1951 at a cost of $2 million. By 1960, the plant had been acquired by Beaunit. (Courtesy of the Elrod Collection, Greenville County Historical Society.)

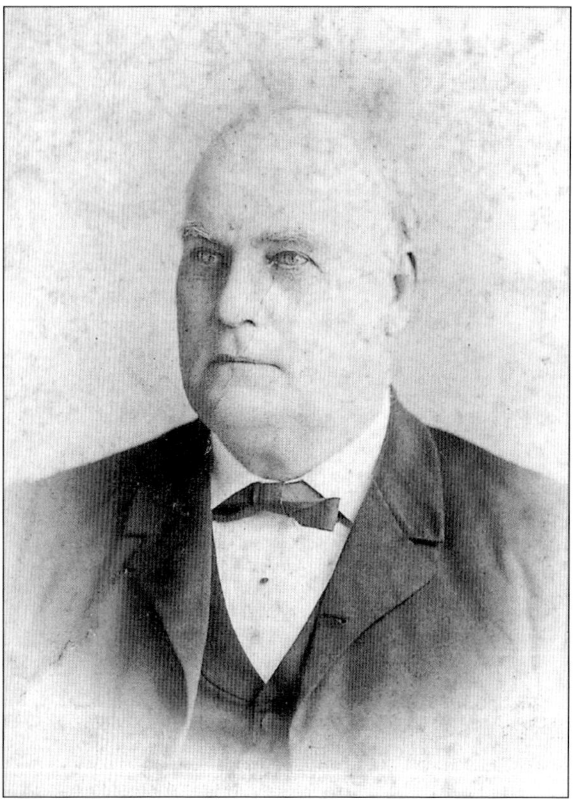

**Henry Pinkney Hammett.** Born in Laurens County in 1822, Hammett got his start in the textile industry as a bookkeeper for Batesville Cotton Mill, established by William Bates. He married Bates's daughter in 1848 and was made partner in the company a year later. Hammett and Bates sold the company in 1862 and went on to purchase 255 acres at Garrison Shoals along the Saluda River to establish a new mill. Bates died in 1872, before the mill was built. H.P. Hammett lived close to another 20 years, passing on May 8, 1891. (Courtesy of the Piedmont History Collection, Greenville County Library System.)

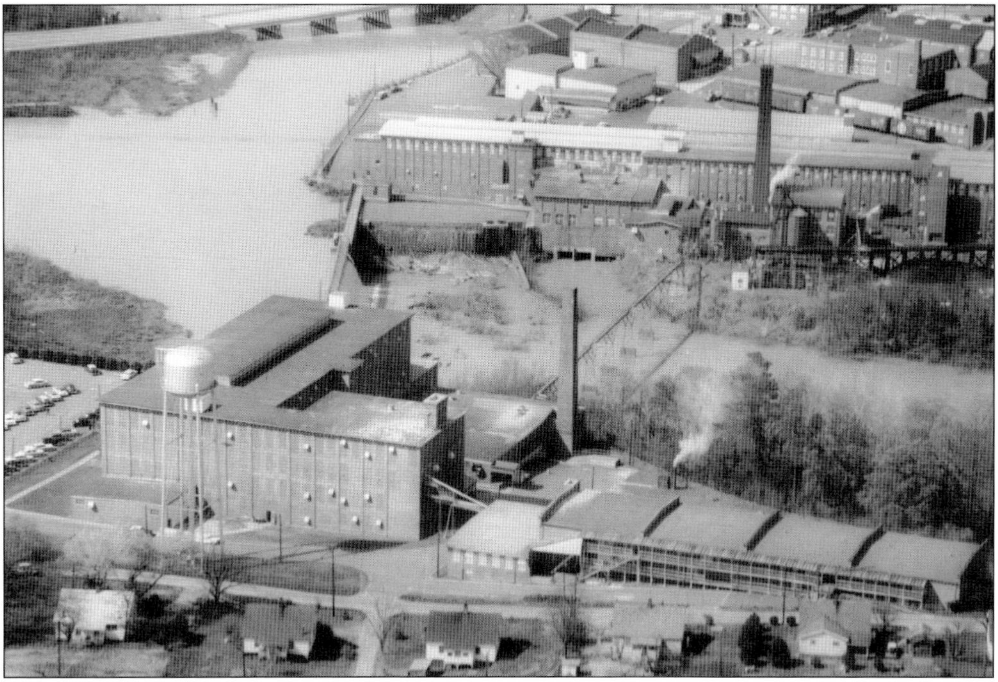

**Piedmont Manufacturing Company.** Established by Henry Pinkney Hammett in 1873, the mill and village were situated at Garrison Shoals along the Saluda River. Hammett had many of the building materials made on site, including brick and steel. Piedmont No. 1 opened in 1876 with No. 2 opening in 1888. As it was situated on a river, the mill was powered by a waterwheel. By 1892, the mills operated 47,000 spindles and 1,300 looms. (Courtesy of the Coxe Collection, Greenville County Historical Society.)

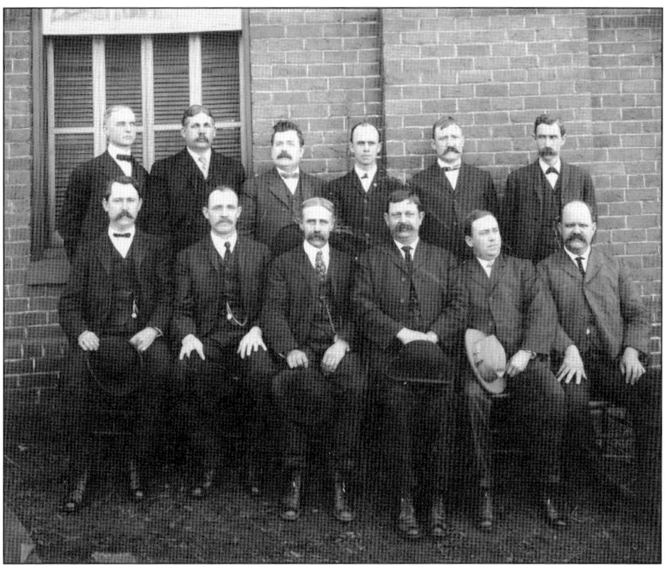

**Piedmont Manufacturing Officers and Overseers, 1910.** Included in this photograph are W.E. Beattie, S.T. Buchanan, R.W. Sloan, Lewis Jewell, Judge Picklesimer, G.L. Doggett, M. Roberts, Ollie Haynes, John Eskew, Arthur Duncan, and Horie Cobb. (Courtesy of the Greenville County Library System.)

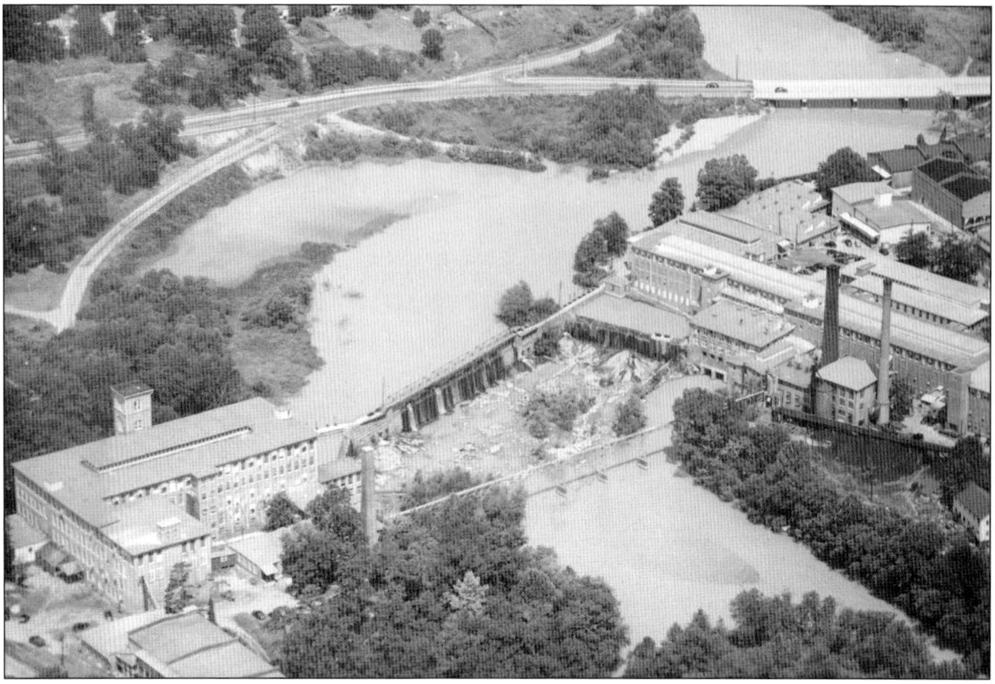

**Piedmont Manufacturing Company.** In 1946, the mill was sold to J.P. Stevens and Company. With the modern Estes Plant opening, production was gradually shifted to the new plant until operations ceased at Piedmont in 1977. The No. 1 mill was placed in the National Register of Historic Places on June 2, 1978. In October 1983, a fire destroyed almost all of the building, resulting in its ruins being demolished and losing its National Register designation on March 5, 1986. (Courtesy of the Coxe Collection, Greenville County Historical Society.)

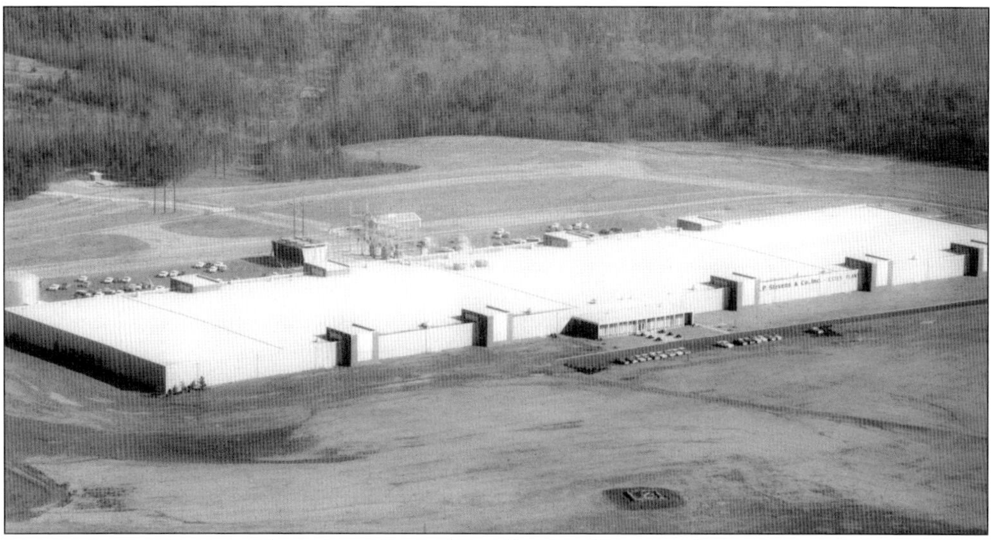

**Estes Plant.** At a cost of over $6 million, the mill opened in 1964 by J.P. Stevens and Company and was named a top-10 plant in the United States. The new mill quickly replaced production at Piedmont Manufacturing, and the older facilities were converted to warehouse space. In 1986, the Estes Plant was sold to the Delta Mills Marketing Company. (Courtesy of the Coxe Collection, Greenville County Historical Society.)

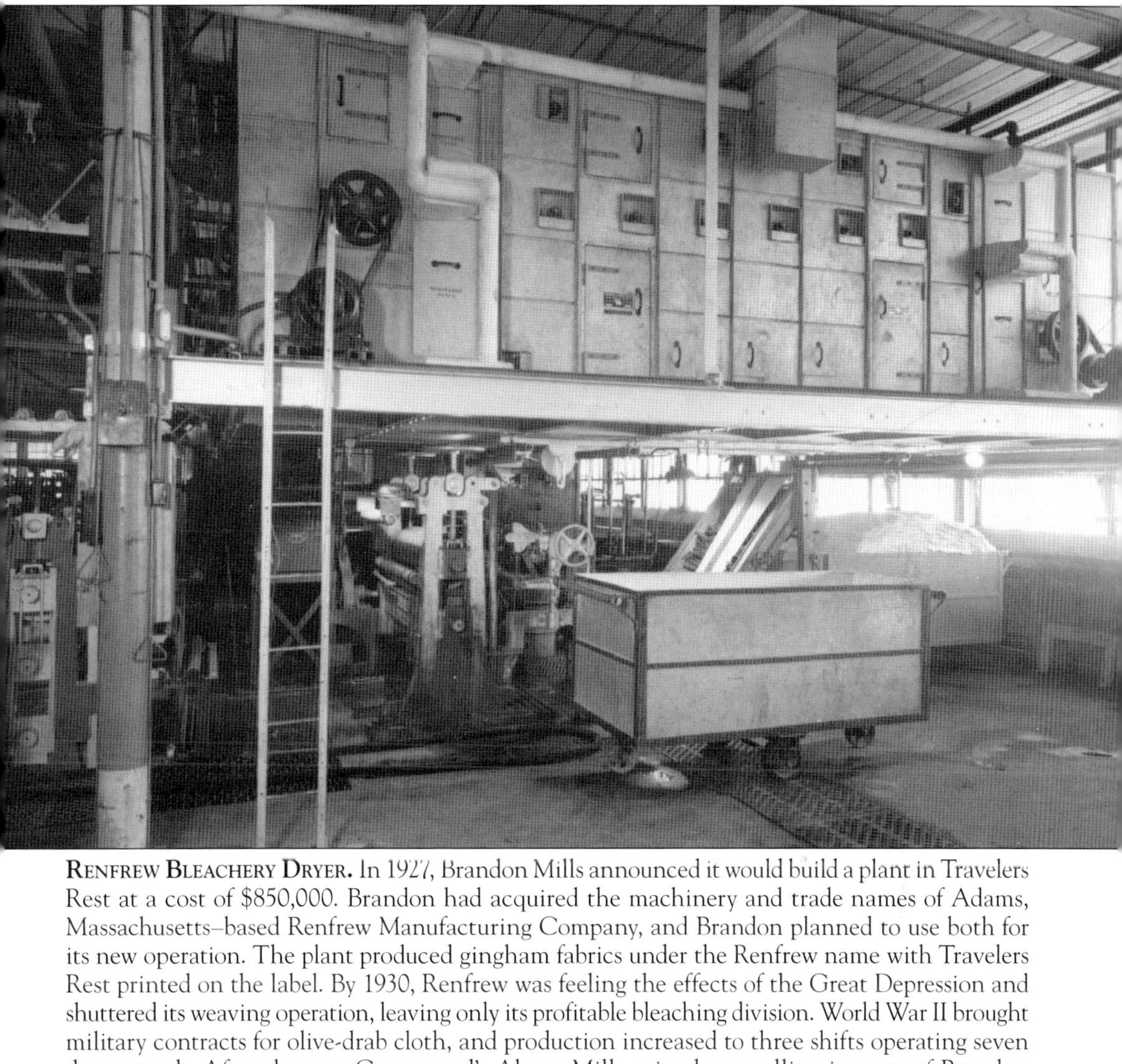

**Renfrew Bleachery Dryer.** In 1927, Brandon Mills announced it would build a plant in Travelers Rest at a cost of $850,000. Brandon had acquired the machinery and trade names of Adams, Massachusetts–based Renfrew Manufacturing Company, and Brandon planned to use both for its new operation. The plant produced gingham fabrics under the Renfrew name with Travelers Rest printed on the label. By 1930, Renfrew was feeling the effects of the Great Depression and shuttered its weaving operation, leaving only its profitable bleaching division. World War II brought military contracts for olive-drab cloth, and production increased to three shifts operating seven days a week. After the war, Greenwood's Abney Mills gained controlling interest of Brandon Corporation, and in 1949, the two companies merged. As a result of overseas competition, the mill was sold several times starting in 1979 to Allied Product's Kerr Division, and then to Rocky Mountain Industries in 1984, before finally closing in 1988. (Courtesy of the Coxe Collection, Greenville County Historical Society.)

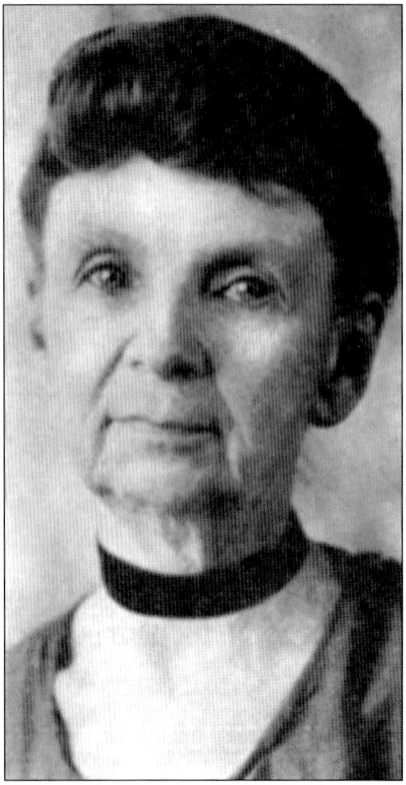

**Mary Putnam Gridley.** In the 1870s, George Putnam moved his family from Massachusetts to Greenville to take a position as superintendent of Camperdown Mill. By 1880, he had purchased Batesville Cotton Mill and made his recently widowed daughter Mary Putnam Gridley secretary. When Gridley's father died in 1890, she became president, making her the first woman to hold such a position in the South. As president, she purposely signed official correspondence with her initials, M.P., to not let on to business colleagues that she was a woman. Mary Putnam Gridley ran Batesville Cotton Mill for over 20 years before selling the company. (Courtesy of the Greenville County Library System.)

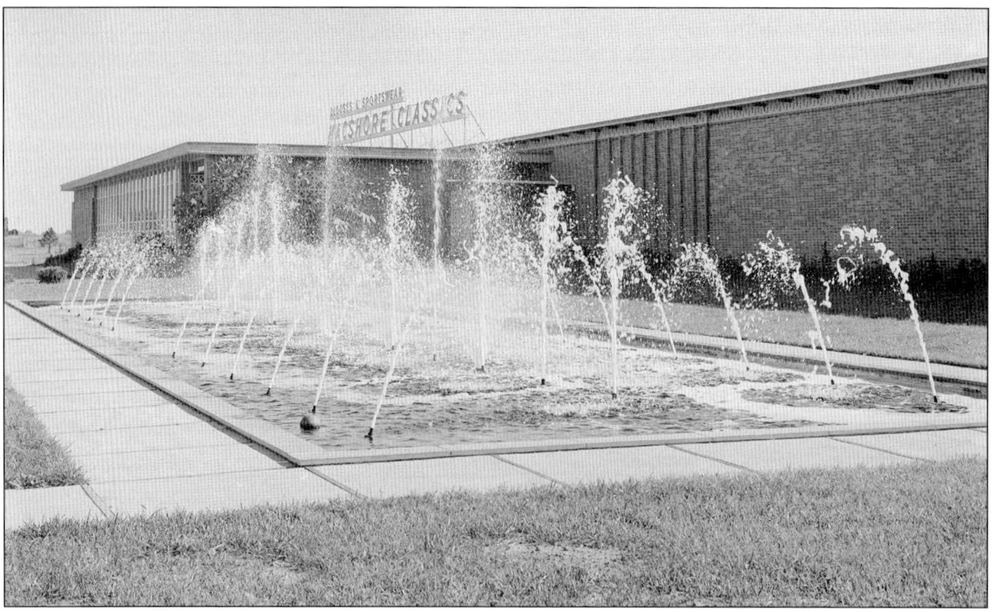

**Macshore Classics.** Founded in 1943, the company first manufactured women's blouses and sportswear. The third generation–run company is still located in its 150,000-square-foot facility on Laurens Road. It remains a cut-and-sew operation, although now it manufactures products for the home furnishing and hospitality industries. (Courtesy of the Wilson Collection, Upcountry History Museum.)

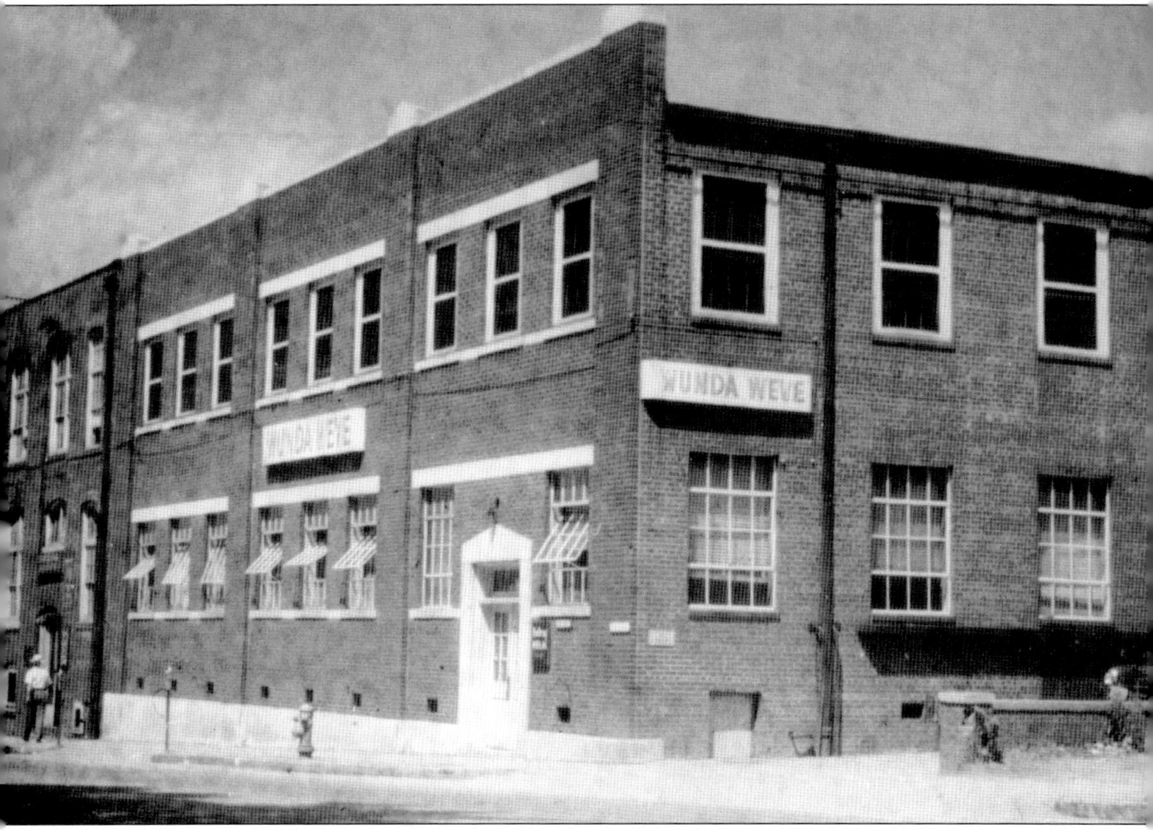


**WUNDA WEVE CARPET COMPANY.** Located at the corner of River and Hammond Streets, the company began producing cotton throw rugs in the early 1900s and later grew to become one of the largest carpet manufacturers in the United States, with products in more than 500,000 homes. Wunda Weve later built a multimillion-dollar facility on Poinsett Highway that manufactured cotton, nylon, and wool carpet. In the 1970s, the company was one of the first to apply Scotchgard and antistatic chemicals to carpet. After buyouts by Dan River in 1965 and World Carpets in 1995, the company ultimately became part of Dalton-based Mohawk Carpet in 1998. The Greenville plant had close to 750 employees at the time of its closing. (Courtesy of the Landing Collection, Greenville County Historical Society.)

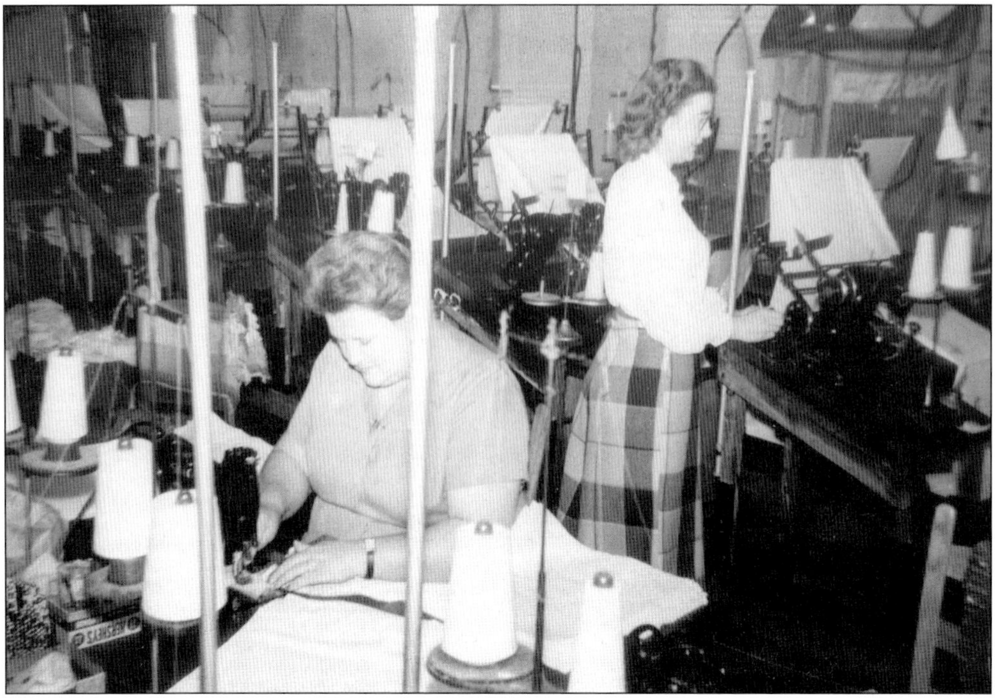

**CAROLINA MANUFACTURING.** Better known for its Hav-A-Hank brand handkerchiefs, the company began in a garage on Townes Street by Malcom P. "Mack" Niven in 1948. The company's humble beginnings started with shipping goods in discarded shipping crates found in downtown alleys. However, quality was second to none, and the company grew to become the largest handkerchief manufacturer in the world. Due to the continued growth, Carolina first moved into a larger plant built on Laurens Road and then to its Augusta Road facility in 1984. (Courtesy of the collection of Mack P. Niven Sr. and family.)

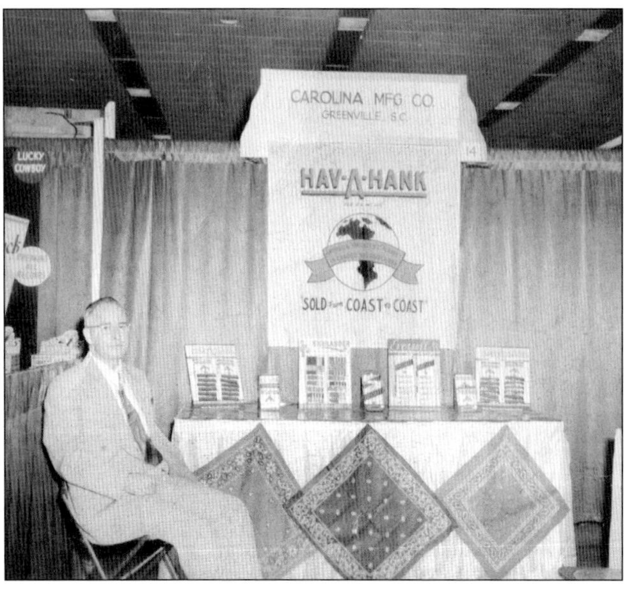


**HAV-A-HANK.** Malcolm P. Niven sits in front of a sales booth at the SWCA Convention in Atlanta in July 1951. Carolina became the largest manufacturer of handkerchiefs and bandanas in the world, selling over 1.5 million packages a month. They are also responsible for producing the original Tiger Rag for Clemson University. In 1986, the company entered the promotional-products industry by adding custom-printed bandanas, aprons, head wraps, and pet triangles to its offerings. (Courtesy of the collection of Mack P. Niven Sr. and family.)

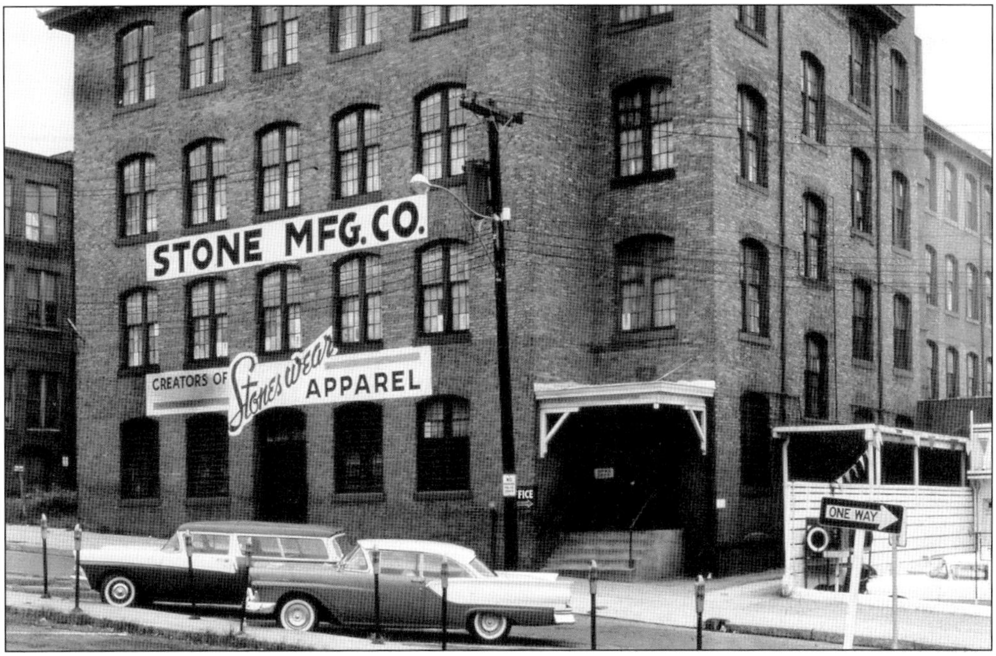


**STONE MANUFACTURING COMPANY.** Opening at 154 Rivers Street on July 9, 1933, by Eugene "Gene" Stone III, labor and equipment included five seamstresses and eight sewing machines, with Gene handling all fabric cutting, packaging, and shipping as his wife, Allene, also known as "Linky," designed the apparel. The business may never have happened if it were not for Stone resigning from his current job with a textile company after not being compensated while on his honeymoon, as promised. By the late 1930s, the company was producing ladies' wear, including sunsuits that sold at Woolworth's for 10¢. Later, the company moved to its Court Street location seen here. (Courtesy of Don Koonce.)

**STONE MANUFACTURING COMPANY.** In 1951, Stone opened its Cherrydale Plant and was heralded as the largest apparel production facility in the world; it was equipped with over 1,000 sewing machines. Over the next three decades, the company continued to develop and expand its product line to offer apparel for the entire family. In the mid-1980s, the company began to manufacture soccer clothing under the Umbro label and officially changed its name to Umbro International in 1997. After the sale of the Umbro line in 1999, the company reverted back to its original name. (Courtesy of Don Koonce.)

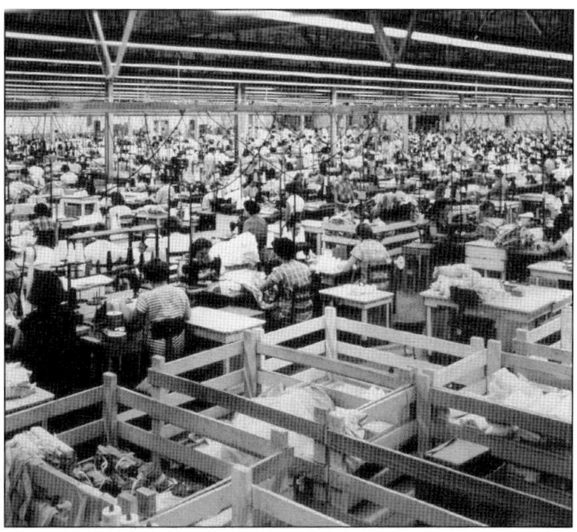

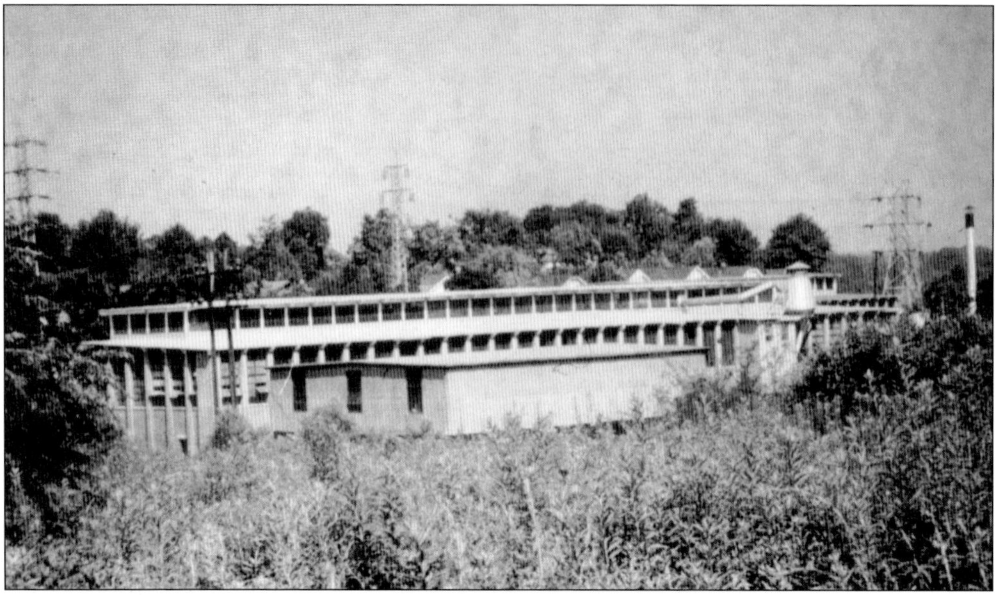

**Riverdale Mill.** Located off Cedar Lane Road, the mill was organized out of Okeh Manufacturing in January 1920. It was equipped with 2,500 spindles, and its authorized capitalization had been increased to $200,000. Started by F.H. Cunningham, he acted as president until 1922. (Courtesy of the Landing Collection, Greenville County Historical Society.)

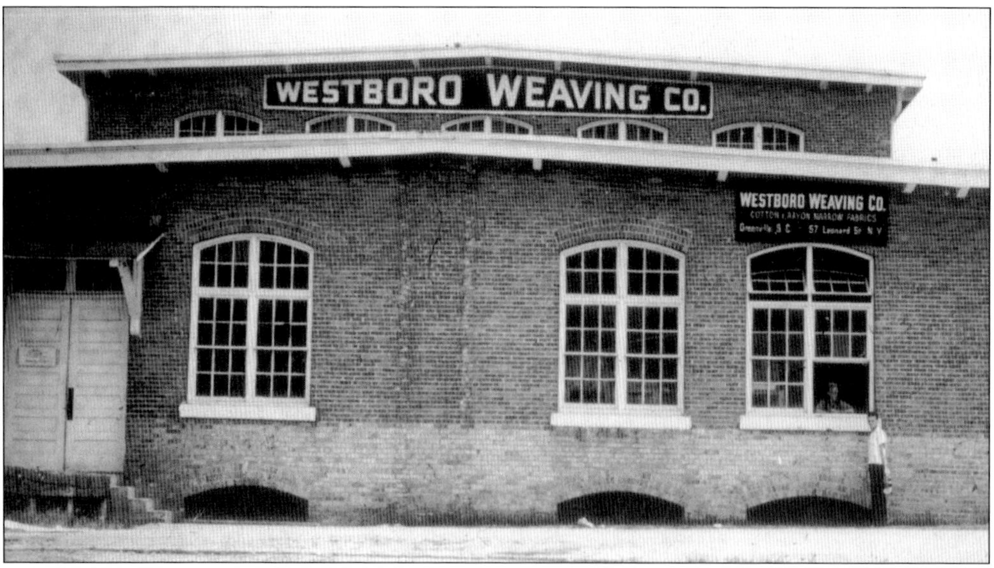


**Westboro Weaving Company.** Located on Laurens Road, the mill building was originally constructed in 1903 by Henry McGee to produce coarse yarns from mill waste, and in 1907, it became the only woolen mill in the state. In 1918, the mill was sold to Atlanta-based Beaver Duck Mills and produced cotton duck cloth. The mill was transferred to Couch Cotton Mills on June 26, 1920, with S.A. Burns a president. The company ceased in 1923, and the National Bank of Charleston assumed ownership of the building but later sold it to New York–based Lullwater Manufacturing Company. In September 1934, it was sold to Westboro, Massachusetts–based Westboro Weaving Company. Westboro produced cotton and rayon narrow fabrics. (Courtesy of the Landing Collection, Greenville County Historical Society.)

# *Two*

# VILLAGE LIFE

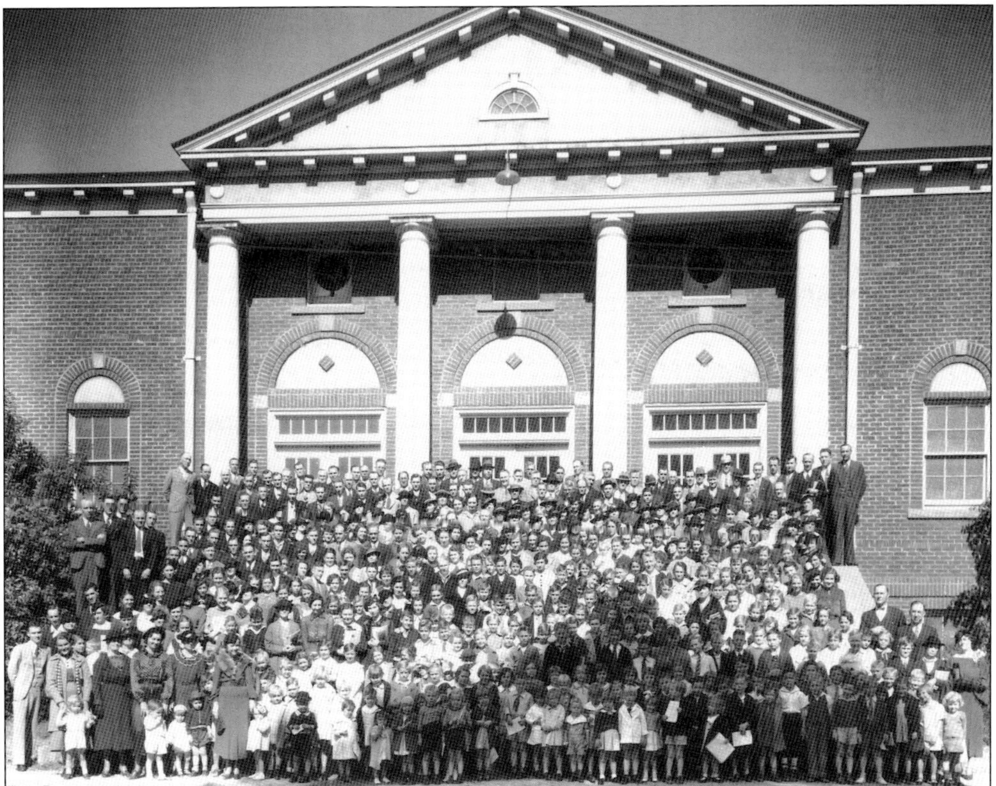

**BRANDON BAPTIST CHURCH.** Built after a fire in 1923, the new sanctuary seen here sat 800. In March 1929, over 1,700 Brandon employees went on strike due to stretch-outs and low wages. Without salaries during the strike, many families went hungry. In response, Brandon Baptist pastor John Wrenn set up a relief fund and urged the mill and workers to reach a settlement. It was not until May that a settlement was negotiated by the United Textile Workers Union. The church was also "Shoeless Joe" Jackson's home church. When Jackson passed in 1951, his funeral was attended by hundreds of admirers. (Courtesy of the Coxe Collection, Greenville County Historical Society.)

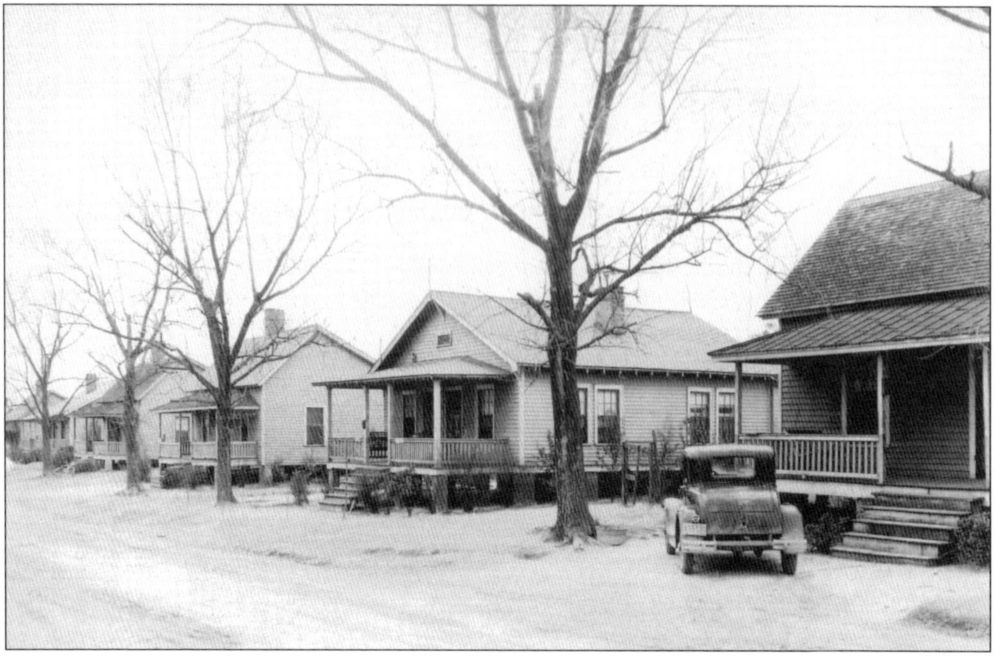

**BRANDON VILLAGE.** By the end of 1899, there were 66 houses built for operatives, prior to the construction of the mill. From 1900 to 1903, the number of houses had reached 450 to meet the needs of the ever-increasing workforce. Each house had space for a garden and electricity, including one outlet per household. In 1949, Greenwood-based Abney Mills had controlling interest of Brandon and decided to sell off the houses. A large number of employees had saved up enough during the war years and others had GI benefits, which made it possible to purchase a house. (Courtesy of the Brandon Historical Society Collection, Greenville County Library System.)

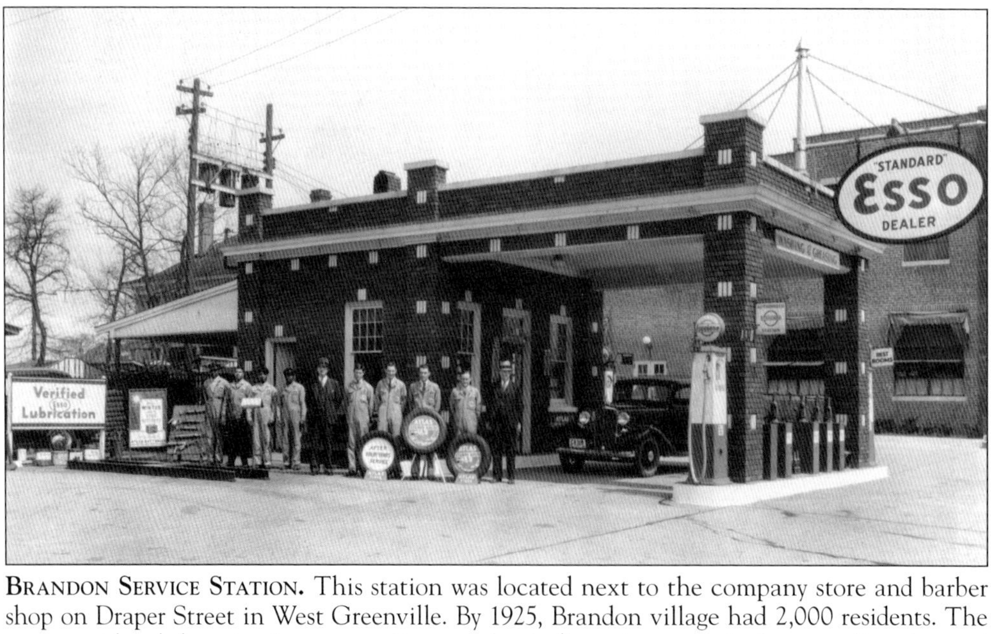


**BRANDON SERVICE STATION.** This station was located next to the company store and barber shop on Draper Street in West Greenville. By 1925, Brandon village had 2,000 residents. The area considered changing its name to Branwood to indicate its proximity between Brandon and Woodside Mills. (Courtesy of the Coxe Collection, Greenville County Historical Society.)

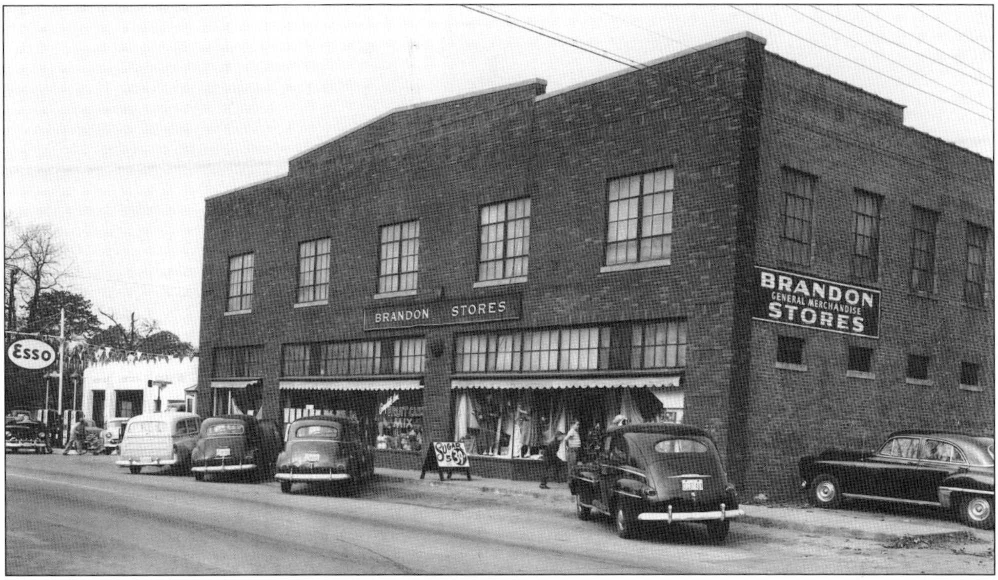


**BRANDON MILL STORE.** The mill store was located at the corner of Cooper and Draper Streets. Seen here during the holiday season, storefront window displays are decorated with Christmas ornaments and mannequins donning ladies fashion. Promotional signage encourages shoppers to buy fruitcake mix and sugar for 39¢. (Courtesy of the Coxe Collection, Greenville County Historical Society.)

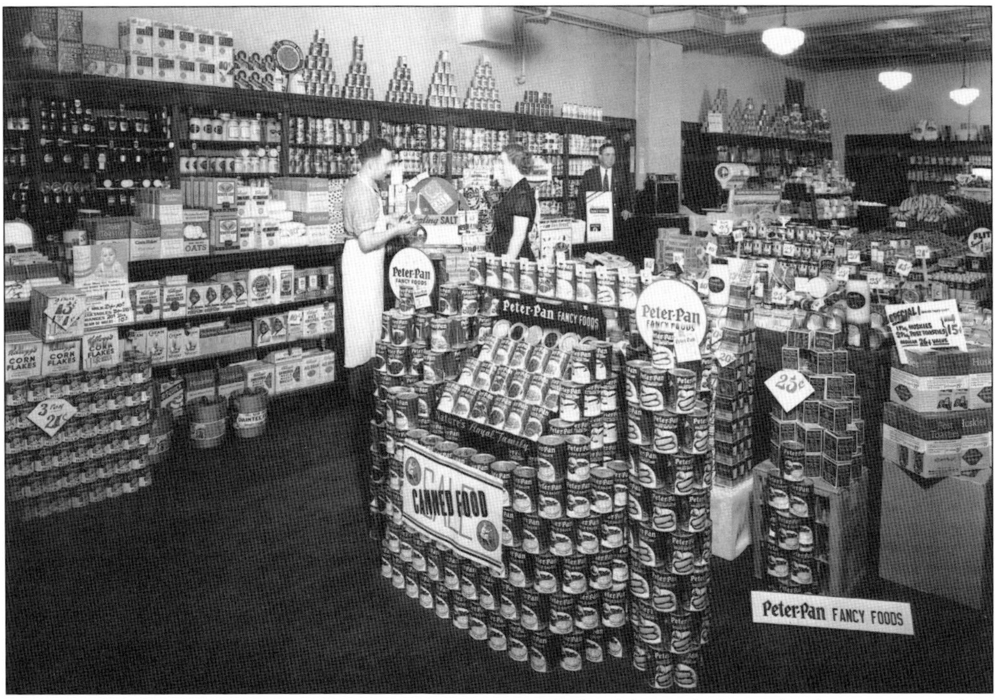


**SHOPPING AT BRANDON MILL STORE.** A customer is helped by a clerk inside the store. Familiar brands such as Post Toasties, Kellogg's Corn Flakes, White Lily, and Duke's Mayonnaise alongside names no longer offered, such as Flit, are neatly displayed on shelves. (Courtesy of the Coxe Collection, Greenville County Historical Society.)

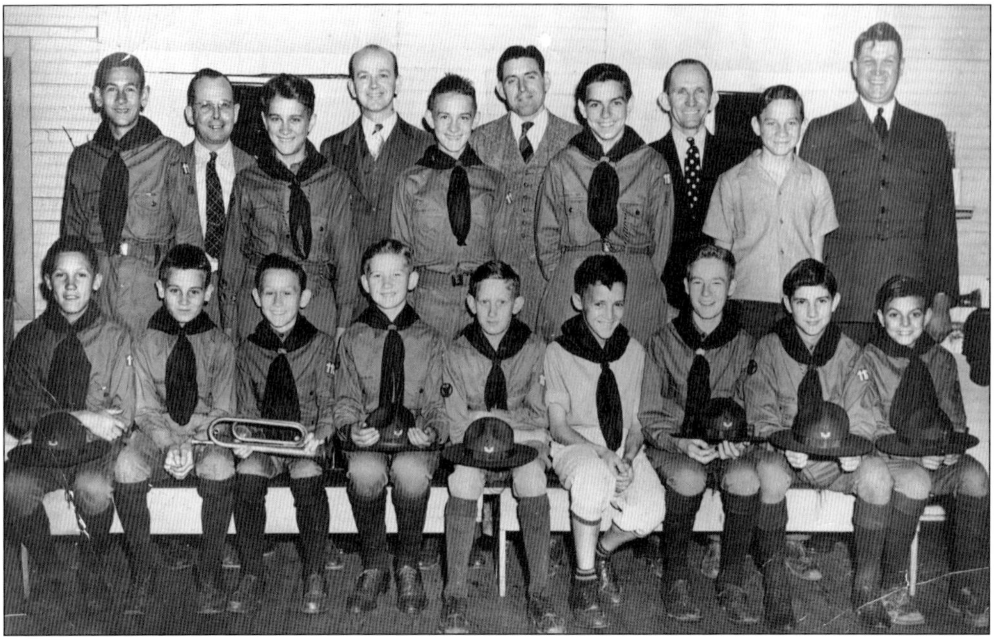

**Brandon Boy Scout Troop.** Brandon Mill built a log cabin for South Carolina's first Boy Scout troop. The cabin is located at the bottom of the hill behind the mill at the corner of Jones and Waco Streets. The cabin still stands today. (Courtesy of the Brandon Historical Society Collection, Greenville County Library System.)

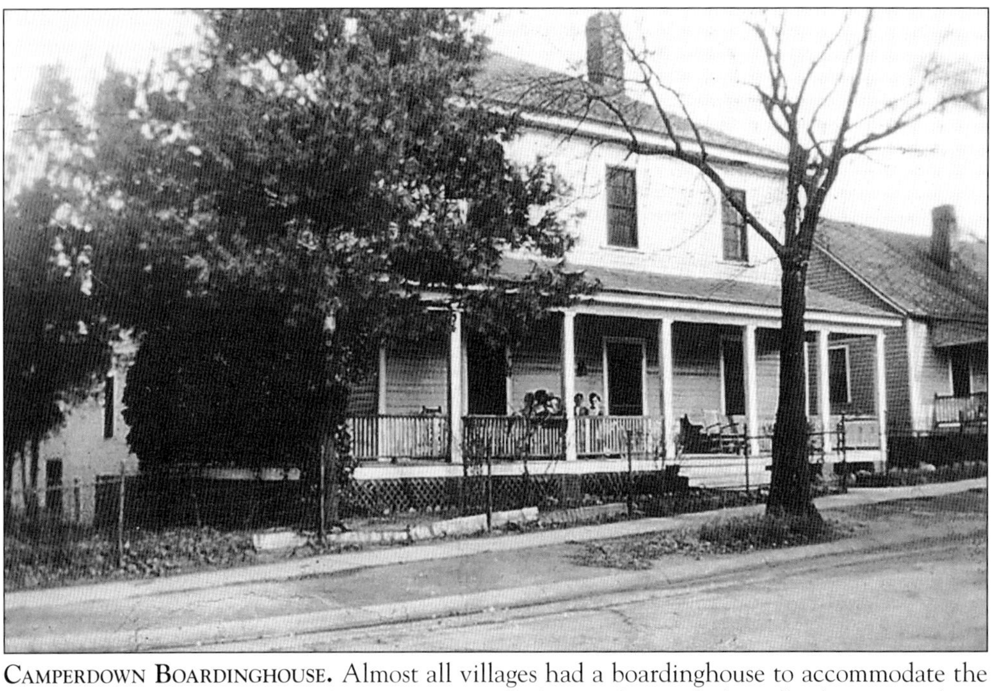

**Camperdown Boardinghouse.** Almost all villages had a boardinghouse to accommodate the great migration of workers from the mountains and other rural areas to the mill. The Camperdown boardinghouse was located at 13 Choice Street. (Courtesy of the Camperdown Historical Society Collection, Greenville County Library System.)

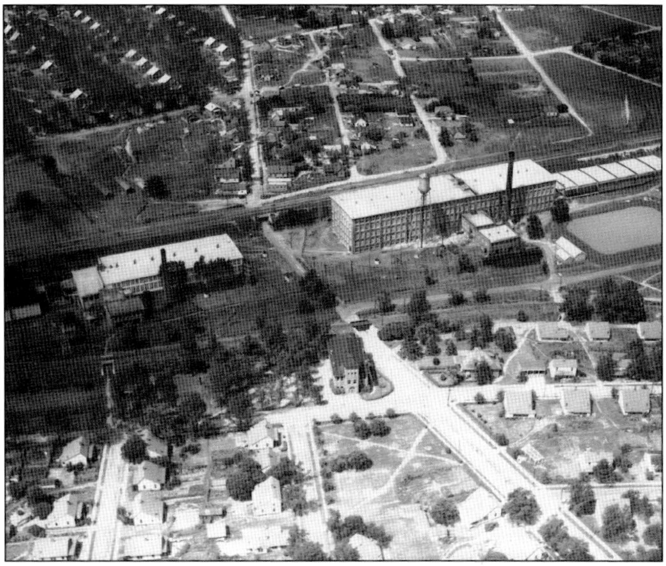

**American Spinning Village.** The town consisted of three villages built at three separate times. Seen in this William Coxe aerial are the American Spinning school and American Spinning office building in the center of the photograph. The Sampson Mill on the left was later razed, and the space was used for employee parking for the American Spinning Mill across Hammett Street. (Courtesy of the Coxe Collection, Greenville County Historical Society.)

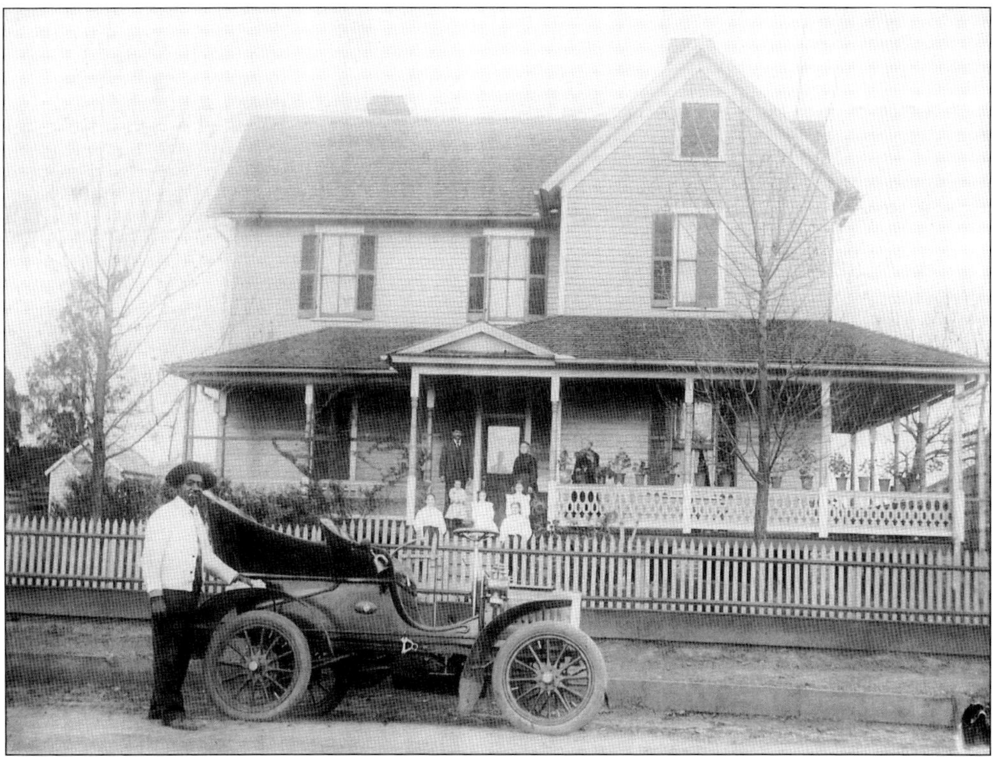

**Tom Sizemore House.** Pictured on the porch with his family at their house, located on Sizemore Street (named in his honor), Tom Sizemore became superintendent of the American Spinning Company in 1898. This c. 1910 photograph shows the family's Oldsmobile parked out front. (Courtesy of the Robert H. Duke Collection, Greenville County Library System.)

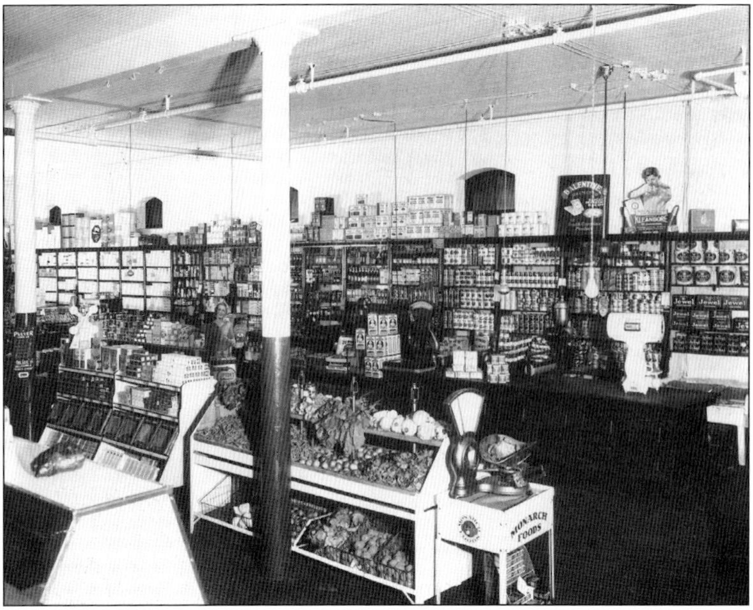


**Inside the Poe Mill Store.** Built before 1900, the store provided the village with staple items, canned goods, toiletries, and toys. Local companies such as Balentine's supplied meats and Monarch Foods provided fresh produce. (Courtesy of the Coxe Collection, Greenville County Historical Society.)

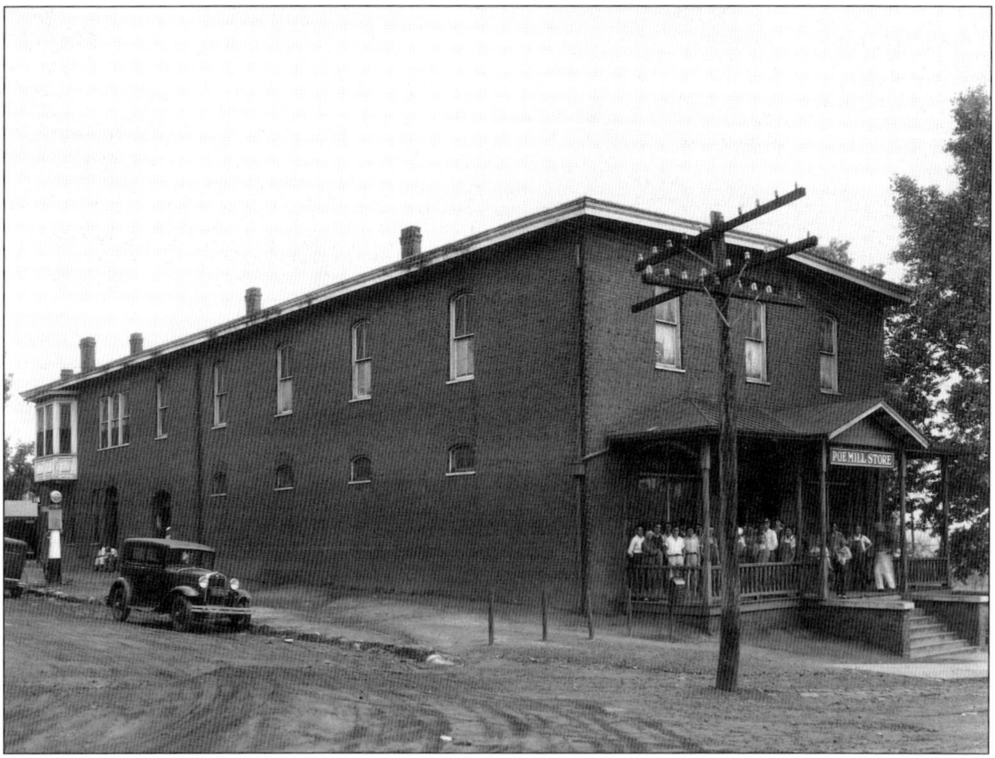


**Poe Mill Store.** The building consisted of two stories and a basement. General mercantile was operated on the first floor and basement, and the second floor provided meeting space for social clubs. The company office was also located in the building. In April 1945, when Pres. Franklin D. Roosevelt's body passed through Greenville by train, the store closed, and a wreath was hung in observance. Hundreds of Poe Mill residents stood on Buncombe Road to watch the train pass. (Courtesy of the Coxe Collection, Greenville County Historical Society.)

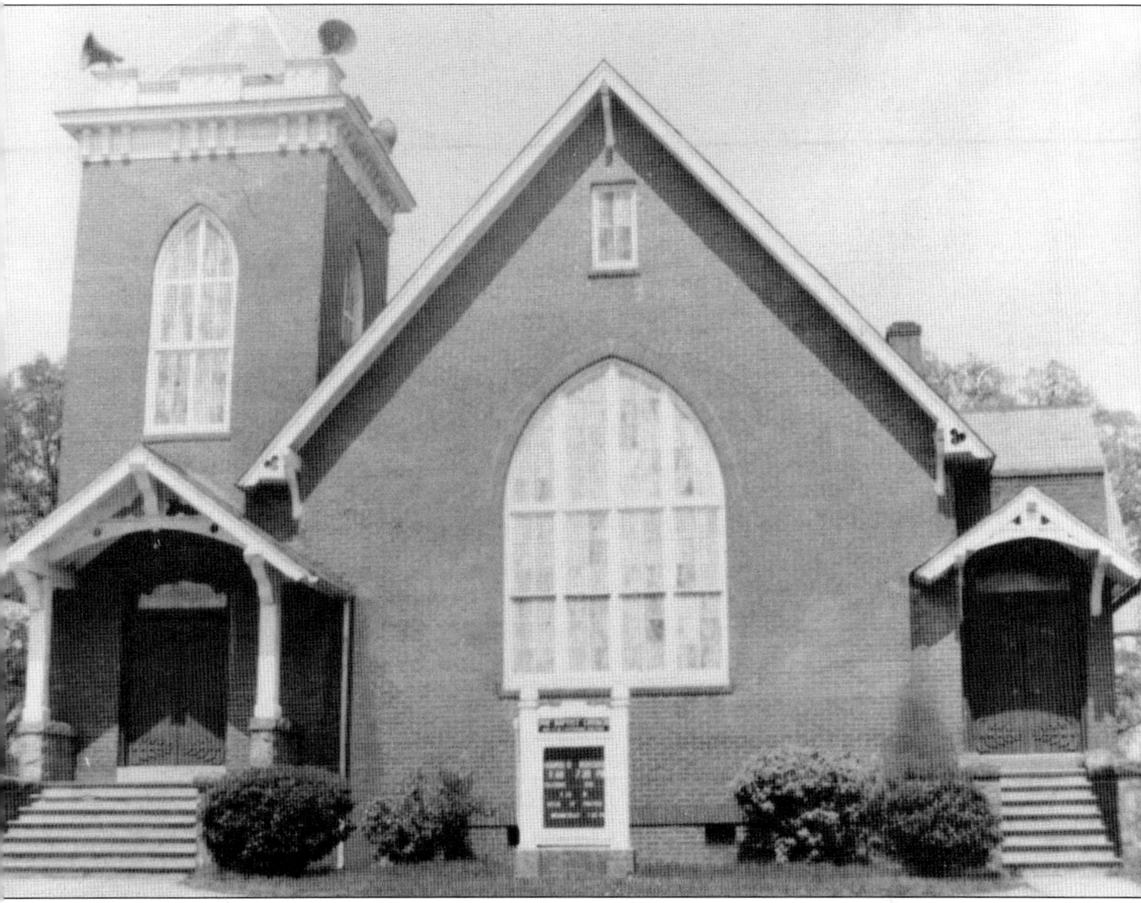

**Poe Baptist Church.** Organized in 1903, this sanctuary was built in 1924. In 1929, with the onset of strikes in textile mills throughout the South, Poe Baptist's Preacher Anderson sided with the mill operatives instead of his salary-paying management. As a result, he was locked out of the church. When he began to preach from the porch of his mill home he was evicted, and a new minister was hired in his place. (Courtesy of the Poe Historical Group Collection, Greenville County Library System.)

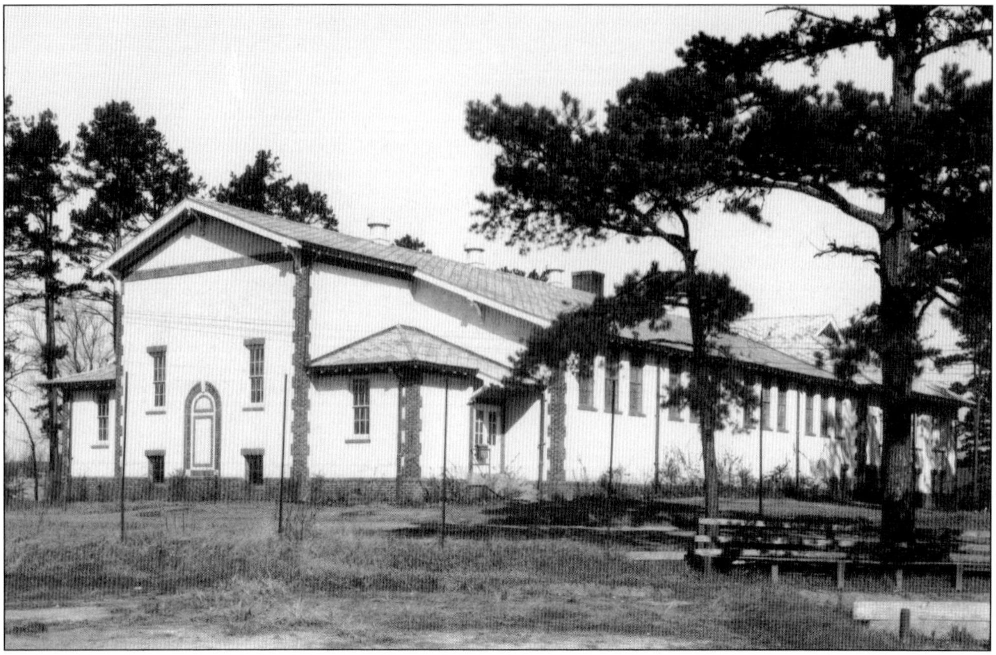

**Monaghan Mill YMCA.** Designed within the original layout of the Monaghan Mill village, it was the first industrial YMCA in the South, costing $18,000. I.E. Umger, a former missionary to China, was named its first director. Umger left in 1905, making assistant L.P. Hollis, director. Under Hollis, the YMCA became a recruiting tool for Monaghan and served as the center of the community. It offered many programs to the village residents, including Bible study, athletics, adult education, dramatic productions, and health talks. The building burned in 1927 and was replaced with the building seen here. (Courtesy of the Coxe Collection, Greenville County Historical Society.)

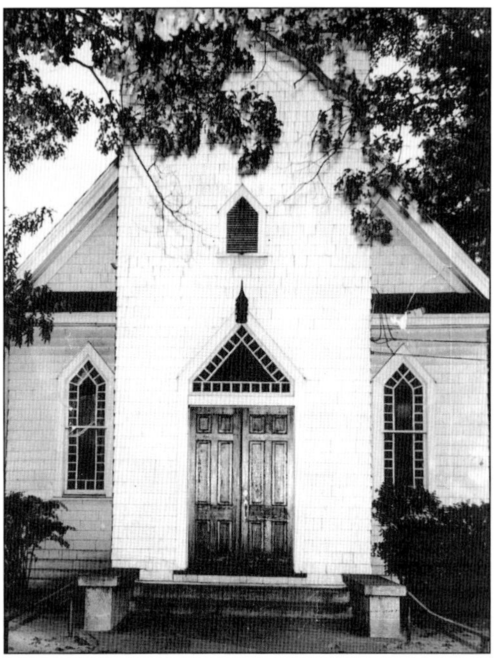

**Monaghan Presbyterian Church.** Monaghan Village originally had a union church with denominations alternating Sunday worship services. Soon after, Baptists, Methodists, and Presbyterians built their own wooden churches, as seen here. (Courtesy of the Monaghan Historical Society Collection, Greenville County Library System.)

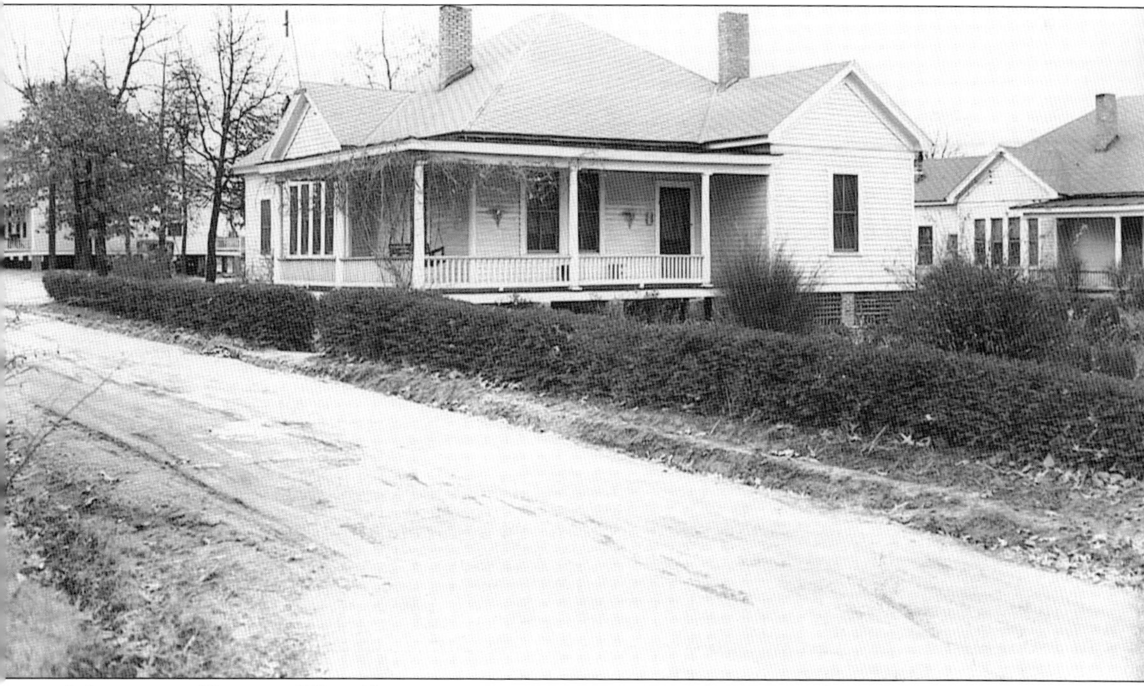

**MONAGHAN VILLAGE, WEST PARKER AND SPEED STREETS.** In the 1920s, a four-room house rented for 85¢ a week, while a five-room rented for $1.10 a week. The mill provided water and electricity at no charge. Civic leaders used Monaghan Village as a model for visitors looking to invest in Greenville. In 1948, new owner J.P. Stevens and Company sold the village houses to operatives at prices ranging from $2,300 to $5,000, with total sales topping $100,000. (Courtesy of the Monaghan Historical Society Collection, Greenville County Library System.)

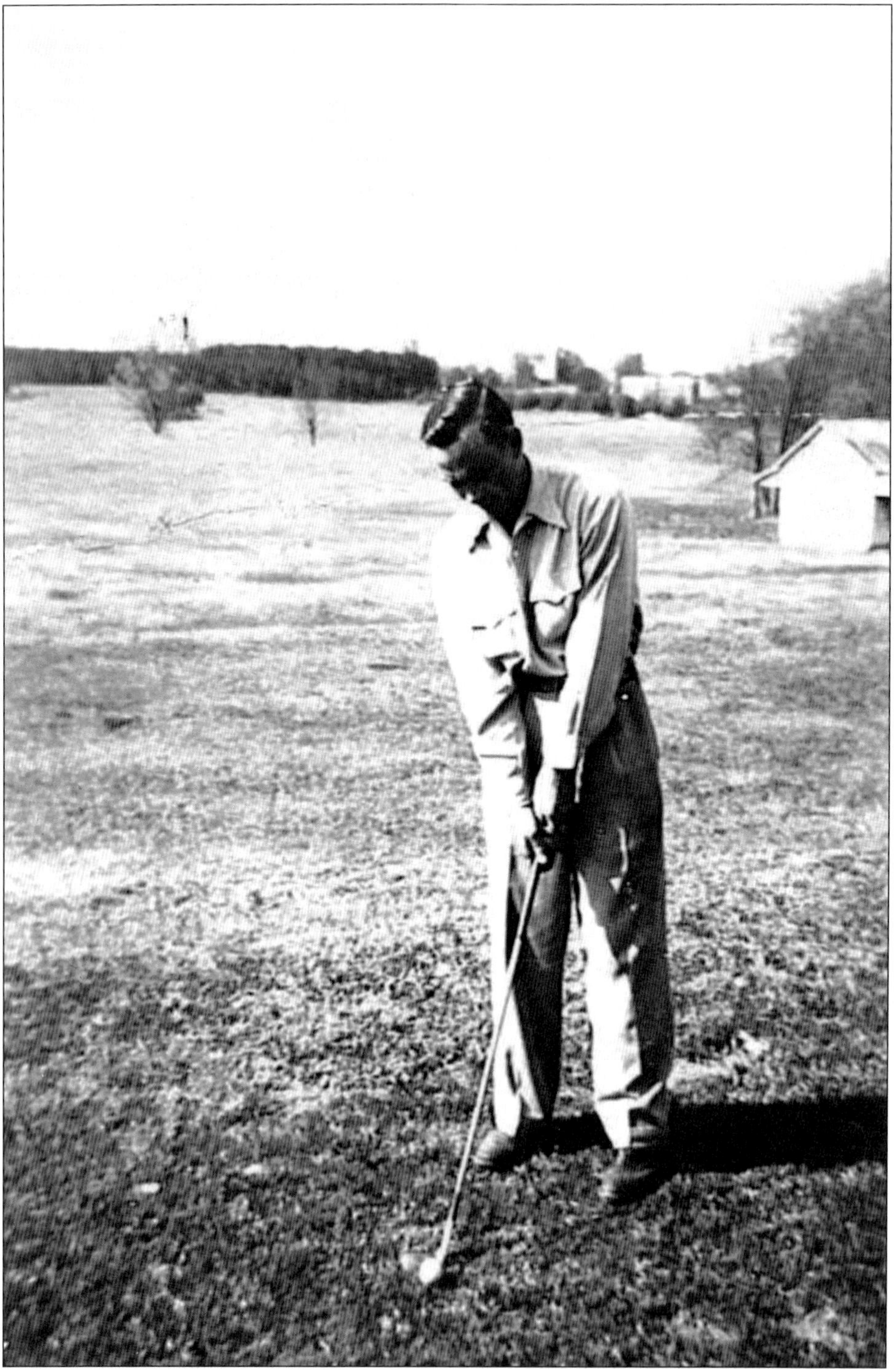

MONAGHAN GOLF COURSE. Ike Murray is seen in this 1955 photograph playing golf on the Monaghan nine-hole golf course. The course was laid out on the mill pasture, and Monaview Elementary is located on the land today. (Courtesy of the Monaghan Historical Society Collection, Greenville County Library System.)

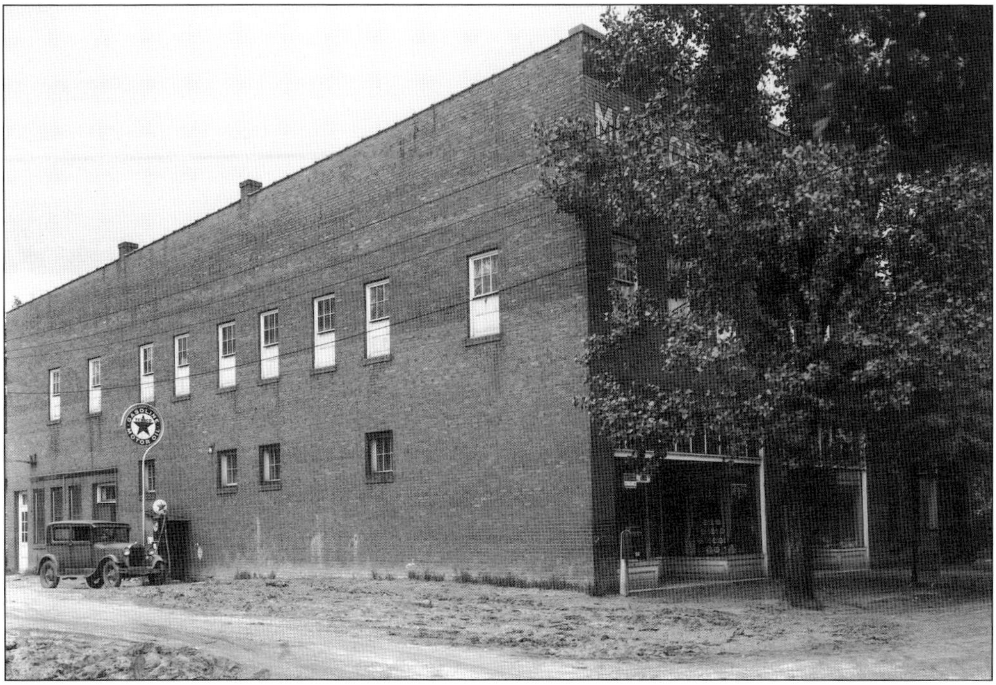

**Monaghan Mill Store.** The two-story brick building sold just about anything one would need. Texaco gasoline could be purchased along with household supplies, such as rakes, mops, brooms, soaps, and detergents. A National Recovery Administration (NRA) member sign can be seen in the rear of the store. The NRA was a New Deal agency established by the Franklin D. Roosevelt administration to bring labor, government, and industry together to form fair practices. The hardest challenge the NRA had to deal with was the General Textile Strike of 1934. (Both, courtesy of the Coxe Collection, Greenville County Historical Society.)

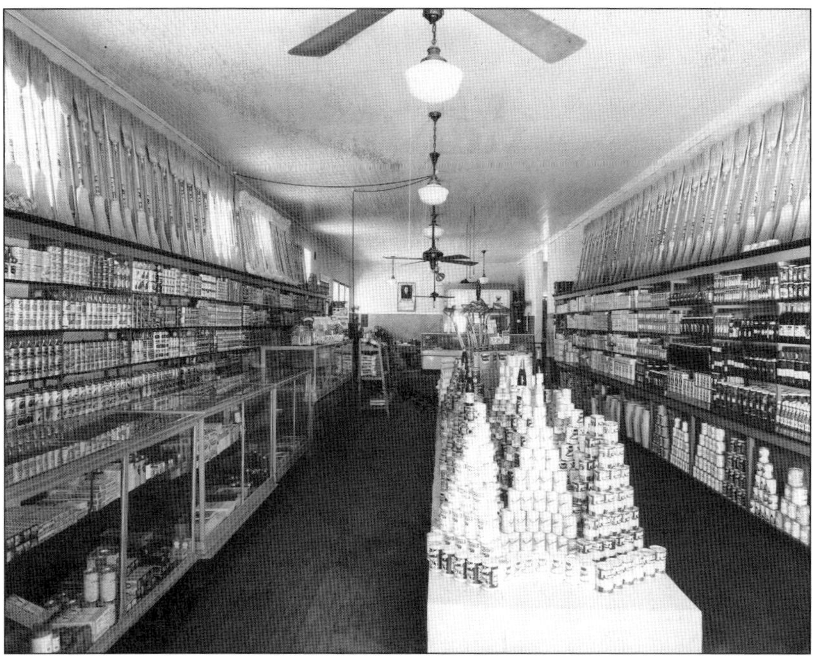

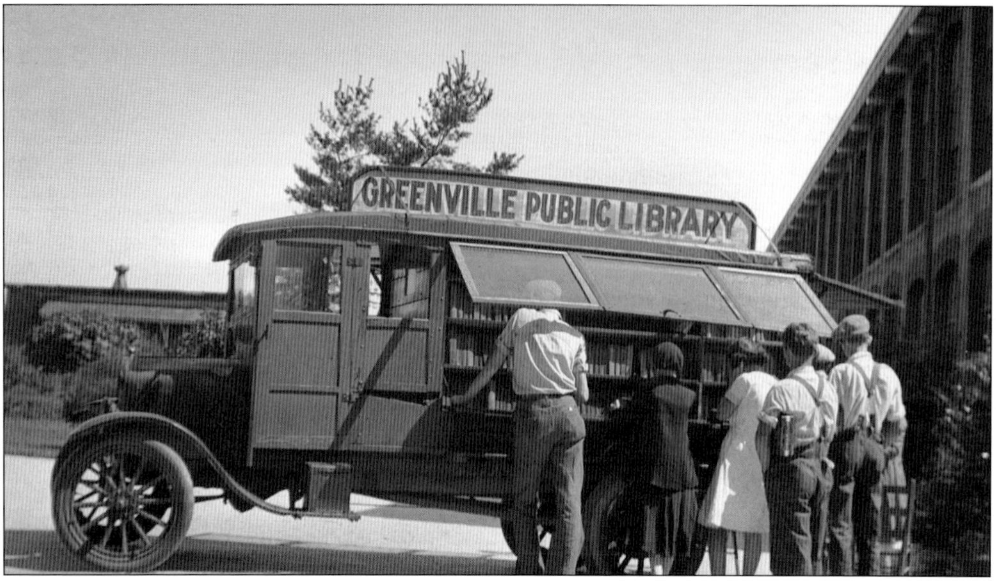


**Monaghan Mill Book Stop.** In 1923, the Greenville County Public Library converted a Ford truck to a bookmobile and named it "the Pathfinder." It began service to the textile-mill communities within the Parker District in September of that year. (Courtesy of the Greenville County Library System.)

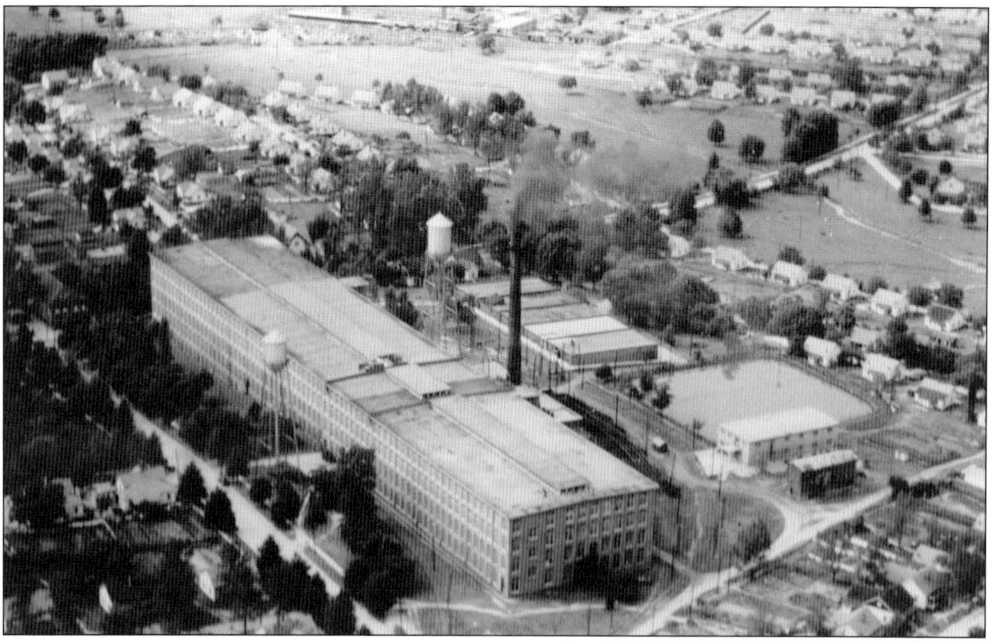

**Woodside Village.** The mill and village were designed by Joseph E. Sirrine on 220.25 acres situated between Brandon and Monaghan Mills. The village included a three-teacher schoolhouse, company store, and union church used by the Baptist and Methodist congregations on alternating Sundays. In the following years, a YMCA, swimming pool, zoo, baseball field, tennis courts, and other schools were added. In July 1950, the village voted 63-6 to incorporate as a town with a mayor and police chief serving with minimal salaries. The village was placed in the National Register of Historic Places in 1987. (Courtesy of the Coxe Collection, Greenville County Historical Society.)

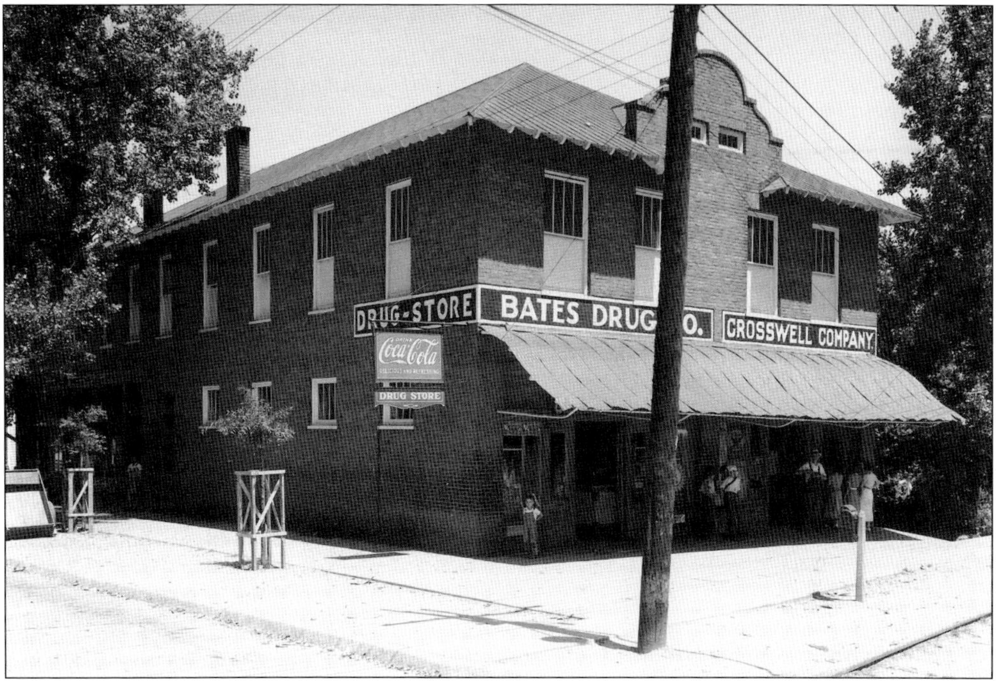


**CROSWELL BROTHERS.** Along with other textile companies, Woodside provided its villages with a company store where employees could purchase goods. However, in the case of their West Greenville Village, Woodside owned the building but leased the space to the three Croswell brothers to own and operate the mercantile store alongside Bates Drug Company. The two-story 8,400-square-foot building was erected by Woodside in 1905 and stood until the mid-1960s. (Courtesy of the Coxe Collection, Greenville County Historical Society.)

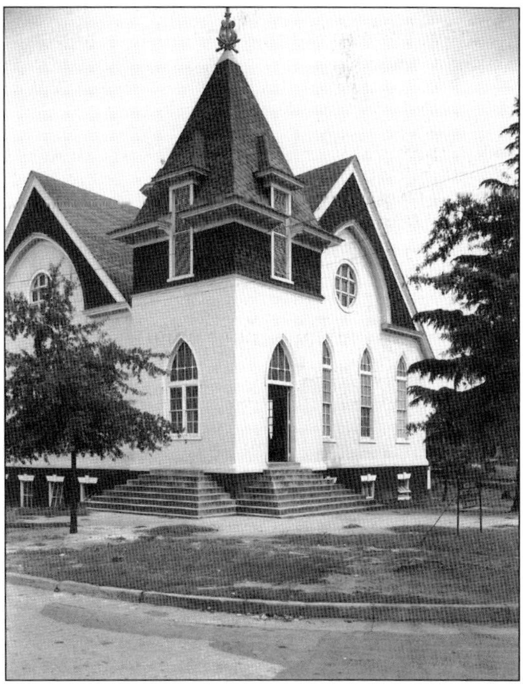

**WOODSIDE BAPTIST CHURCH.** Designed by Joseph E. Sirrine and built in 1910, the church was constructed at a cost of $21,000. The church burned after the first service and was rebuilt. One entrance was also enclosed, as seen in this photograph. In 1961, the congregation built a new, larger sanctuary. (Courtesy of the Coxe Collection, Greenville County Historical Society.)

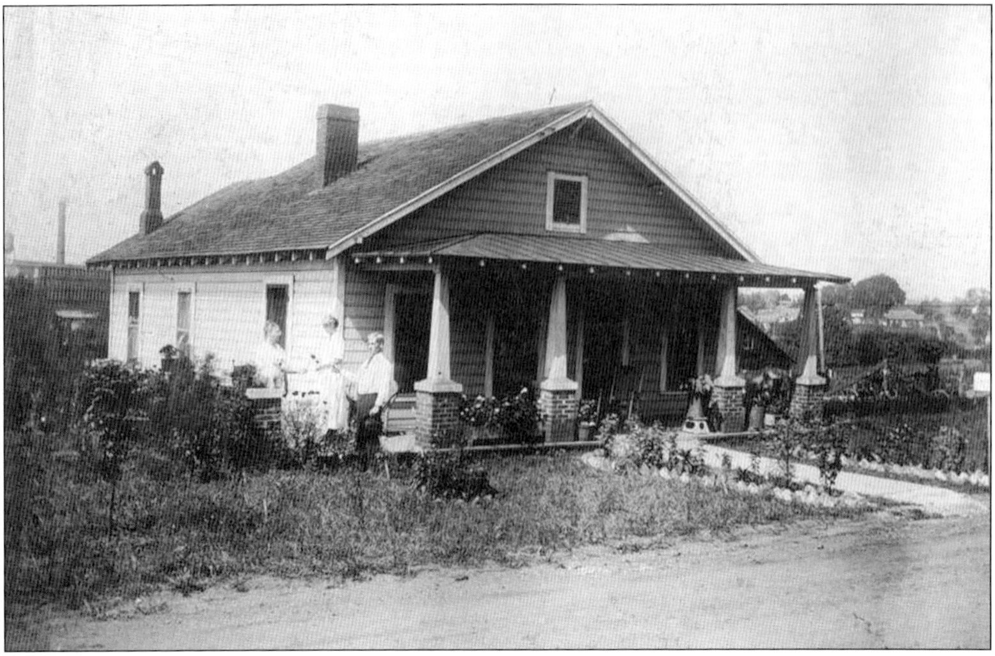

**Woodside Village.** Construction of the homes began in 1902, with additional homes being built over the following 22 years. In all, a total of 442 homes were built using 11 different floor plans. The company rented the homes at a rate of 25¢ to 50¢ per room per week. In the early 1950s, Woodside sold the homes to the public. (Courtesy of the Greenville County Library System.)

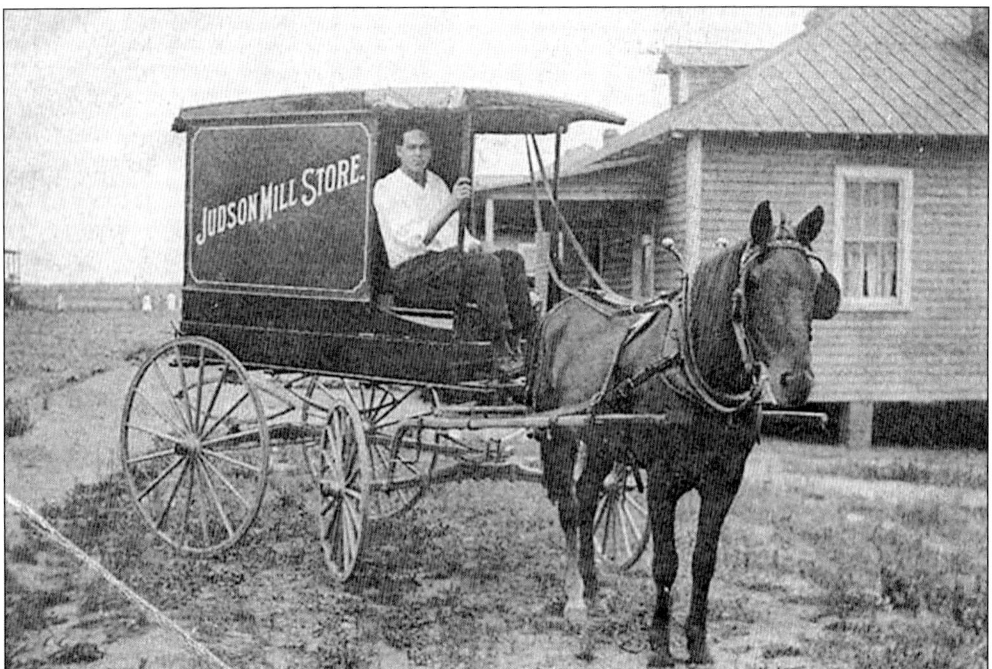


**Judson Mill Store Wagon.** This horse-drawn wagon is seen making deliveries in the Judson community. Judson Village was constructed in 1912 with 75 millhouses, built at a cost of $500 each. (Courtesy of the Greenville County Library System.)

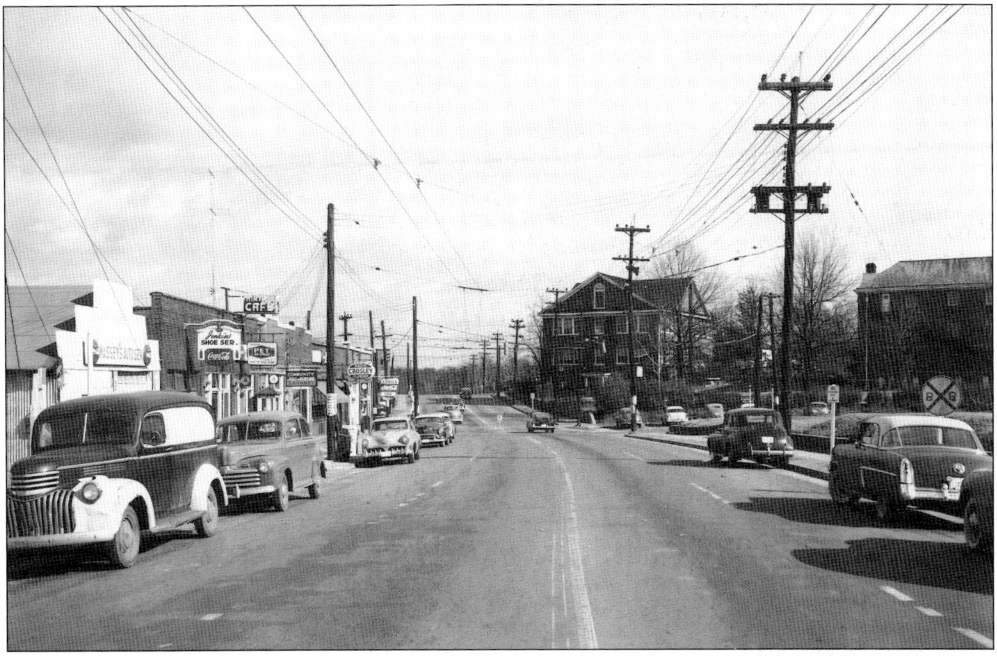


**JUDSON CROSSING.** The intersection of Easley Bridge Road and Third Avenue was the business district for the Judson Village. Stores lined the street, including Massey's Auto Service, Jenkins Shoe Service, Hinton's Café, Community Laundry, Crosley Radio and Television, and Dacus Brothers Drug Store. (Courtesy of the Coxe Collection, Greenville County Historical Society.)

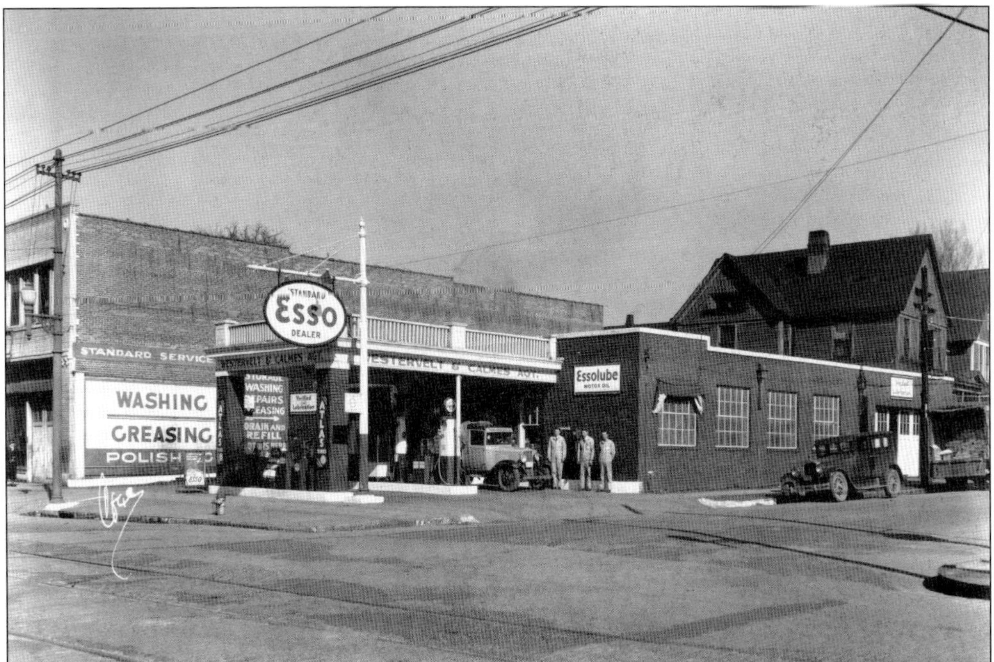


**WESTERVELT AND CALMES ESSO STATION.** At this full-service filling station in Judson, attendants and mechanics offered automotive service, cleaning, and repair. The station was also an Atlas Tire distributor. (Courtesy of the Coxe Collection, Greenville County Historical Society.)

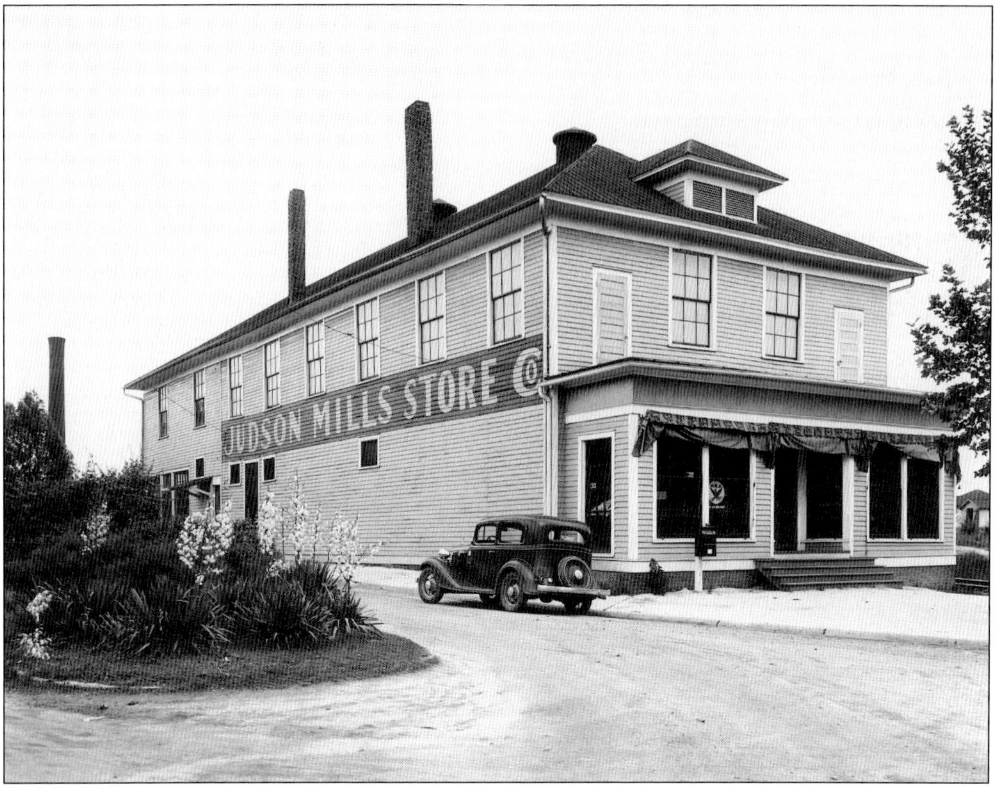


**JUDSON MILL STORE.** Before 1930, many mill operatives received an envelope, instead of a paycheck, listing their wages and deductions for rent, utilities, and purchases at the company store. If the deductions did not erase all earnings, workers would then receive tokens for use at the company store. If they did use up all of their earnings, their pay envelope would simply contain a sheet with a written squiggle that was known as "drawing the worm." (Courtesy of the Coxe Collection, Greenville County Historical Society.)

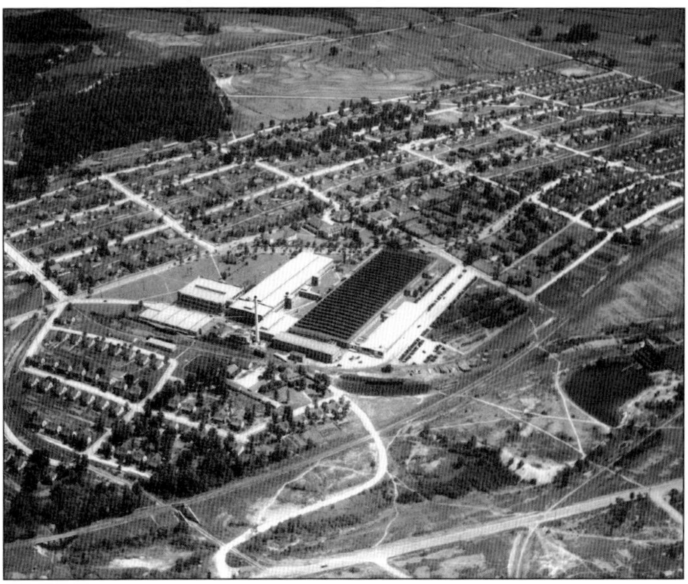

**DUNEAN VILLAGE.** Dunean was a 180-house village with a curving main street. The streets were named after directors of the plant. The six overseers' houses were located on the first block of Smyth Street. (Courtesy of the Coxe Collection, Greenville County Historical Society.)

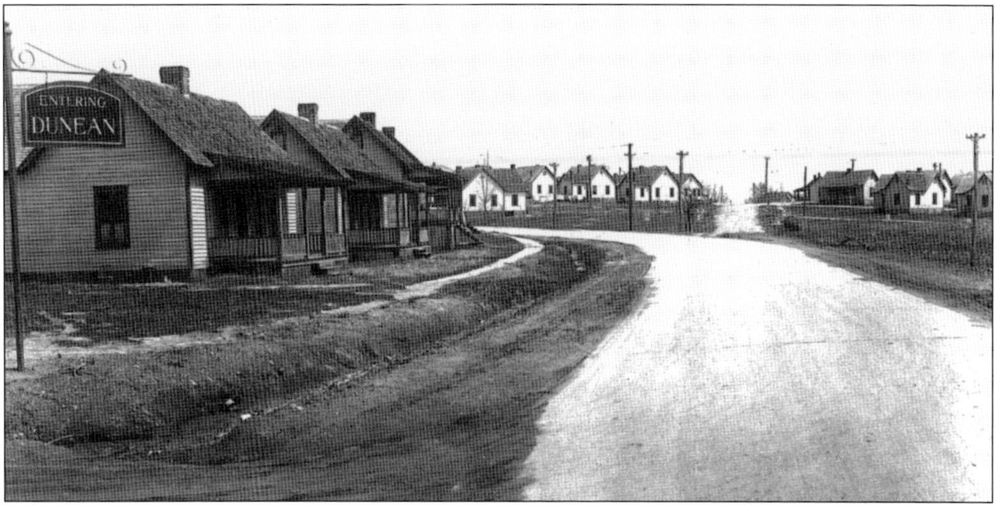


**Dunean Village, Allen Street at Atlanta Highway.** Three different housing styles alternated on relatively large lots. Sewer, water, and electricity were provided by the mill at no charge. Although housing was free, by the 1920s, a surcharge of 25¢ per room a week was created to subsidize police protection and maintenance. (Courtesy of the Coxe Collection, Greenville County Historical Society.)

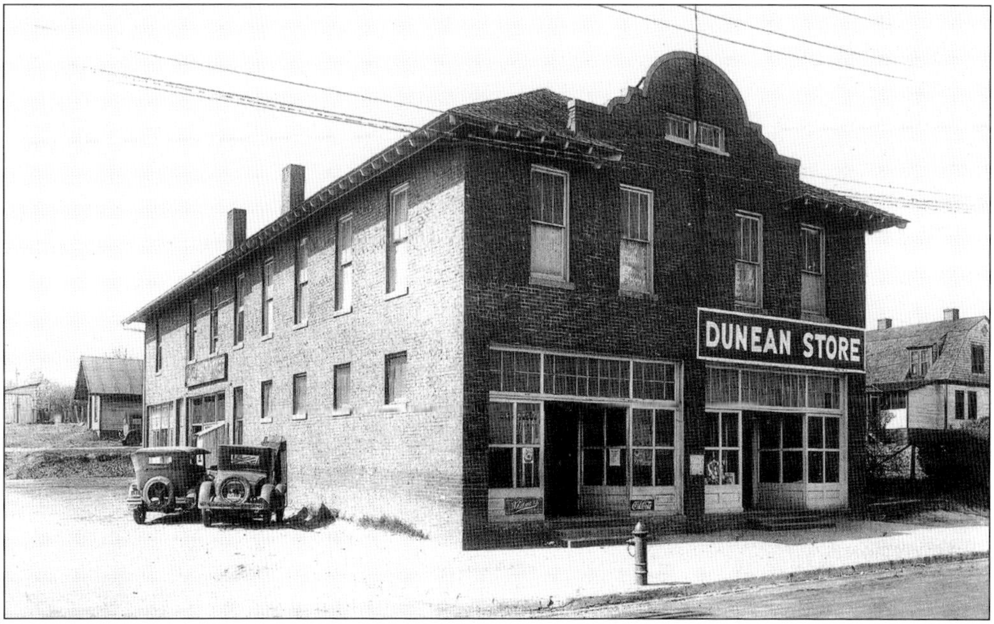


**Dunean Store.** The community store was run for many years by the firm of Rice and Cleveland. Essential goods were sold on a cost-plus basis, but nonessentials such as tobacco and sodas were sold at an exorbitant rate. Dunean-produced fabrics could also be purchased, and all items could be bought with a coupon book. The building was the center of community life due to the second floor's use as an all-purpose meeting room. In 1912, the Methodist and Baptist churches were organized in the meeting room. It was there that they alternated Sundays for conducting worship while holding a combined weekly Sunday school class. In addition to holding religious services, the meeting room was also used for the Dunean School in 1913, with an enrollment of 147 pupils. (Courtesy of the Coxe Collection, Greenville County Historical Society.)

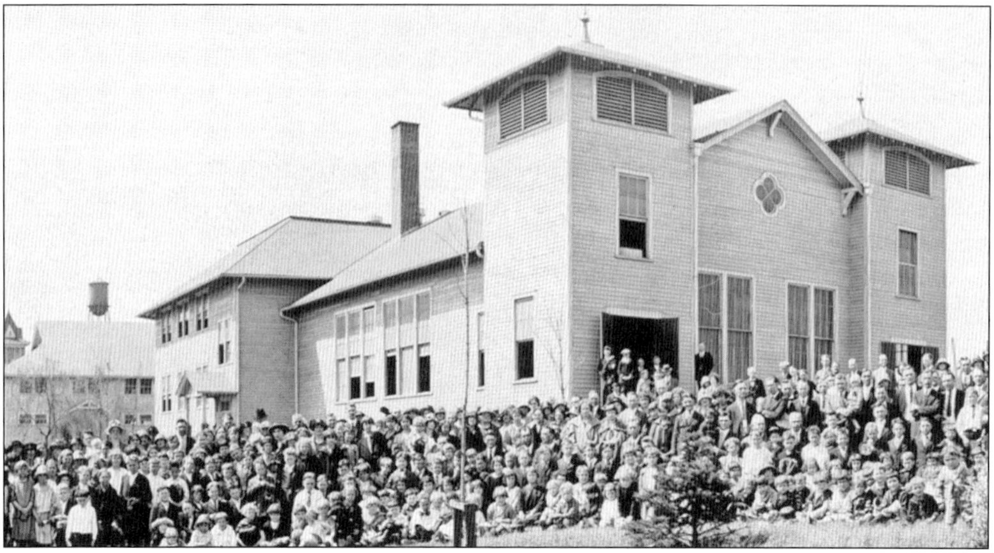

**Dunean Baptist Church.** On November 17, 1912, some 18 men and women met at the second-floor meeting room at the Dunean Company Store and organized the Dunean Baptist Church, naming G.B. Lee as pastor. Baptisms were performed at nearby Brushy Creek. Originally constructed as a wooden clapboard building, the sanctuary was later enlarged by removing the two towers, adding a four-columned front with a steeple, and bricking the entire façade. (Courtesy of the J.P. Stevens-Clemson Collection, Greenville County Library System.)

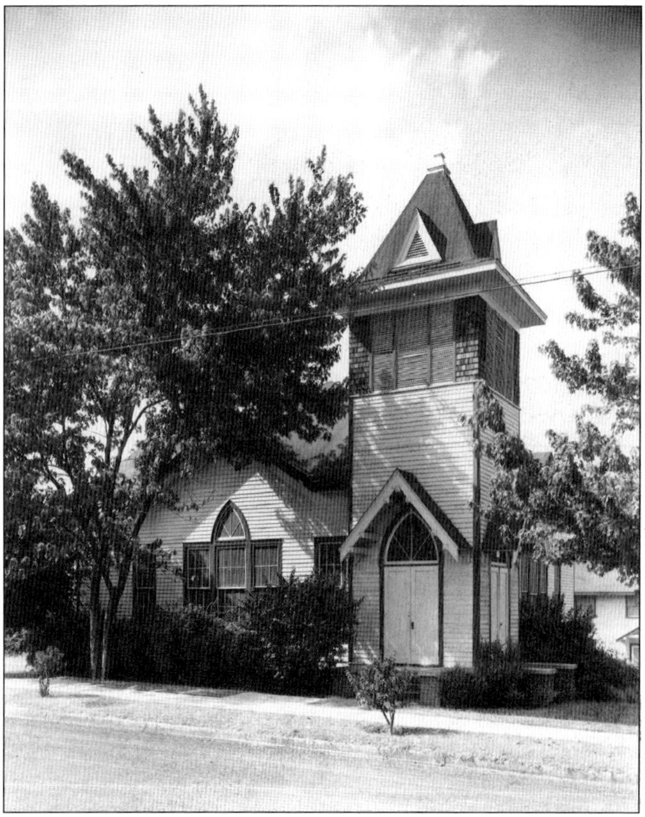

**Dunean United Methodist Church.** Soon after the Baptist congregation was organized, the Methodist Church at Dunean was formed. The church was built in 1918, as seen here. Later, the church was bricked, and the hip and gable roof was removed for a Gothic facade. (Courtesy of the Coxe Collection, Greenville County Historical Society.)

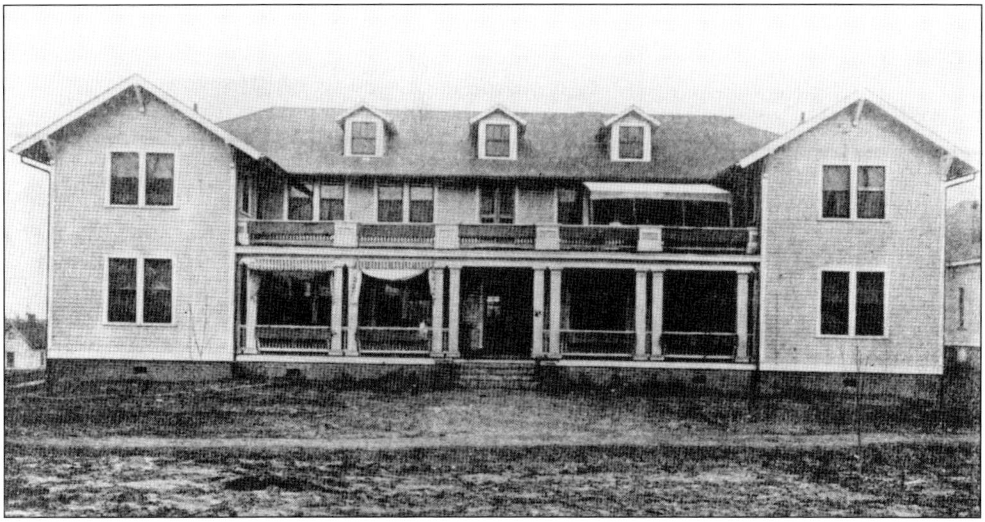

**DUNEAN GUESTHOUSE.** Located on the square across from the mill, it was originally constructed in 1919 as a YMCA, the first at a South Carolina textile mill. The two-story structure had large activity rooms on the first floor and living quarters on the second. Programs held at the building included sewing, gymnastics, and community nights featuring movies and reading. A resident nurse was on site, as was two resident secretaries. (Courtesy of the Coxe Collection, Greenville County Historical Society.)

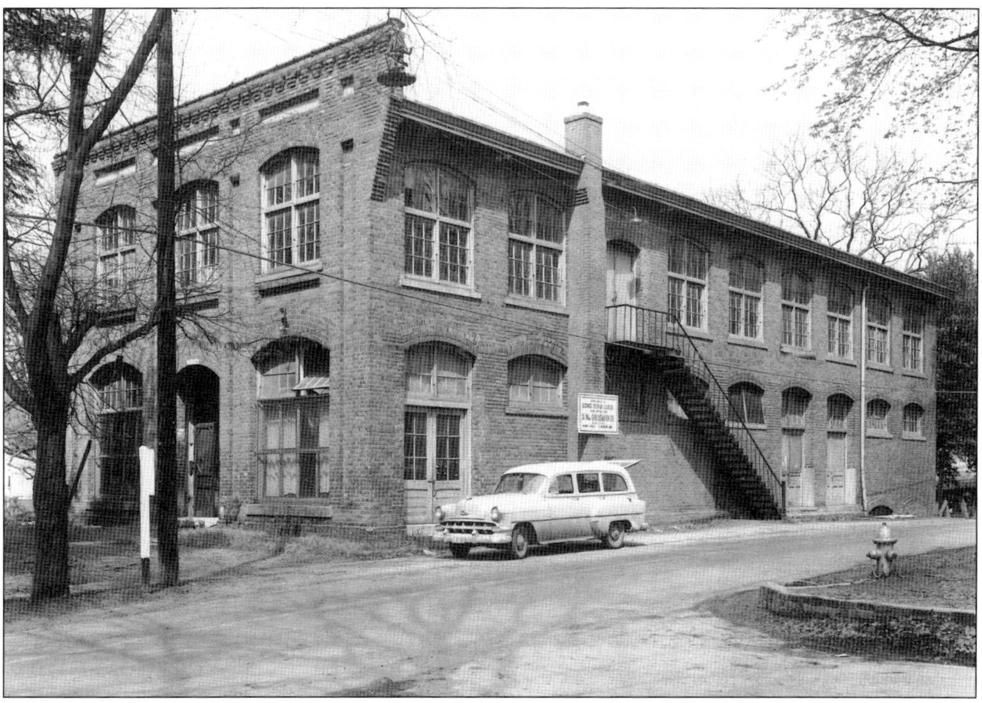

**MILLS MILL COMMUNITY BUILDING.** Designed by Joseph E. Sirrine in 1902 and completed in 1903, the community building was located on Guess Street. Although it was designated as a YMCA on the village plan, it was used as the company store until 1913. It simultaneously served as a YMCA and union church, used on alternate weeks by Baptist and Methodist congregations. (Courtesy of the Coxe Collection, Greenville County Historical Society.)

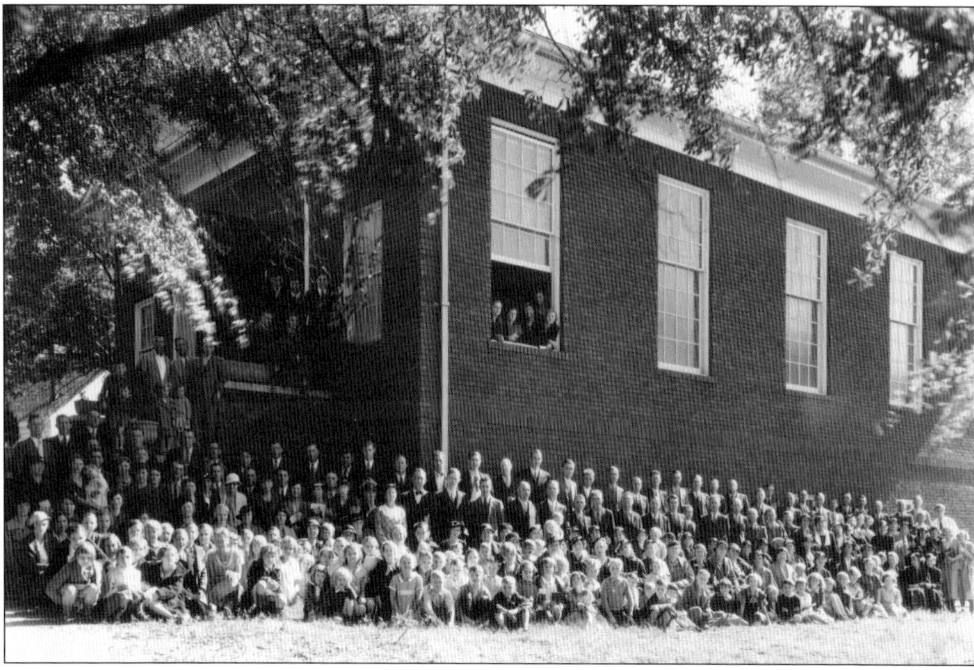

**Mills Mill Baptist Church.** By 1919, the Baptist congregation had built its own church on Green Avenue. It was originally named Mills Mill Baptist, but the name was changed to Emanuel Baptist in the 1920s. (Courtesy of the Coxe Collection, Greenville County Historical Society.)

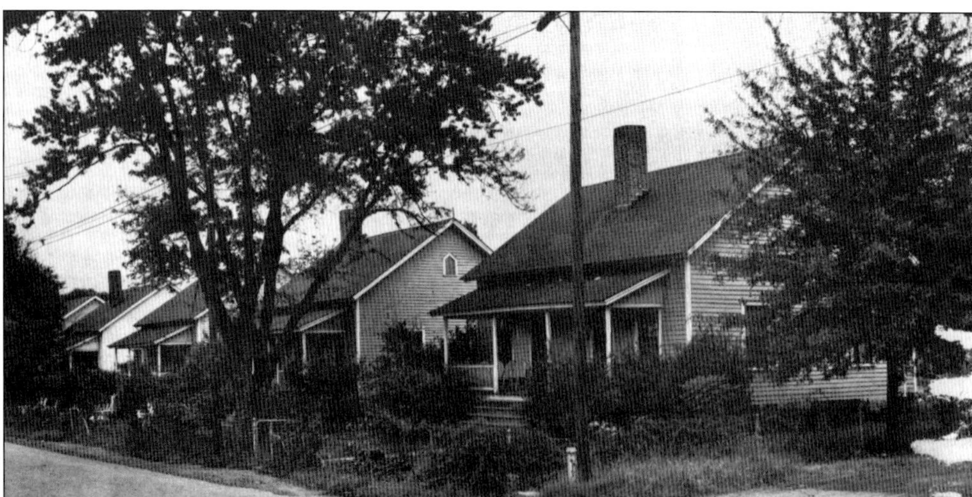

**Union Bleachery Village.** Houses line Arrington Avenue, named for mill president John White Arrington. The village had easy access to water since artesian wells were sunken between houses. Union Bleachery constantly maintained the village, as well as added more houses through the decades. Graded streets, new paint, and landscaping were a common practice, and streetlights were added in the 1920s, illuminated by power generated at the plant. Cone Mills sold off the houses in 1959. (Courtesy of the Union Bleachery Historical Society Collection, Greenville County Library System.)

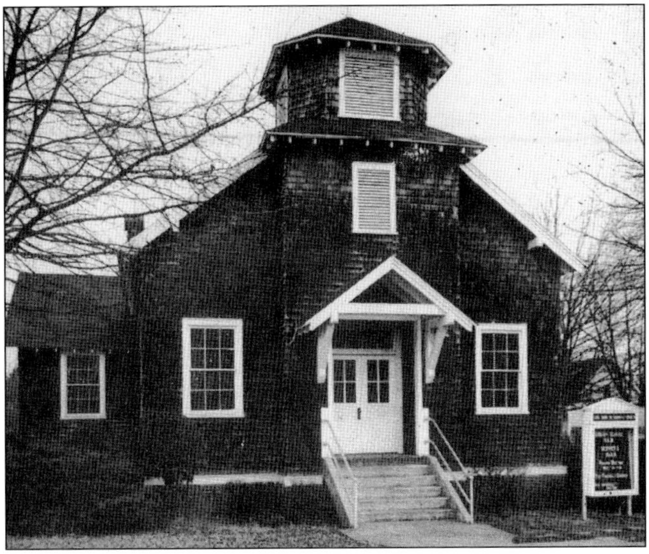

**St. John Methodist Church.** In 1910, Dr. Louis Mulligan organized the Methodist Church in Union Bleachery and chose its name as a nod to the mill's president, John W. Arrington. In 1934, the first sanctuary was built; it a wood-shingled structure with a short octagonal steeple over the front entrance. The church was later renamed Arrington United Methodist Church. (Courtesy of the Union Bleachery Historical Society Collection, Greenville County Library System.)

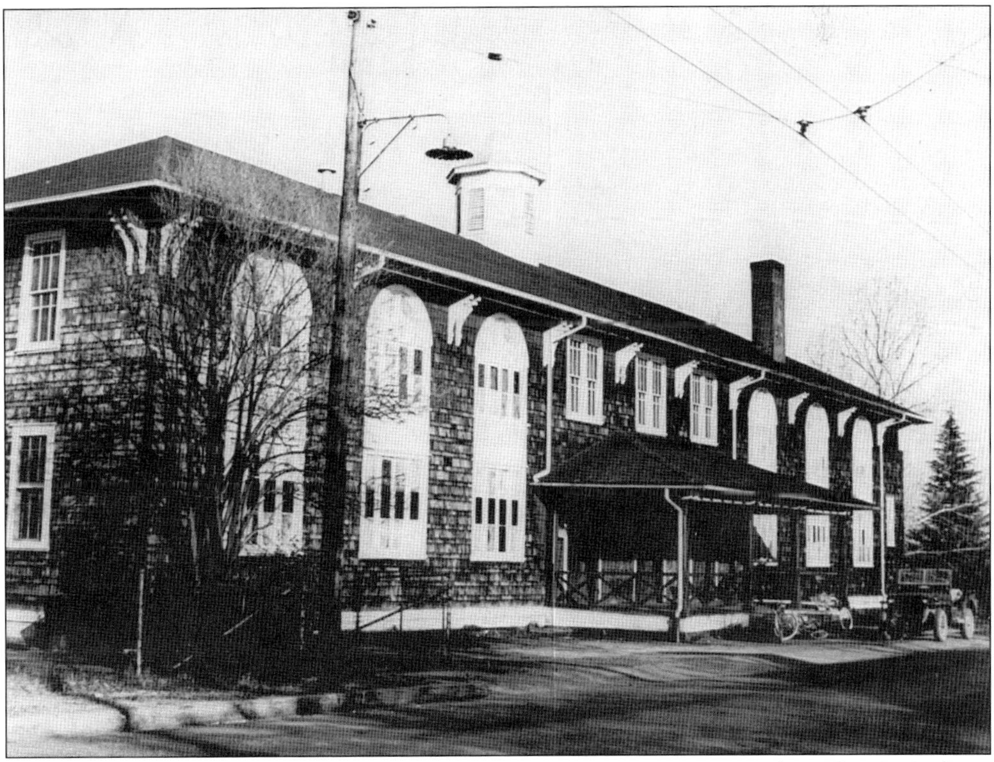

**Union Bleachery Community Building.** By 1923, J.W. Arrington's sons John White Jr., Nelson, and Richard were already working for the company. One goal they had was to improve village life. In order to accomplish this, they hired Clemson University architecture department chair Rudolf E. Lee to design a community building. The $27,000 project included a modern kitchen, meeting rooms, and gymnasium where movies were shown on Saturday evenings and Christmas celebrations were held every December. Children always wondered how Santa, actually mill night watchman Choice Rector, knew each of their names. (Courtesy of the Union Bleachery Historical Society Collection, Greenville County Library System.)

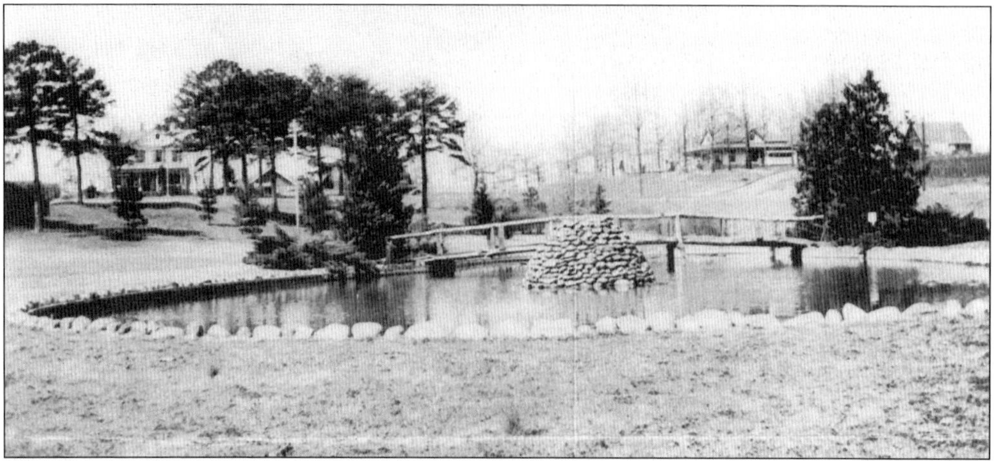

**UNION BLEACHERY FISHPOND.** The company continually encouraged landscaping and maintenance of the grounds around the mill and village. It built an incredible baseball field, a nine-hole golf course, community gardens, and a fishpond complete with an ornamental footbridge located within the village park. The pond was later filled in under the ownership of Cone Mills Corporation. (Courtesy of the Union Bleachery Historical Society Collection, Greenville County Library System.)

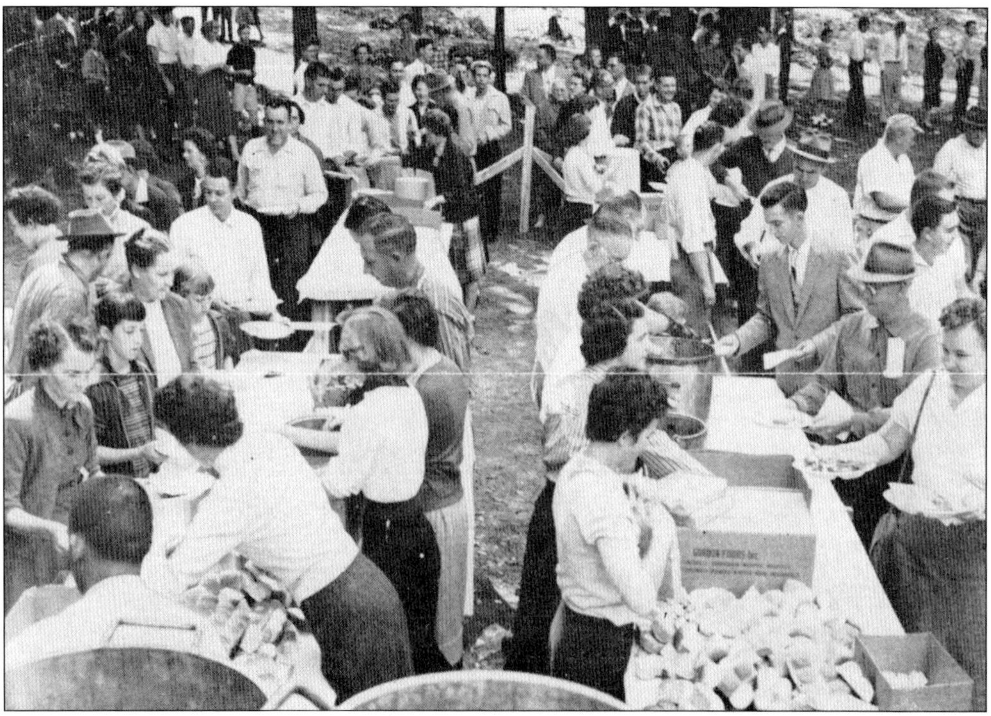

**UNION BLEACHERY ANNUAL BARBECUE.** In 1923, the mill began holding an annual barbecue for all workers and their families. First held at Dukeland Park, the barbecues later took place at either River Falls or Paris Mountain State Park, as seen here in the 1950s. The schedule for the day was always the same: games at 10:30 a.m., ice cream available at 11:30 a.m., meals at 1:00 p.m., and ice cream again at 2:00 p.m. (Courtesy of the Union Bleachery Historical Society Collection, Greenville County Library System.)

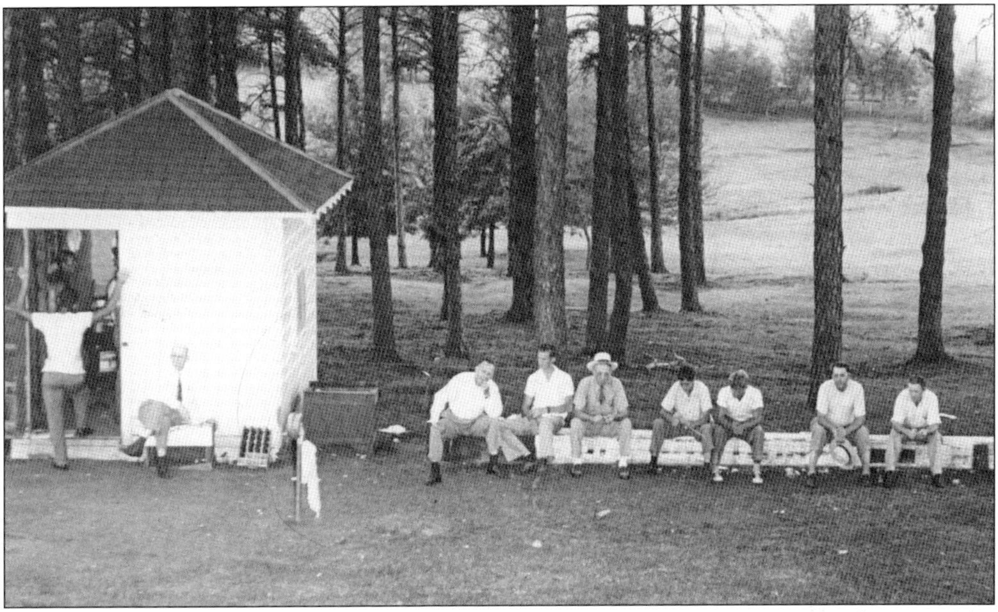

UNION BLEACHERY GOLF COURSE. The mill maintained a nine-hole golf course at the rear of the village in the pasture. All Union Bleachery employees were eligible for membership or could pay green fees. Workers took up the new sport with zest. Later, a new reservoir to supply water to the plant was built on the golf course by Cone Mills Corporation. (Courtesy of the Union Bleachery Historical Society Collection, Greenville County Library System.)

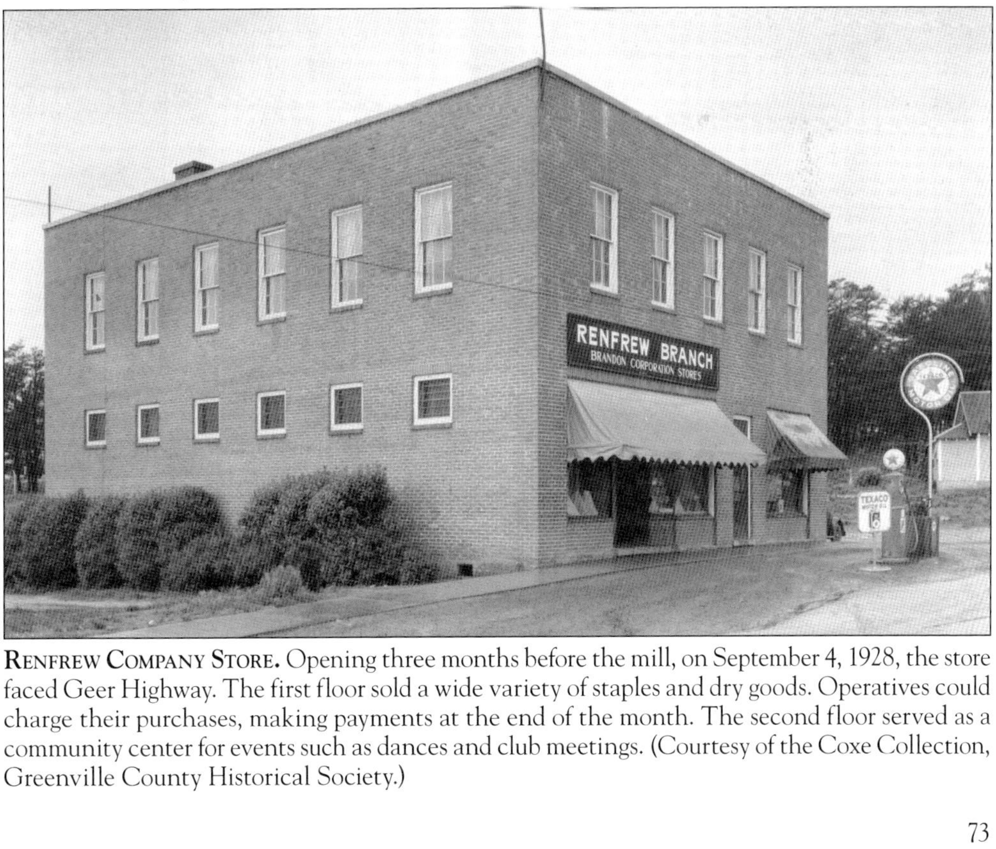


RENFREW COMPANY STORE. Opening three months before the mill, on September 4, 1928, the store faced Geer Highway. The first floor sold a wide variety of staples and dry goods. Operatives could charge their purchases, making payments at the end of the month. The second floor served as a community center for events such as dances and club meetings. (Courtesy of the Coxe Collection, Greenville County Historical Society.)

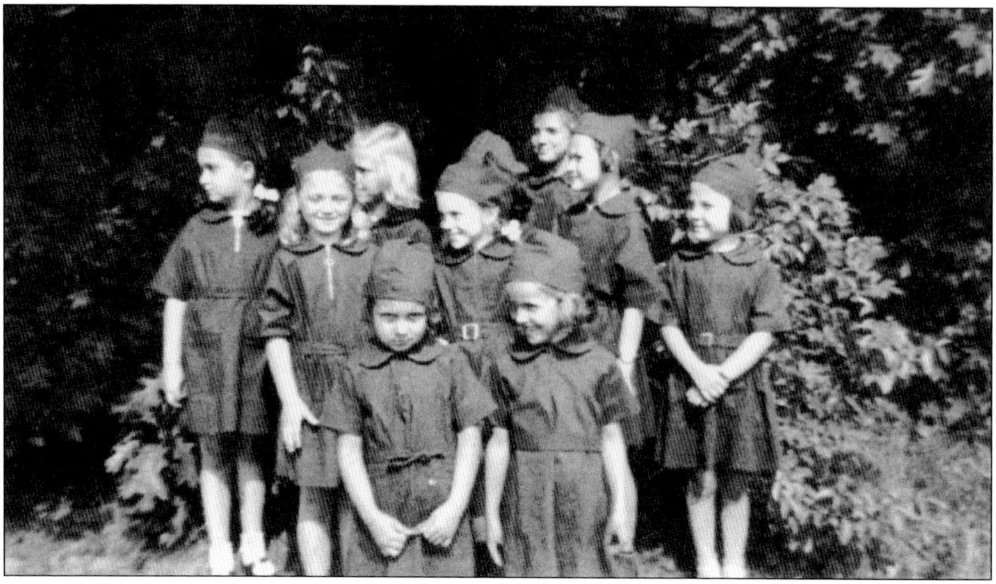

**Renfrew Brownie Scouts.** Renfrew Bleachery sponsored a troop of Girl Scout Brownies. Seen dressed in uniform are, from left to right (first row) Anne Murphy and Betty Clair Bledsoe; (second row) Nell Anderson, Ann Nuckles, Margaret Lockaby, and Peggy McDowell; (third row) Elizabeth Getaz, Barbara Worrell, and Dora Jane Murphy. (Courtesy of the Travelers Rest Historical Society Collection, Greenville County Library System.)

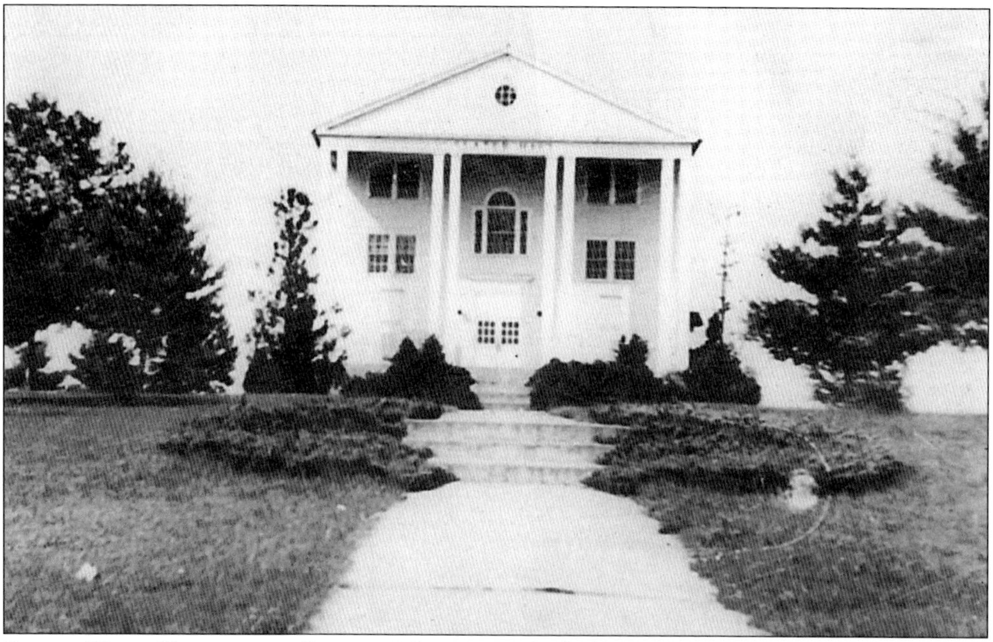

**Slater Hall Community Center.** The two-and-a-half-story white clapboard building was designed by J.E. Sirrine and Company. The main floor provided space for a gymnasium, stage, and auditorium area where the mill would host dances, holiday celebrations, and movie nights. The second and third floors provided the kitchen and meeting space for various clubs and organizations. It also was the site of the union church until separate churches were built. (Courtesy of the Slater Hall Citizens' Committee Collection, Greenville County Library System.)

**McBee Methodist Church.** Also known as McBee Chapel, an octagonal brick church, is located on Main Street in Conestee. Built in 1856, it was designed by millwright John Adams and named for the mill founder and "Father of Greenville" Vardry McBee. The church was added to the National Register of Historic Places on March 23, 1972. (Courtesy of the Landing Collection, Greenville County Historical Society.)

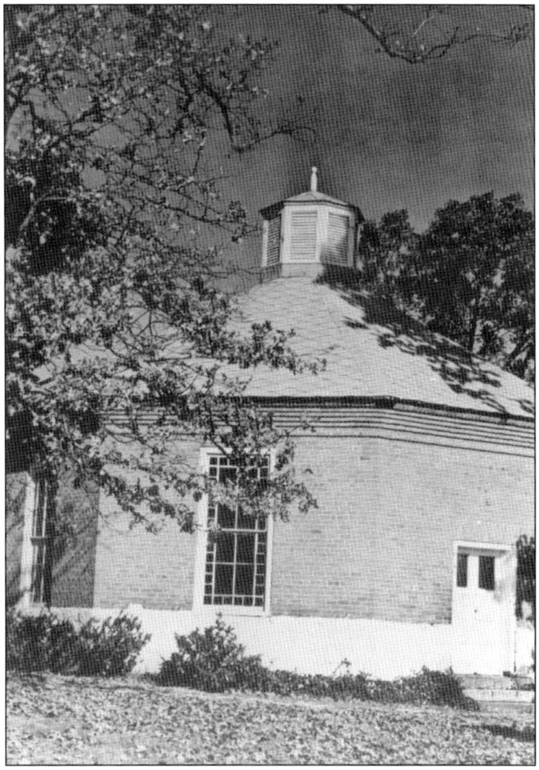

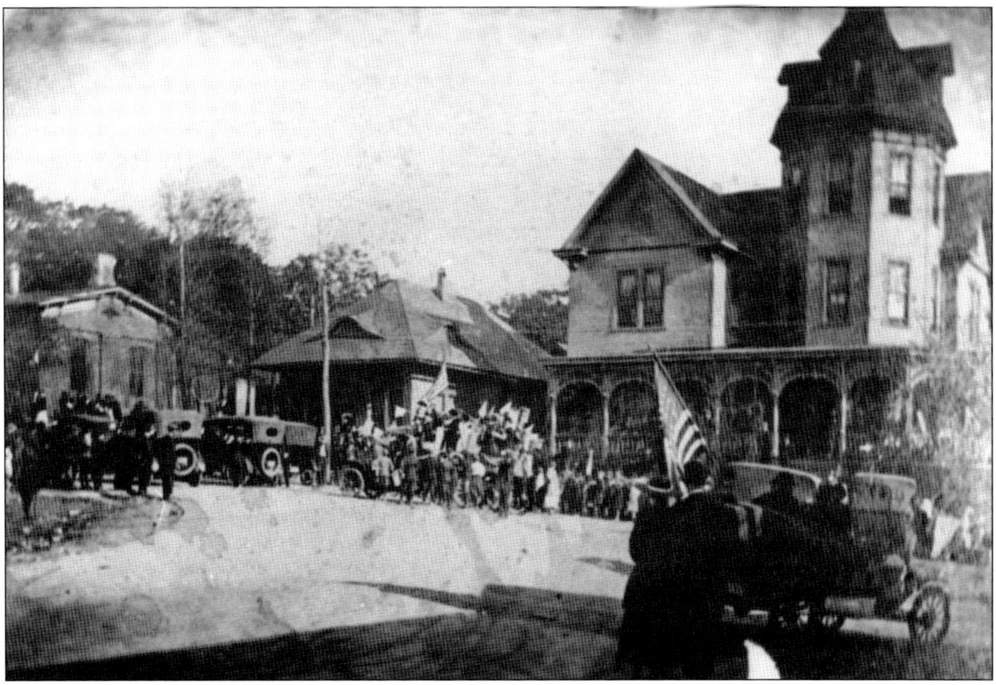

**Piedmont YMCA.** Also known as the Lyceum, the structure was erected in 1902 and served as a community building that was the hub for activity in the village. The building was destroyed by fire in 1943. (Courtesy of the Piedmont History Collection, Greenville County Library System.)

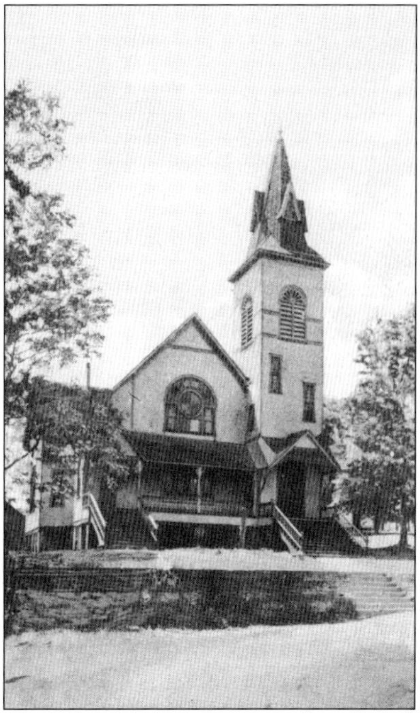

**Piedmont Methodist Church.** The Methodist Church in Piedmont was organized on November 4, 1876. The congregation met at the union church until it could afford to build their own in 1892. The church was destroyed by fire in 1933, and a brick sanctuary was built in its place. (Courtesy of the Piedmont History Collection, Greenville County Library System.)

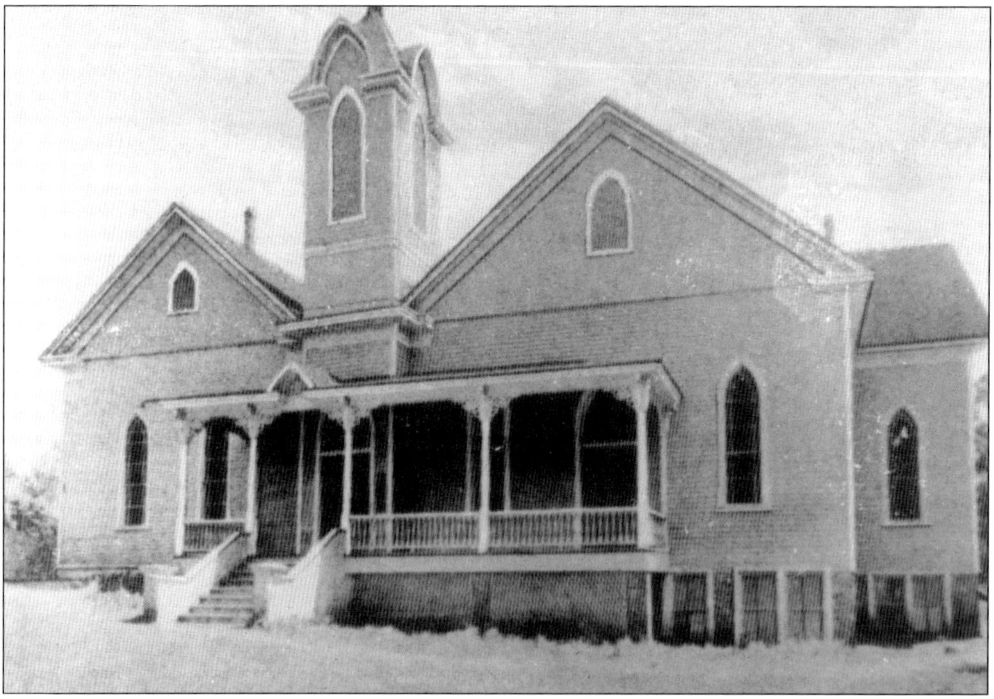

**Piedmont Baptist Church.** Piedmont Manufacturing built a union church for Baptists, Methodists, and Presbyterians to meet for worship until funds were raised for each congregation to build their own. Piedmont Baptist was organized on December 28, 1879. The first chapel, built in 1891, seen here with renovations in 1908, was located on Hotel Hill. In 1937, the congregation began to raise funds for a new church, which opened on December 5, 1941. (Courtesy of the Piedmont History Collection, Greenville County Library System.)

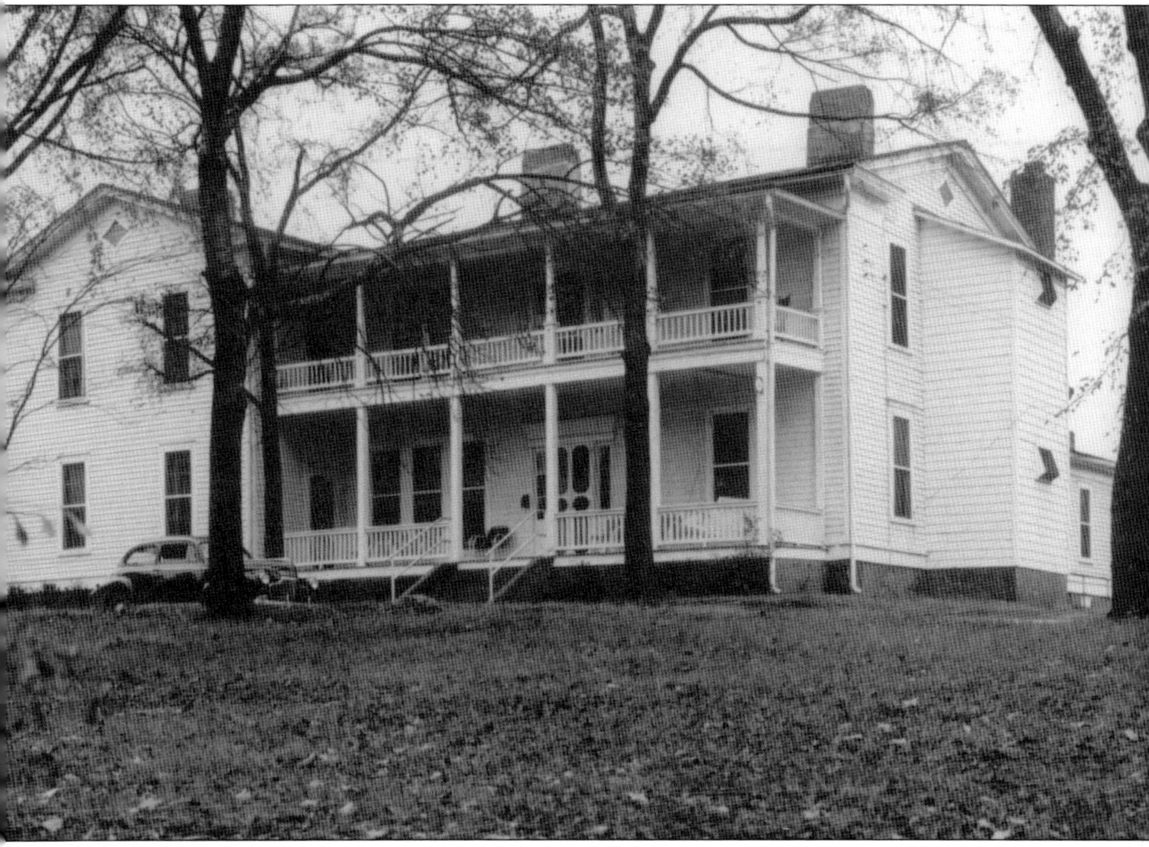

**Piedmont Hotel.** The Piedmont, for which Hotel Hill is named, later became the teacherage, where single female teachers resided. The mill president's house was situated next to the hotel. (Courtesy of the Coxe Collection, Greenville County Historical Society.)

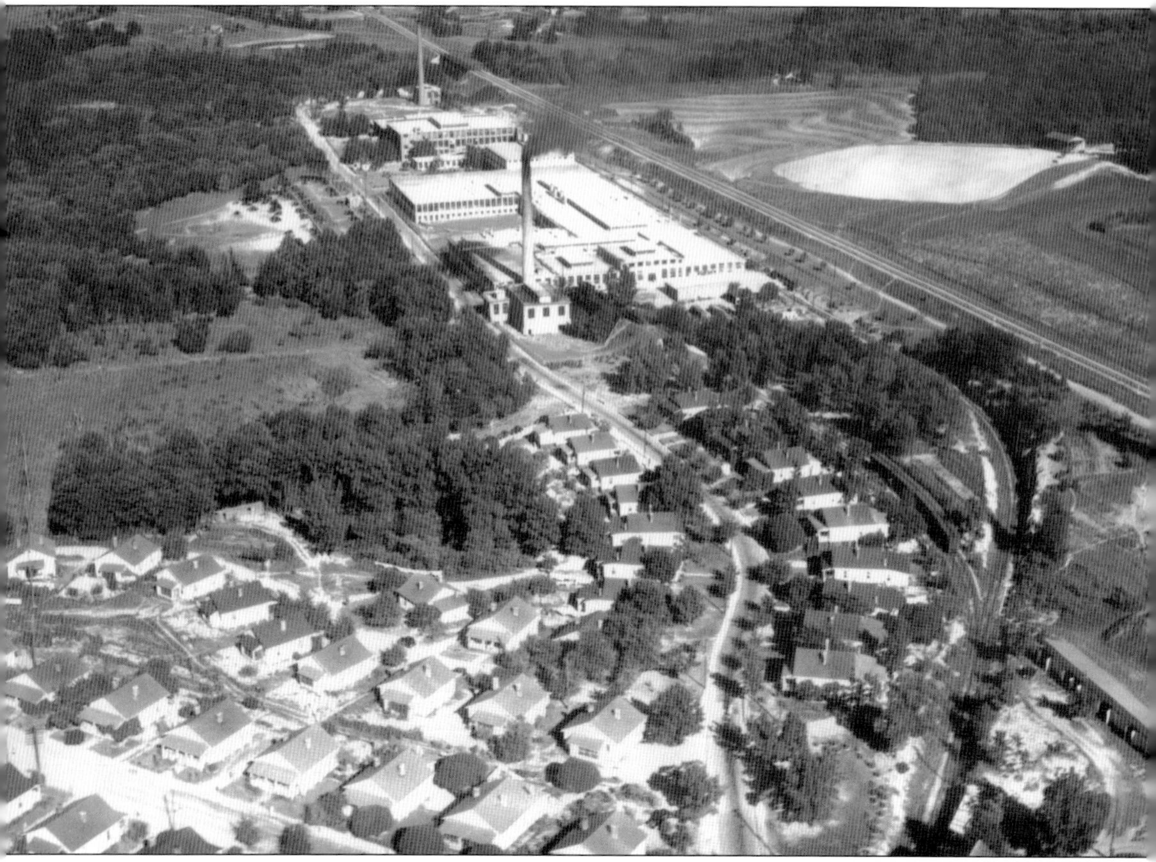

**SOUTHERN BLEACHERY VILLAGE.** Originally, 33 houses were built for the mill. Operatives lived in simple white clapboard houses, while supervisors lived in Craftsman-style houses. The superintendent had an even larger house, located at the corner of School and Main Streets. Twin stone pillars marked the entrance to the village. Duplexes were built two years later with bathroom amenities, shared by both families, located on an enclosed porch. African American employees lived in houses located on Blacktop Road, which was situated across the Enoree River in an area known locally as "Black Bottom." The mill originally offered workers cow barns and pig sties on land next to the Enoree but decided to raze them due to the stench. Garden plots were offered in their place. A mule-drawn wagon provided weekly sanitation pickup. (Courtesy of the Coxe Collection, Greenville County Historical Society.)

*Three*

# Flourishing County

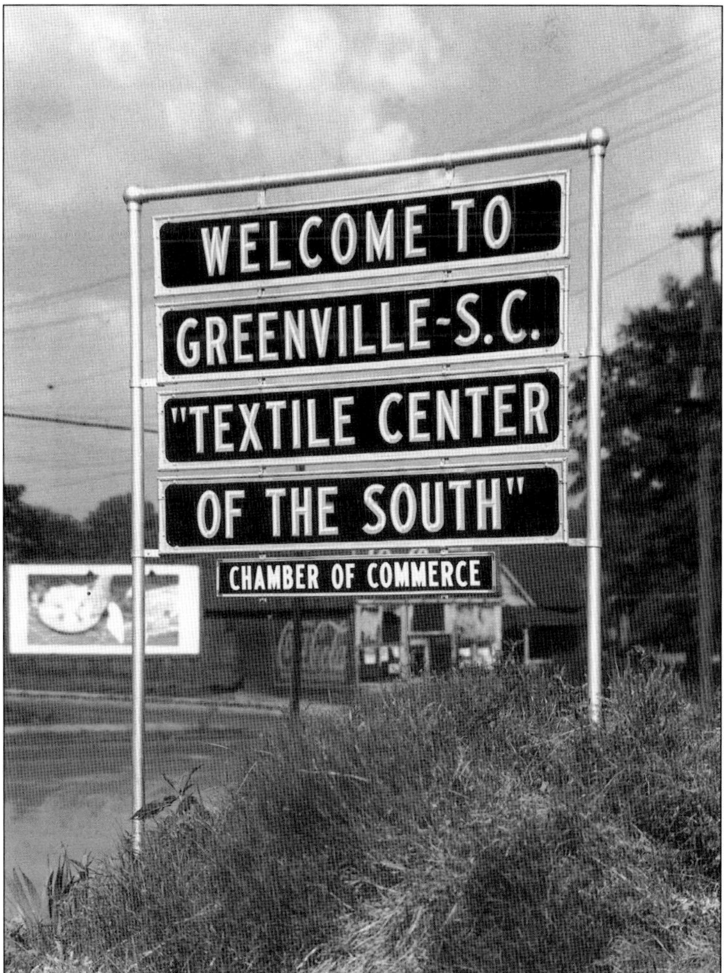


**Welcome to Greenville.** In the 1950s, the Greenville Chamber of Commerce launched a campaign to brand the area as the "Textile Center of the South." By 1960, Greenville grew more audacious and started billing itself as the "Textile Capital of the World." Greenville carried this title for the next 20 years. (Courtesy of the Coxe Collection, Greenville County Historical Society.)

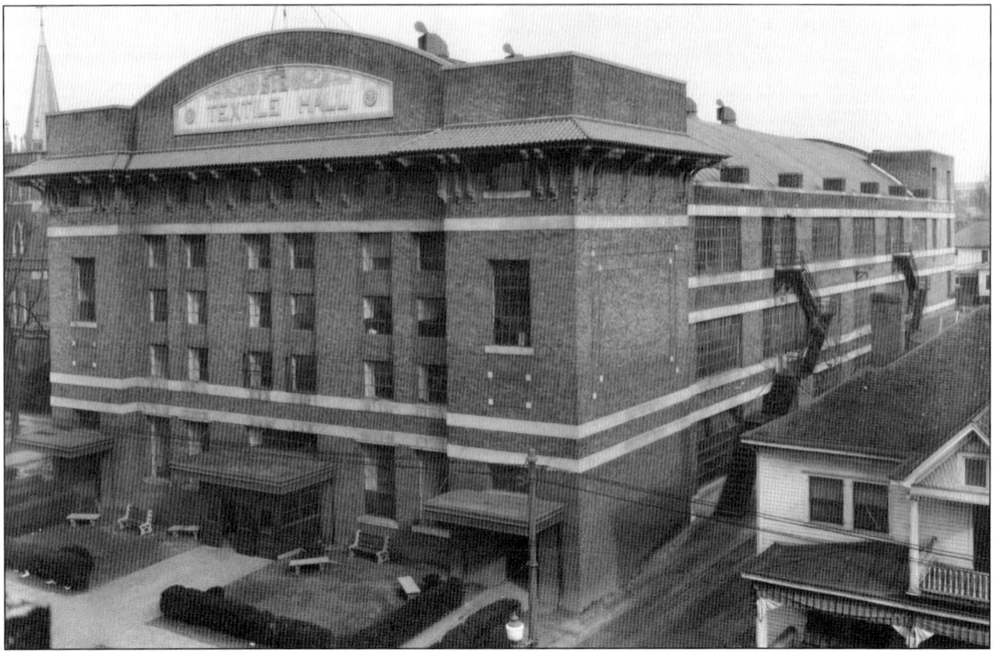


**OLD TEXTILE HALL.** Built in 1917 for the Southern Textile Exhibition, the five-story building was designed by Joseph E. Sirrine and Company and erected by Fiske-Carter Construction Company of Spartanburg. Two one-story annexes were constructed in 1926 and 1952 to provide additional exhibition space. Textile machinery exhibitions were held at old Textile Hall from 1917 to 1962. (Courtesy of the Coxe Collection, Greenville County Historical Society.)

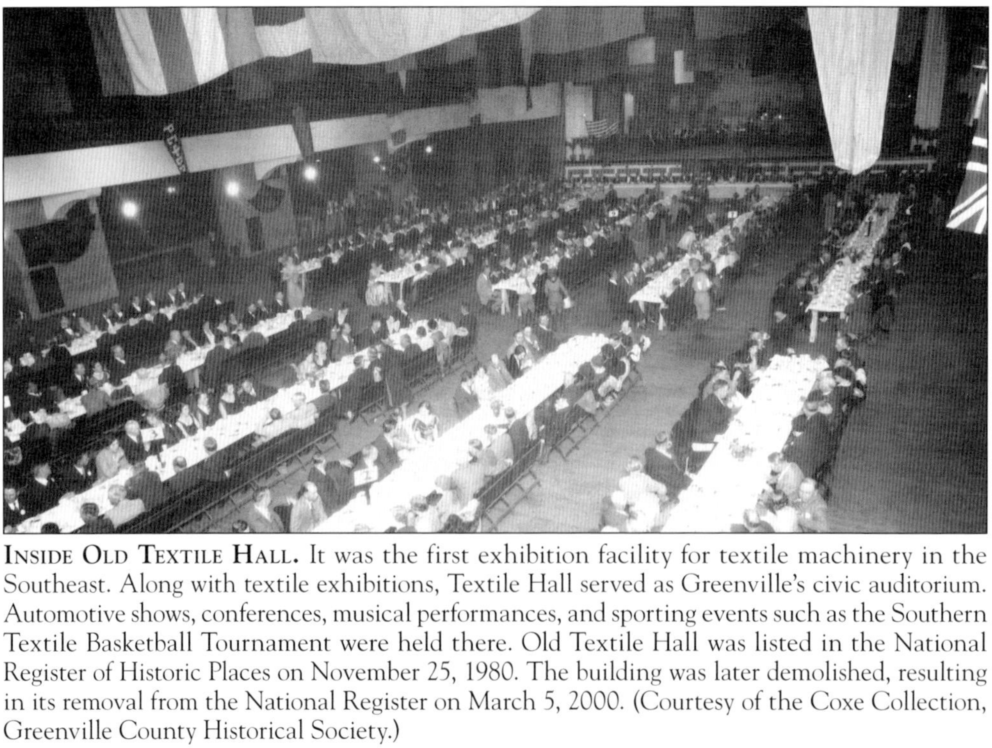

**INSIDE OLD TEXTILE HALL.** It was the first exhibition facility for textile machinery in the Southeast. Along with textile exhibitions, Textile Hall served as Greenville's civic auditorium. Automotive shows, conferences, musical performances, and sporting events such as the Southern Textile Basketball Tournament were held there. Old Textile Hall was listed in the National Register of Historic Places on November 25, 1980. The building was later demolished, resulting in its removal from the National Register on March 5, 2000. (Courtesy of the Coxe Collection, Greenville County Historical Society.)

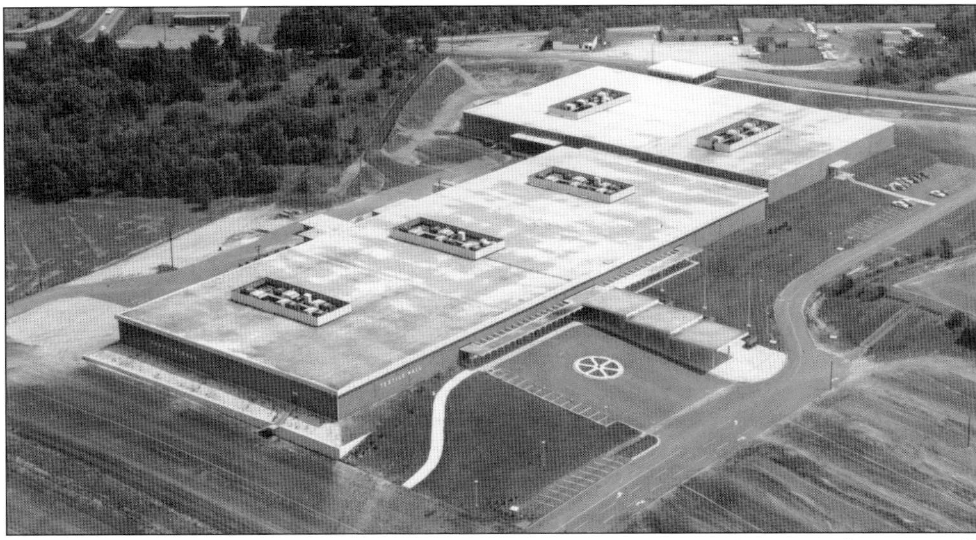

**NEW TEXTILE HALL.** In 1964, a new Textile Hall was built on property adjacent to the Greenville Downtown Airport off Pleasantburg Drive. The building was actually expanded before the first textile exhibition and again two years later. Just as the first Textile Hall, the new exposition center hosted a variety of events, including the Billy Graham Crusade in March 1966. (Courtesy of the Elrod Collection, Greenville County Historical Society.)

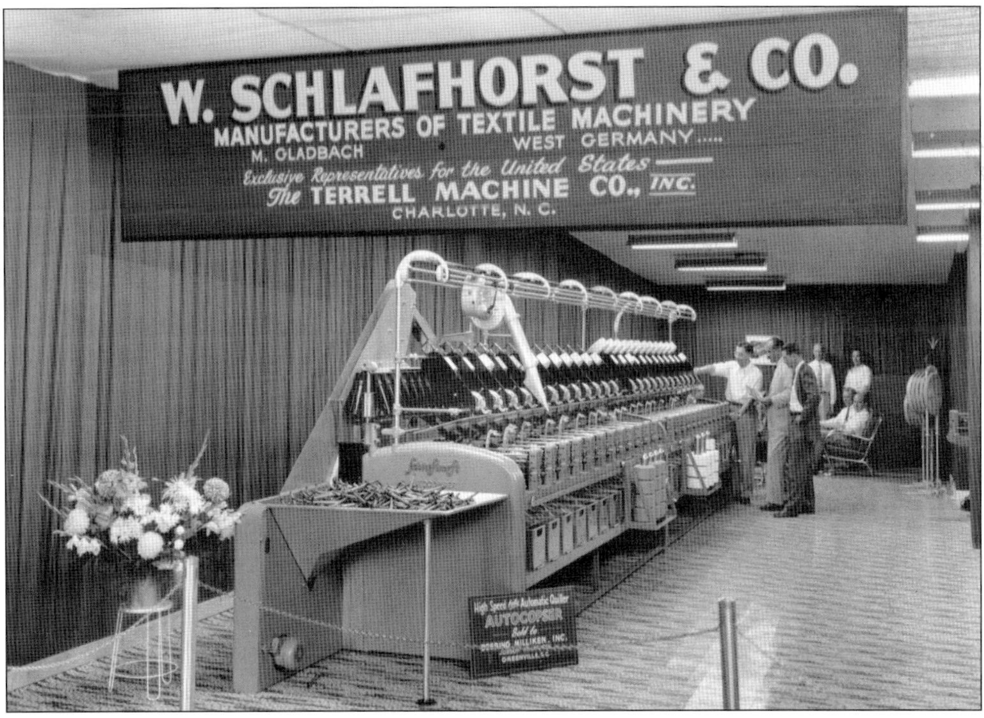


**W. SCHLAFHORST MACHINERY EXHIBIT.** Beginning in 1969, the new Textile Hall hosted the American Textile Machinery Exhibition-International (ATME-I) every fourth and fifth year. Looms and spinning equipment were displayed at the first show, and all other textile equipment was shown at a companion show the following year. The last ATME-I show held in Greenville was in 2004, a combined show. (Courtesy of the Coxe Collection, Greenville County Historical Society.)

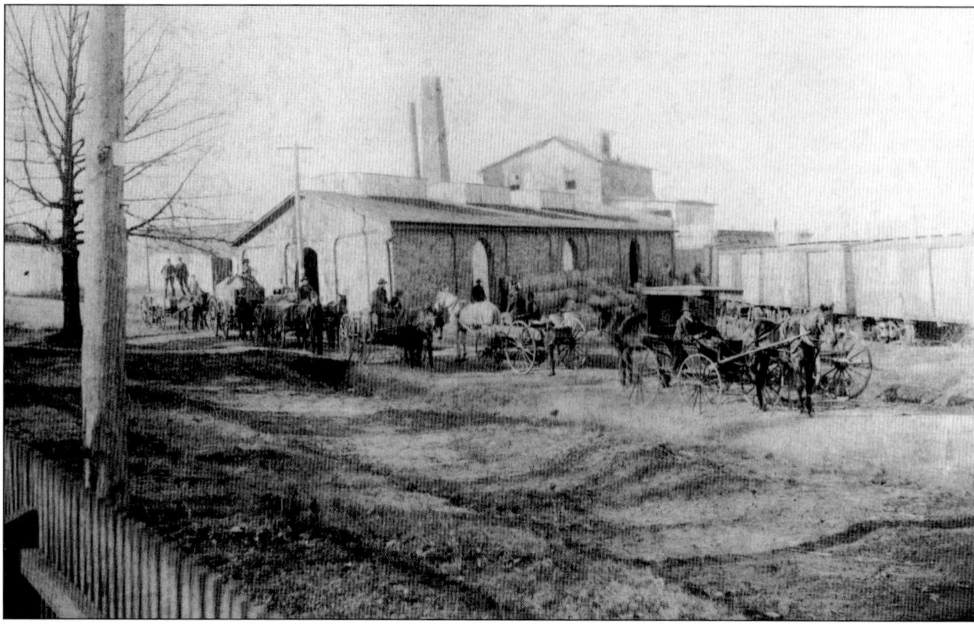

**Cottonseed Oil Company.** Mills Mill owner and entrepreneur Otis Prentiss Mills started the Cottonseed Oil Company at the intersection of Vardry and Augusta Streets in 1872. Although its end-use is not related to textiles, its raw material of cotton was and a natural extension of business for O.P. Mills. The company remained in operation until 1953. (Courtesy of the Landing Collection, Greenville County Historical Society.)

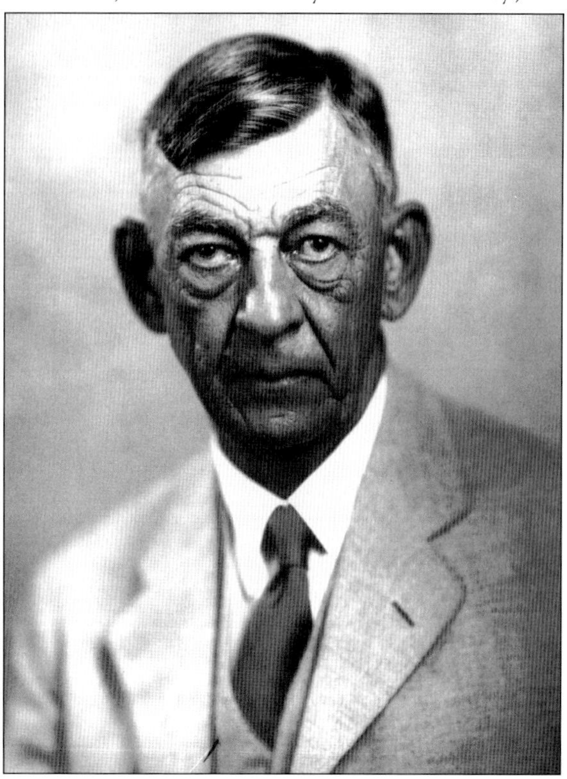

**Joseph Emory Sirrine.** Sirrine began his professional career as an industrial architect and engineer in 1890 and joined New England–based Lockwood, Greene, and Company in their Greenville office in 1894. By 1898, he was in charge of the company's Southern office, supervising the design of dozens of mills. In 1902, Sirrine resumed independent practice, and in 1921, he formed a partnership with eight of his associates named J.E. Sirrine and Company. The company's enterprise spanned from Maine to Texas with projects ranging from textile mills, mill villages, and commercial facilities. Sirrine served on the boards of many major industrial firms, including 19 textile mills. Sirrine kept his office at J.E. Sirrine and Company until his death in 1947. (Courtesy of Tom Finley.)

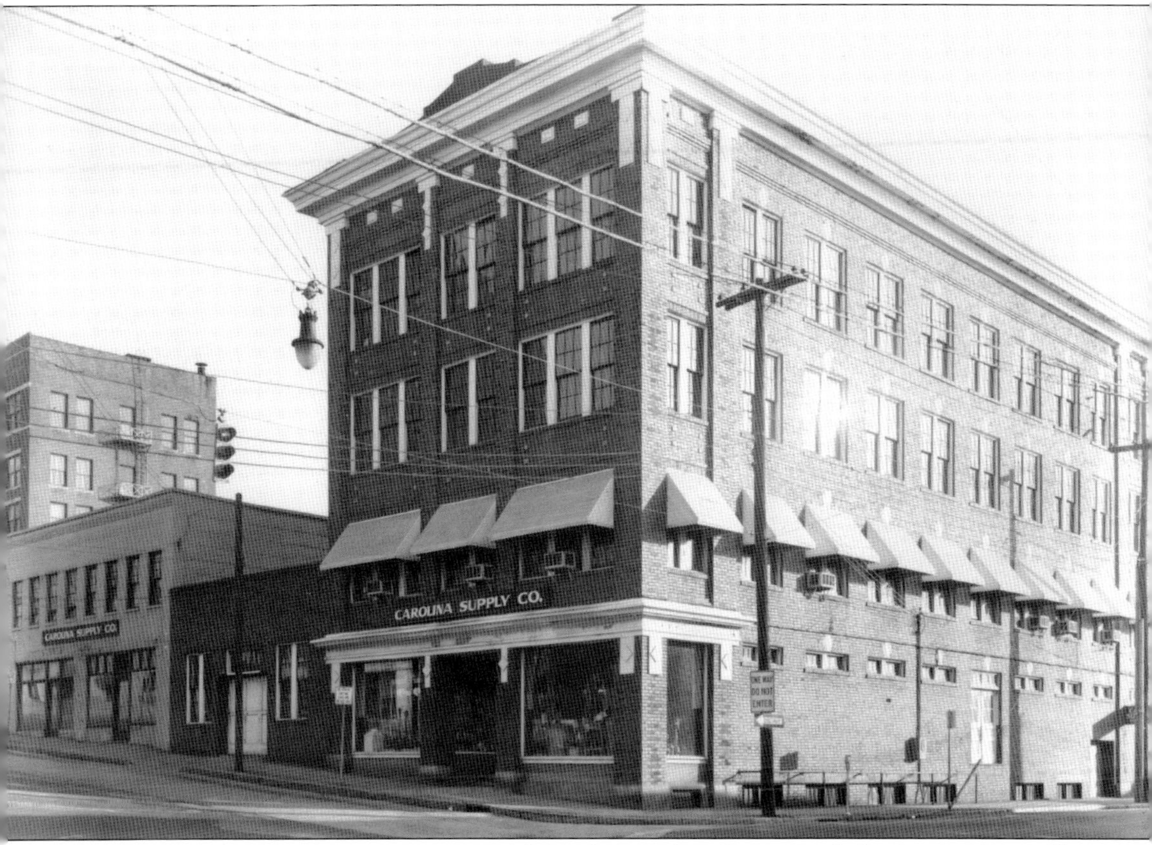


**Carolina Supply Company.** Incorporated in July 1899 by Thomas Inglesby, Francis Cogswell, D.G. Martin, and F.J. Pelzer, the company sold supplies to the area's textile mills. As the company grew with the industry, the firm hired J.E. Sirrine and Company to design a new building to meet their needs. Completed in 1914 by Spartanburg's Carter-Fiske Construction, the four-story brick building was located at 35 West Coffee Street in Greenville's downtown. The company sold in 1990 to Greenville Textile Supply. The building was listed in the National Register of Historic Places on July 3, 1997. (Courtesy of the Coxe Collection, Greenville County Historical Society.)

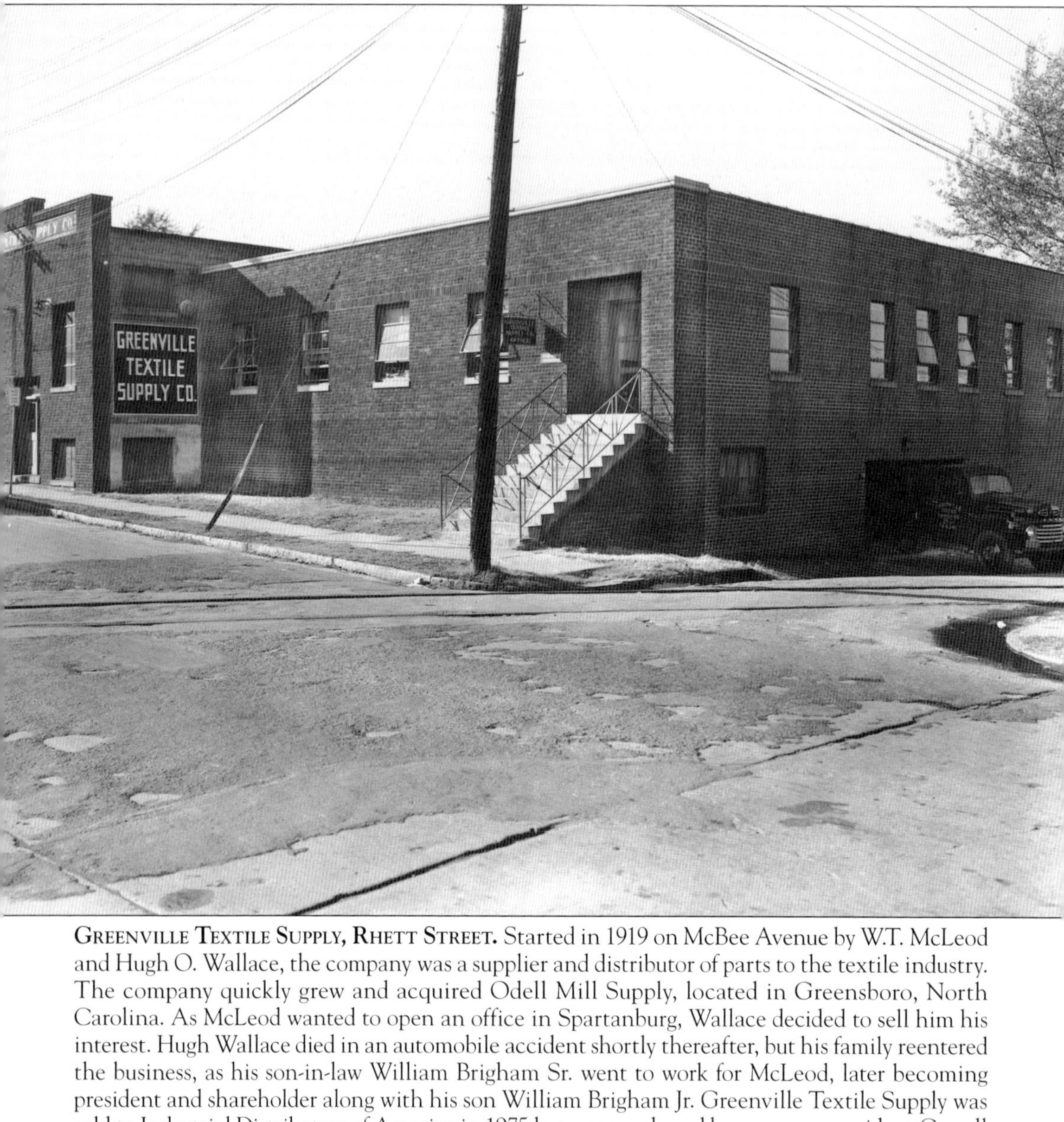


**GREENVILLE TEXTILE SUPPLY, RHETT STREET.** Started in 1919 on McBee Avenue by W.T. McLeod and Hugh O. Wallace, the company was a supplier and distributor of parts to the textile industry. The company quickly grew and acquired Odell Mill Supply, located in Greensboro, North Carolina. As McLeod wanted to open an office in Spartanburg, Wallace decided to sell him his interest. Hugh Wallace died in an automobile accident shortly thereafter, but his family reentered the business, as his son-in-law William Brigham Sr. went to work for McLeod, later becoming president and shareholder along with his son William Brigham Jr. Greenville Textile Supply was sold to Industrial Distributors of America in 1975 but was purchased by company president Carroll L. Stone and three others in 1980. The group later purchased Odell Textile Supply in 1985 and Greenville competitor Carolina Supply in 1990. The company was in operation for 90 years upon its closure in 2009. (Courtesy of the Coxe Collection, Greenville County Historical Society.)

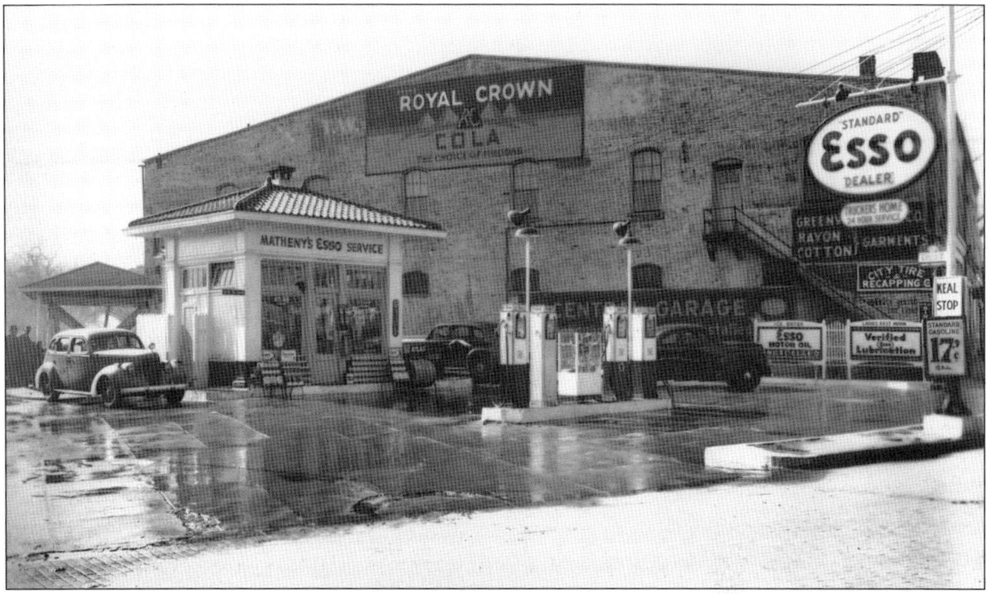


Farmers' Alliance Cotton Warehouse. In 1890, preeminent Greenville builder Jacob Cagle was hired to construct a cotton warehouse at the corner of South Main and Augusta Streets for the Farmers' Alliance. At the time, Greenville County was producing nearly 30,000 bales of cotton per year, so a central warehouse was needed. The Farmers' Alliance came into being as a result of post–Civil War farmers needing to band together for economic survival. The alliance organized in Greenville in the 1880s, and 42 regional alliances came together to build the warehouse in order to cut out the commodity brokers, thus boosting their profits. (Courtesy of the Coxe Collection, Greenville County Historical Society.)

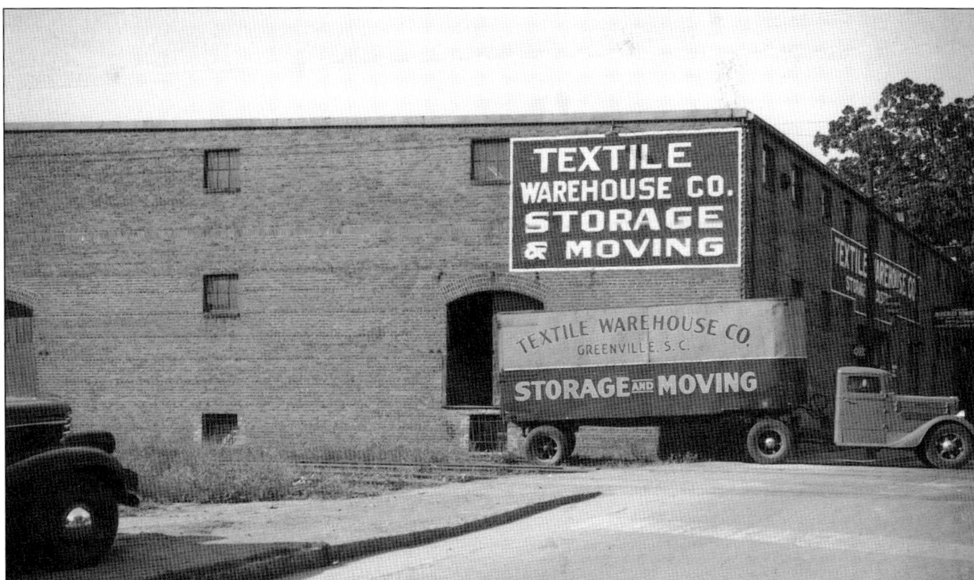


Textile Warehouse Company. Another textile warehouse facility, the Textile Warehouse Company was located at 511 Rhett Street in Greenville's West End. Also located in the building was the Hercules Powder Company, which specialized in industrial chemicals, linseed oil, and turpentine. (Courtesy of the Coxe Collection, Greenville County Historical Society.)

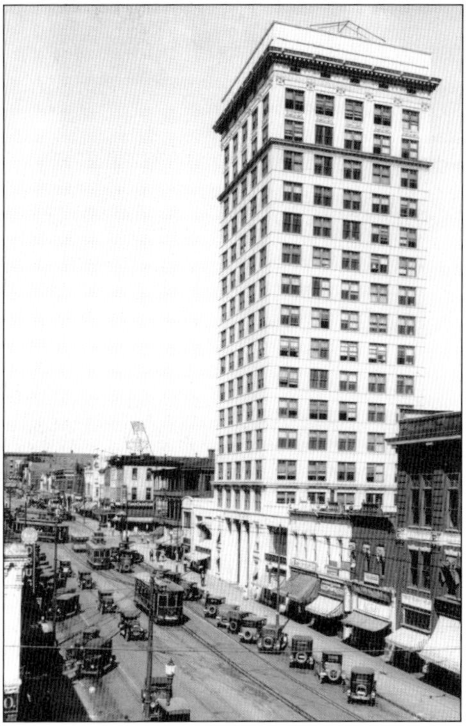

**Woodside Building.** In 1906, the four Woodside brothers started Woodside National Bank. In 1923, the bank moved into a new 17-story building on Main Street, which was the state's tallest building. Two years later, John T. Woodside helped open the Poinsett Hotel, located just south on Main Street. (Courtesy of the Elrod Collection, Greenville County Historical Society.)

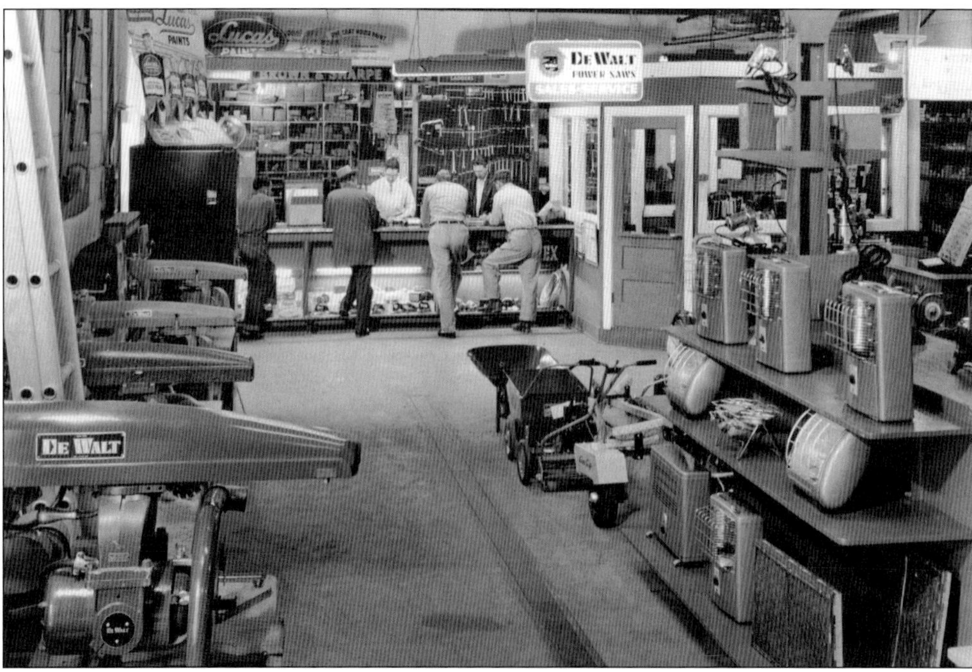


**Poe Hardware and Supply Company.** Started in the 1880s by William T. Wilkins and Nelson Carter Poe, vice president of manufacturing at F.W. Poe Manufacturing, the company provided a wide range of industrial supplies and hardware to the area textile mills. Originally located on Main Street, the company moved to West Greenville for more space and close proximity to the mills in the Textile Crescent. (Courtesy of the Coxe Collection, Greenville County Historical Society.)

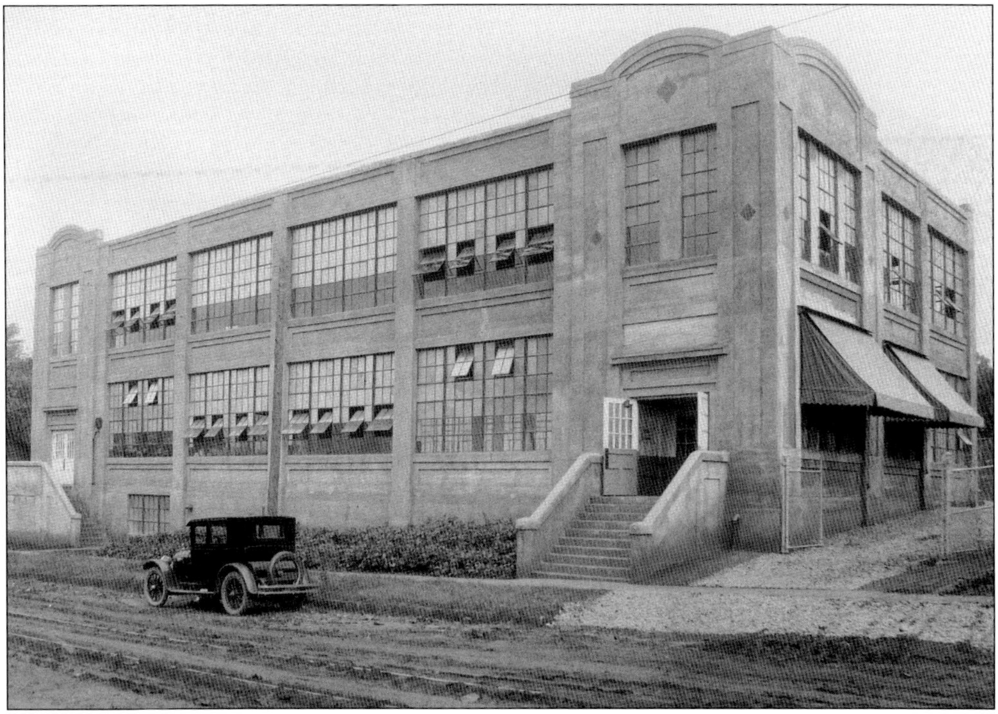

**Steele Heddle.** Originally based in Philadelphia, Pennsylvania, Steele Heddle moved its High Point, North Carolina, operation to Greenville in 1923. The two-story 10,000-square-foot building, located at 617 East McBee Avenue, was the first factory in the South to have every machine powered by electricity. The company produced heddles, which are strips of wires with eyes on both ends used in looms. (Courtesy of the Elrod Collection, Greenville County Historical Society.)

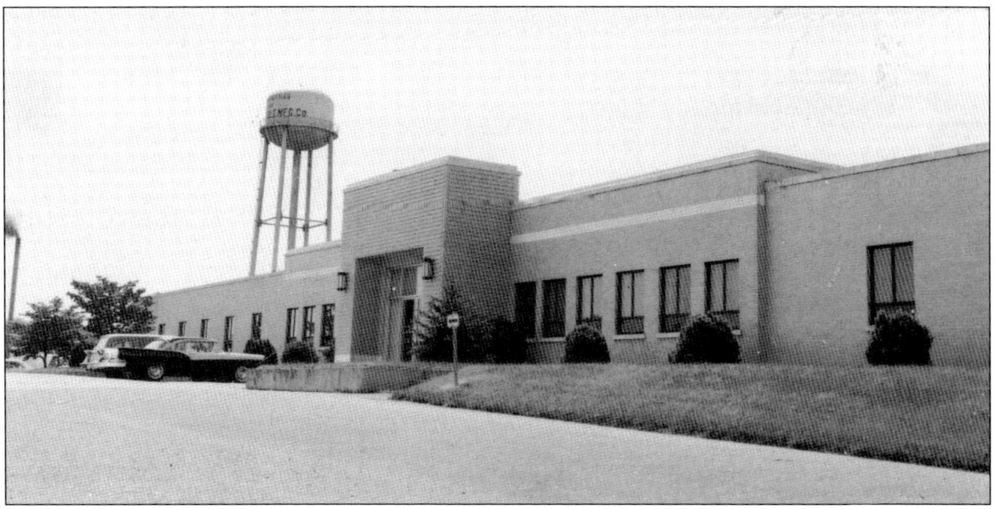

**Steele Heddle Grows.** In 1941, the company acquired 50 acres of land on Rutherford Road near Camp Sevier for its new manufacturing facility. The company became the largest producer of reed and loom winders in the South and made Greenville its new company headquarters. With the decline of the textile industry, the company filed bankruptcy in 2001 and was acquired by Picanol and renamed G.T.P. Greenville-Steele Heddle Division. (Courtesy of the Bill Karst Collection, Greenville County Library System.)

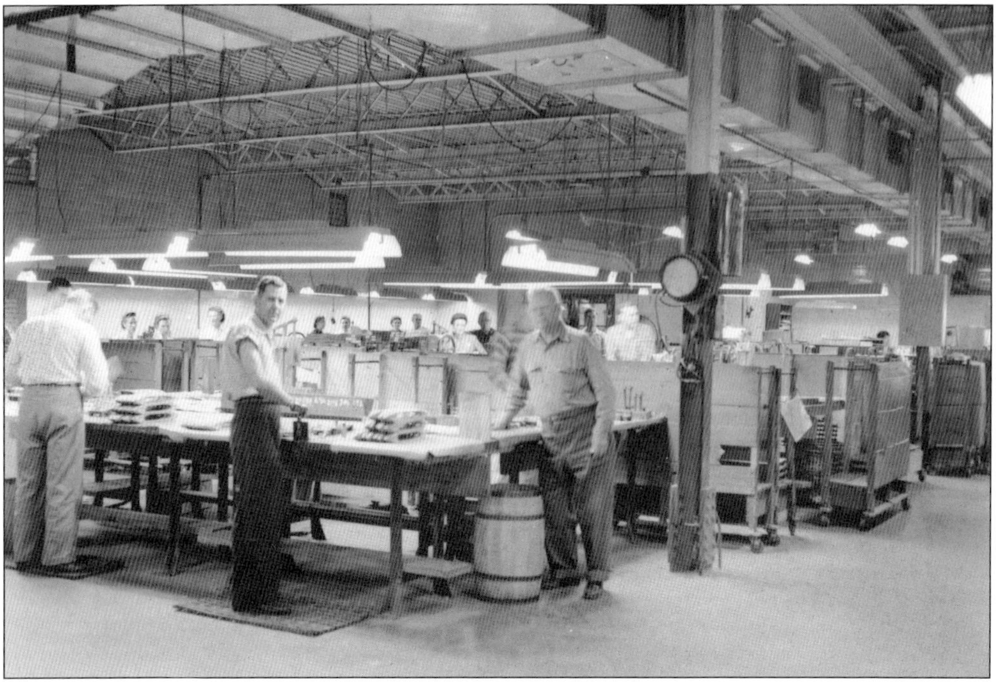

STEELE HEDDLE EMPLOYEES WORKING ON SHUTTLES. Along with heddles, the company also produced shuttles, looms, and reeds. Each of these parts are used in the weaving process on a loom. (Courtesy of the Bill Karst Collection, Greenville County Library System.)

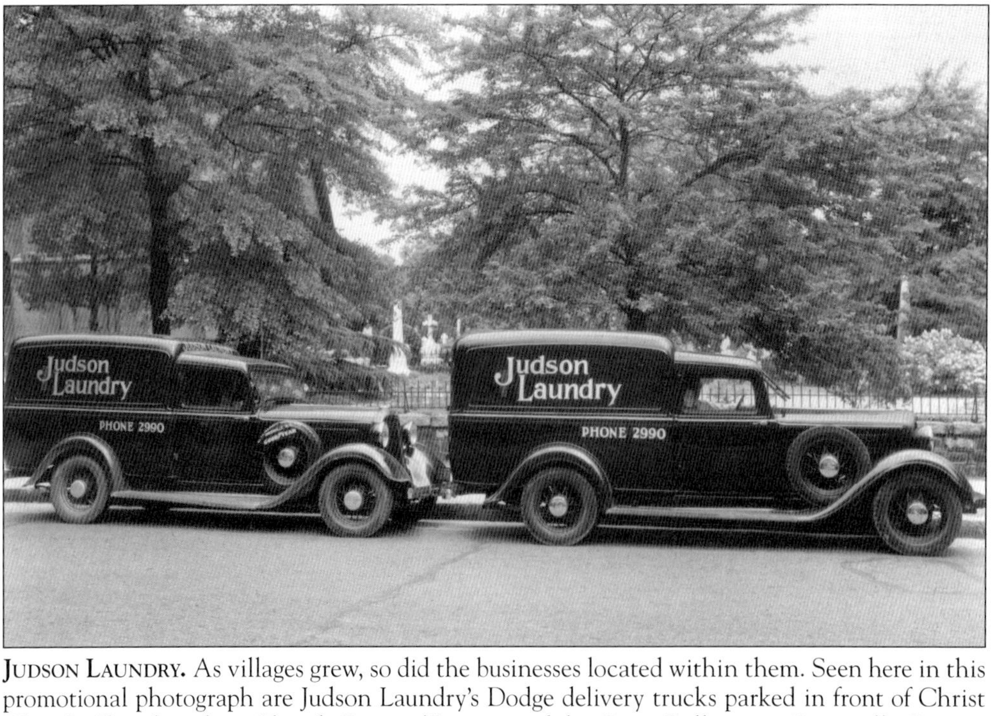


JUDSON LAUNDRY. As villages grew, so did the businesses located within them. Seen here in this promotional photograph are Judson Laundry's Dodge delivery trucks parked in front of Christ Church Churchyard on Church Street. (Courtesy of the Coxe Collection, Greenville County Historical Society.)

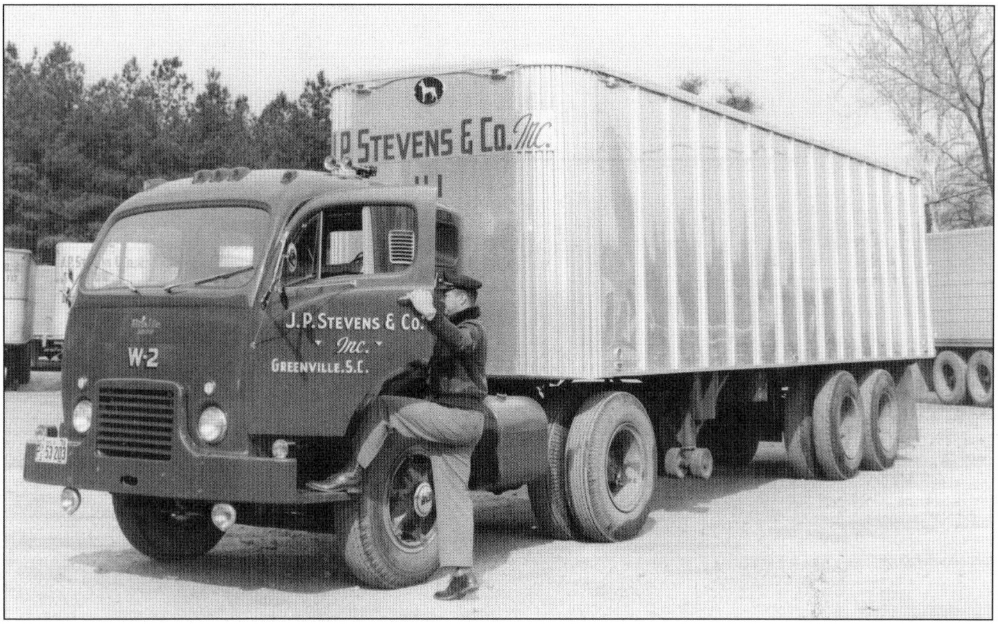


**J.P. Stevens and Company Transportation Division.** J.P. Stevens opened a shipping terminal on White Horse Road to service its many mills. Having an in-house transportation division saved money and created jobs for Greenville residents. The division became part of Westpoint during the 1980s leveraged buyout and is now a part of Rhode Island textile company Cranston Print Works' trucking division. (Courtesy of the Elrod Collection, Greenville County Historical Society.)

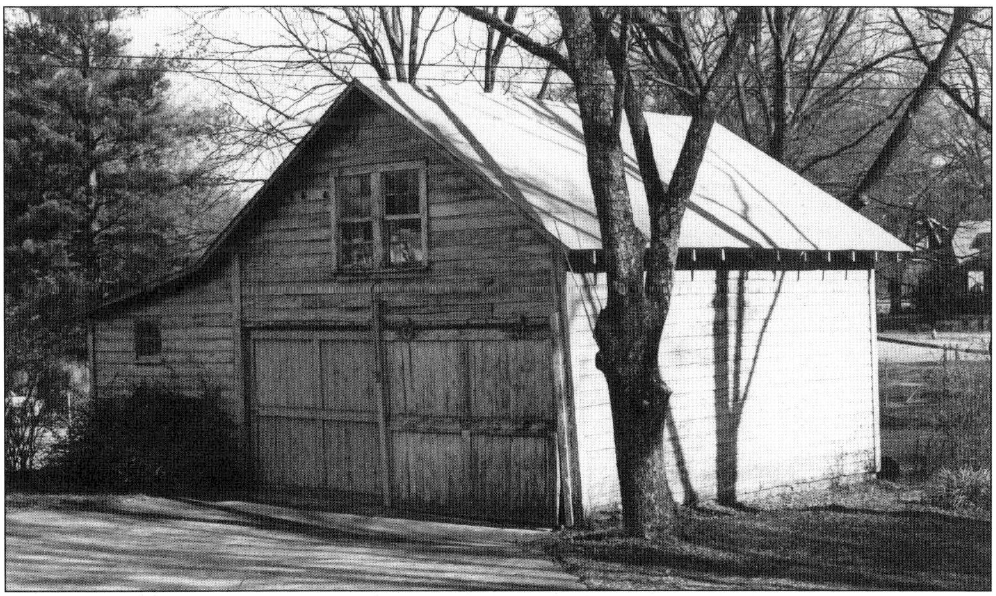

**Louis P. Batson Company.** Founded in 1948 by Louis P. Batson Sr. in the upstairs of his garage, the company began with one product that reduced machinery vibration. One year later, Batson Sr. passed away on Christmas, leaving his wife, Joanna, and daughter, also named Joanna, to run the company while sons Louis Jr. was in the service and Elliott was attending college. Today, the company is run by third-generation family member Caroline Batson Stewart and offers a vast industrial product line. (Courtesy of the Louis P. Batson Company.)

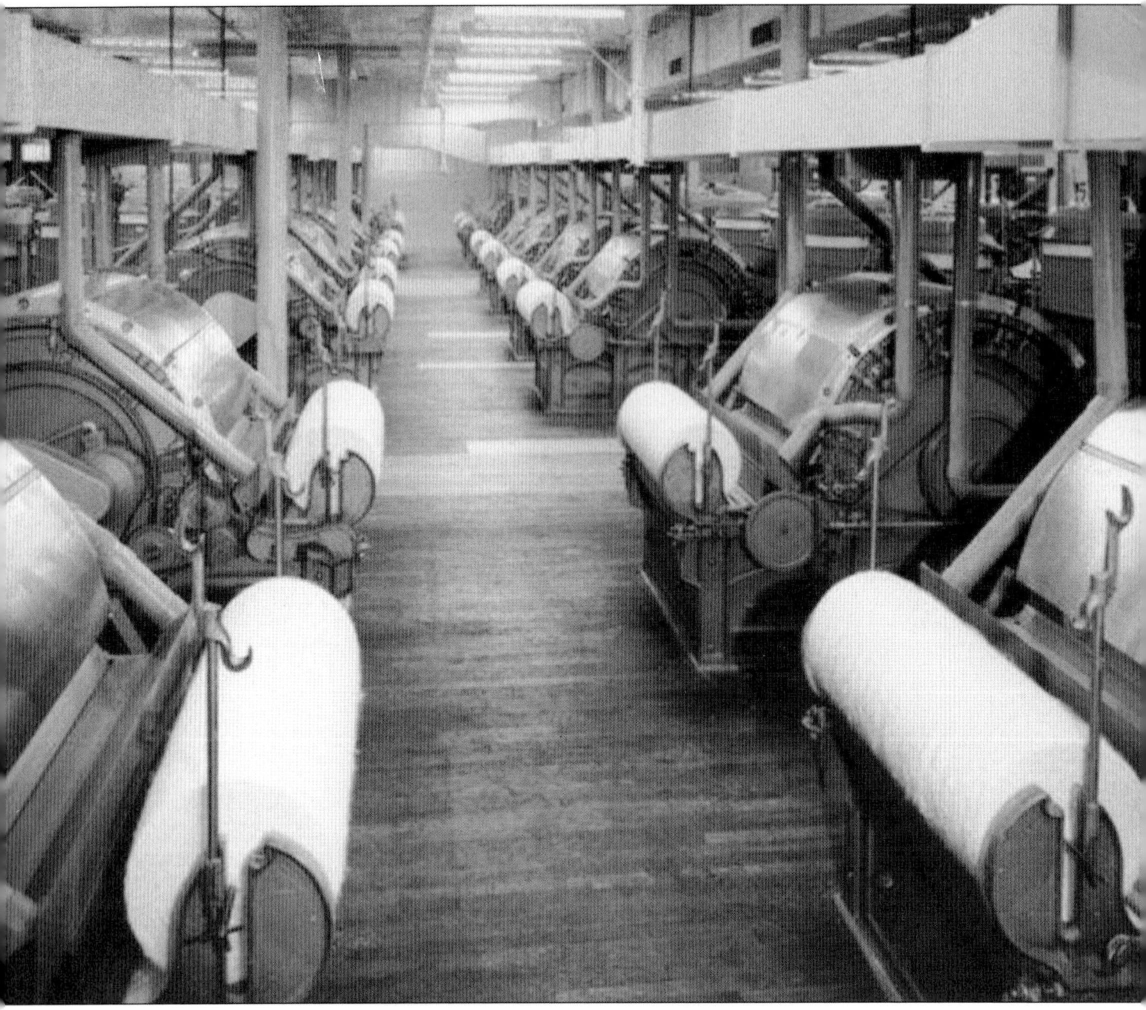

**John D. Hollingsworth on Wheels.** The company's beginnings trace back to 1894 as Pinkney Hollingsworth traveled from mill to mill by mule-drawn wagon offering carding-machine repair. Upon Pinkney's death, his son John D. Hollingsworth Sr. took over the business, running it out of his family home off Augusta Street. In 1919, he traded the wagon for a truck, and his son John D. Hollingsworth Jr., at age 10, began accompanying him on visits to various mills. Hollingsworth Jr. took over the family's business upon his father's passing in 1942. He revolutionized the fiber-processing industry by inventing machinery that separated fibers 10 times faster than earlier machines. Along with its machinery, the company's level of customer support was considered second to none. (Courtesy of the Greenville County Historical Society.)

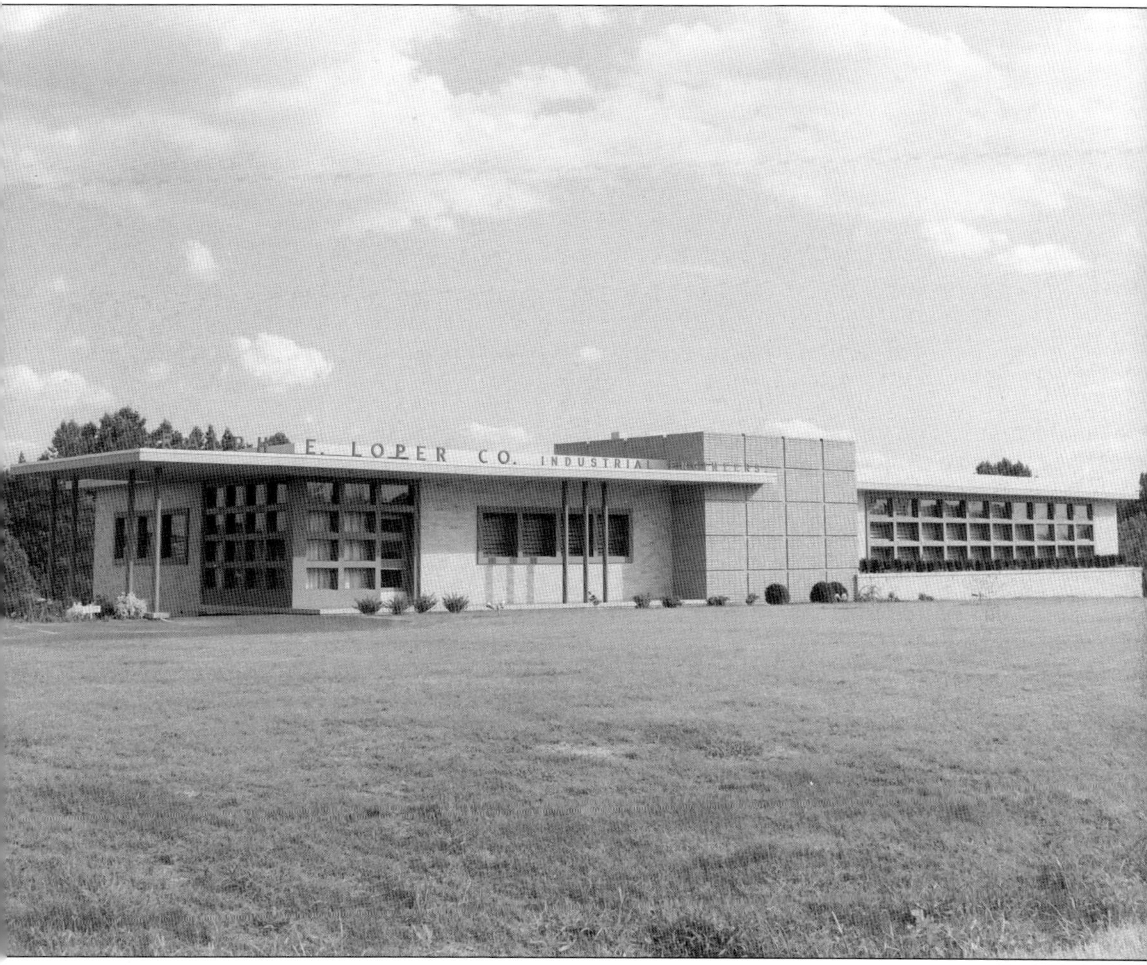


**Ralph E. Loper Company.** The textile-engineering firm based in Fall River, Massachusetts, moved to Greenville in 1953, opening an office on Wade Hampton Boulevard. The industrial engineering and accounting company specialized in textile cost methods. (Courtesy of the Elrod Collection, Greenville County Historical Society.)

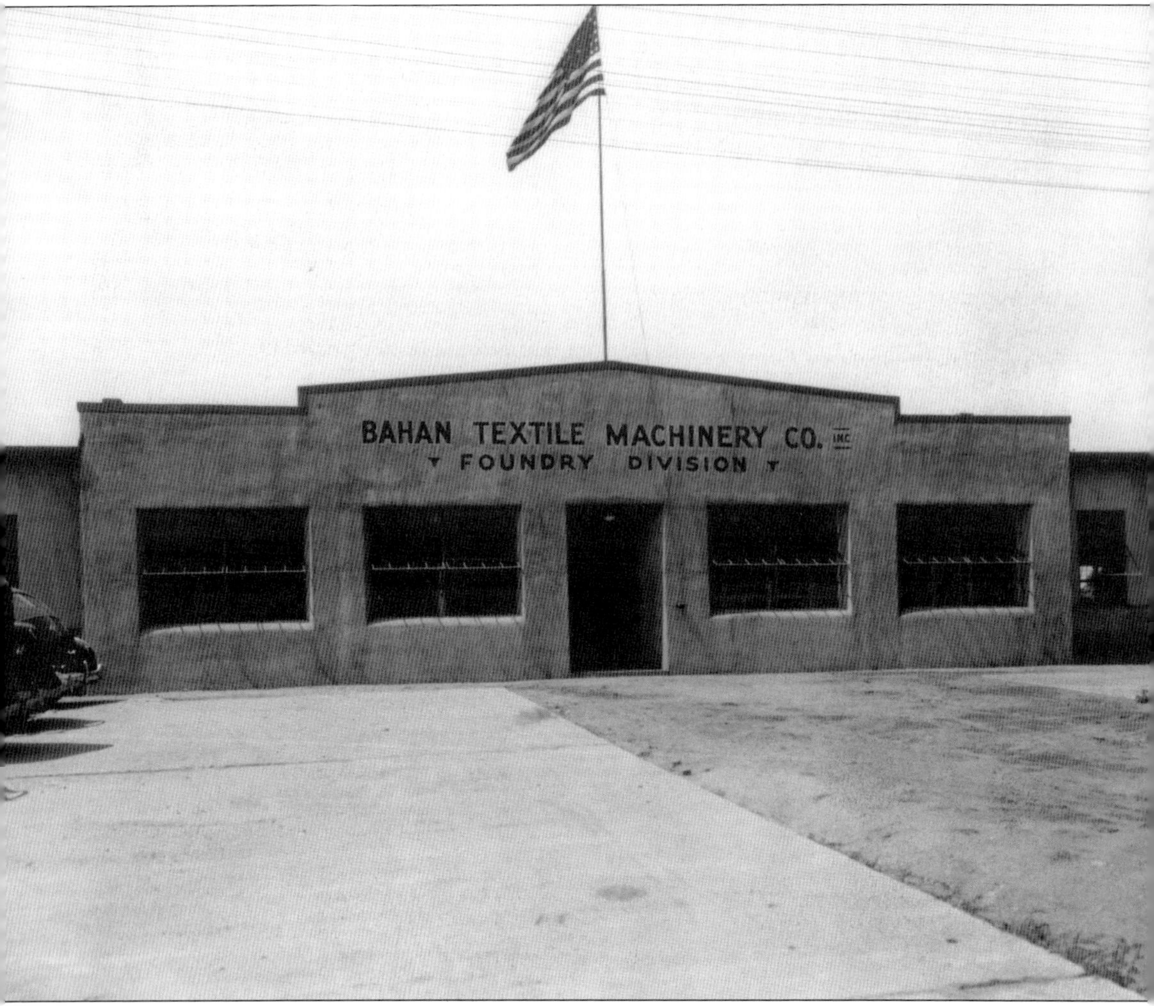


**Bahan Textile Machinery Company.** Founded in Lawrence, Massachusetts, the Greenville Foundry Division was located on Rutherford Road across from Steele Heddle. The company produced replacement parts for looms. (Courtesy of the Coxe Collection, Greenville County Historical Society.)

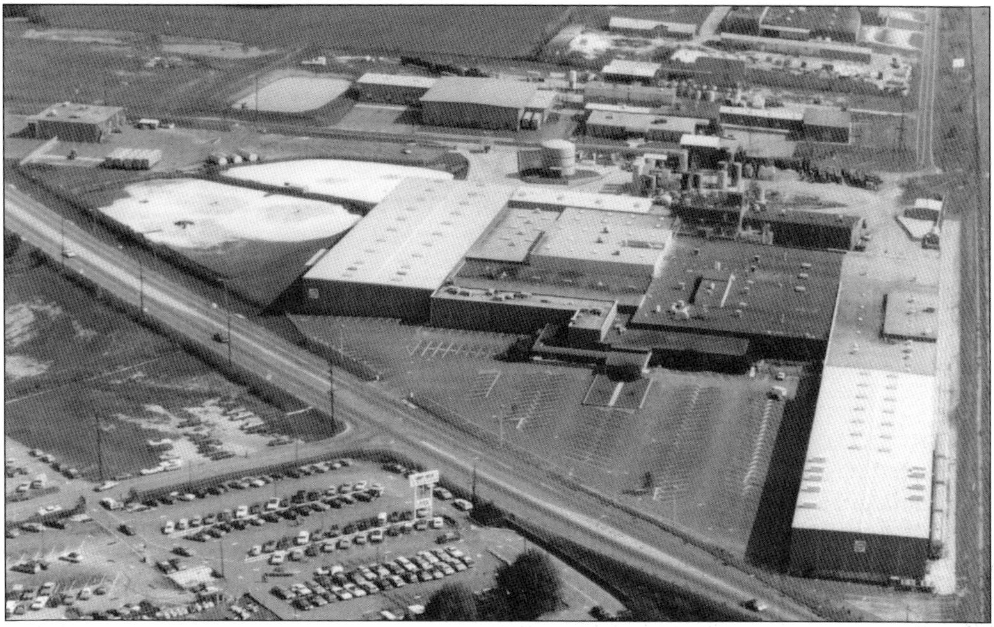

**Texize Chemical Company.** First incorporated in the 1940s, the company sold industrial cleaners to textile mills. It was also one of the first accounts of Henderson Advertising Agency, founded by James M. Henderson in 1946. It was Henderson who persuaded Texize founder Jack Greer to market the company's products for household use. The consumer line was sold to Dow Chemical in 1986. (Courtesy of the Elrod Collection, Greenville County Historical Society.)

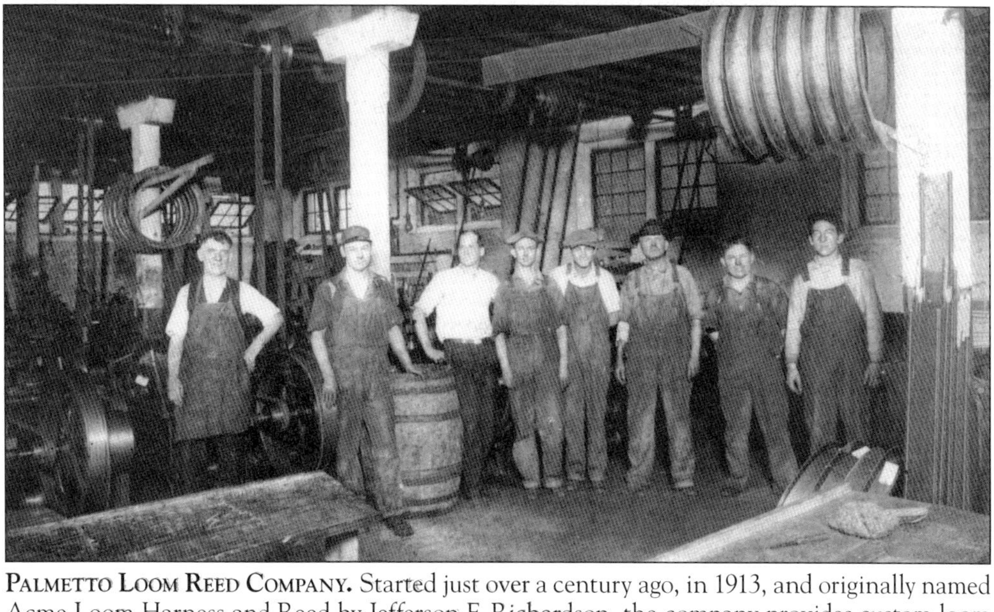

**Palmetto Loom Reed Company.** Started just over a century ago, in 1913, and originally named Acme Loom Harness and Reed by Jefferson F. Richardson, the company provides custom loom reeds as well as service and repair to loom beams through its subsidiary, Palmetto Beam Works. In 1951, the company transferred its entire operation from Acme to Palmetto with a 50-percent partner whose shares were purchased by the Richardson family in 1987. Throughout the company's history, it has been continuously managed by a member of the Richardson family, currently in its fourth generation with Gladys Richardson. (Courtesy of Palmetto Loom Reed Company.)

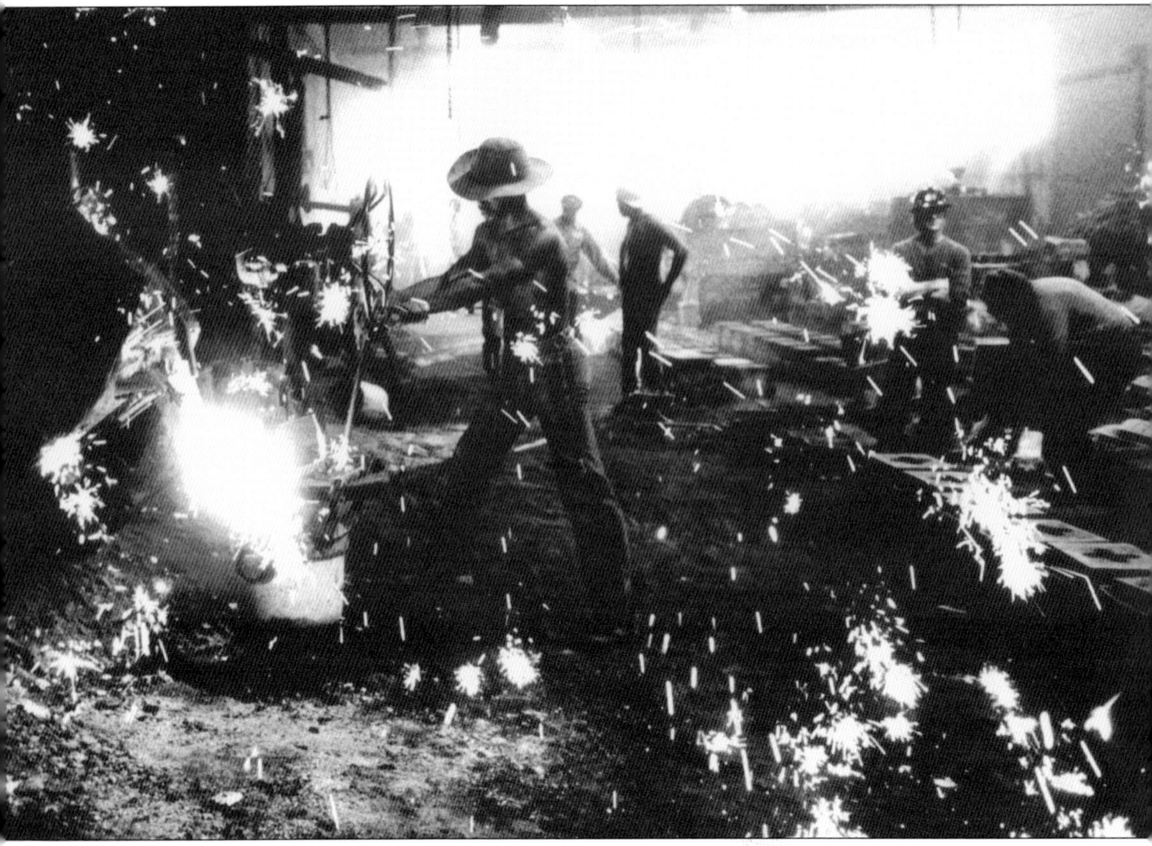

**Eagle Iron Works.** Incorporated in 1919 by Jefferson Pierce Thompson, the business was comprised of a foundry and machine shop, which manufactured mostly textile machine parts for mills in the area. Gears, sprockets, rollers, and pulleys were cast of molten iron that was poured into individual molds to turn out a part, which was then smoothed and polished. In 2008, Eagle Iron Works acquired its Hollywood claim to fame when a portion of George Clooney's movie *Leatherheads* was filmed there. Three generations of Thompsons worked for this thriving company until the demise of the local textile industry. The business closed in 2012, and the property was sold. (Courtesy of the Thompson Collection, Greenville County Historical Society.)

# Four

# Schools

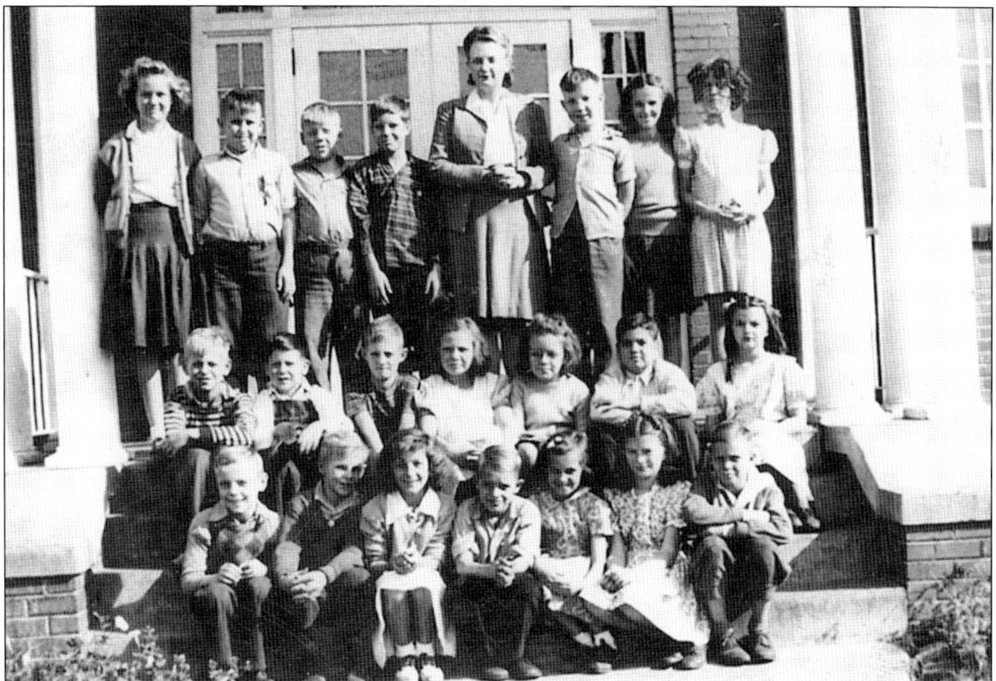

**Graham School.** Started in 1904 by Camperdown Mills, the school was named for mill president Charles E. Graham. When school attendance was made mandatory by the state, the school was turned over to the Greenville City School System. The school system built a new school, seen here on then-named Choice Street (now East Camperdown Way), across from Second Baptist Church. (Courtesy of the Camperdown Historical Society Collection, Greenville County Library System.)

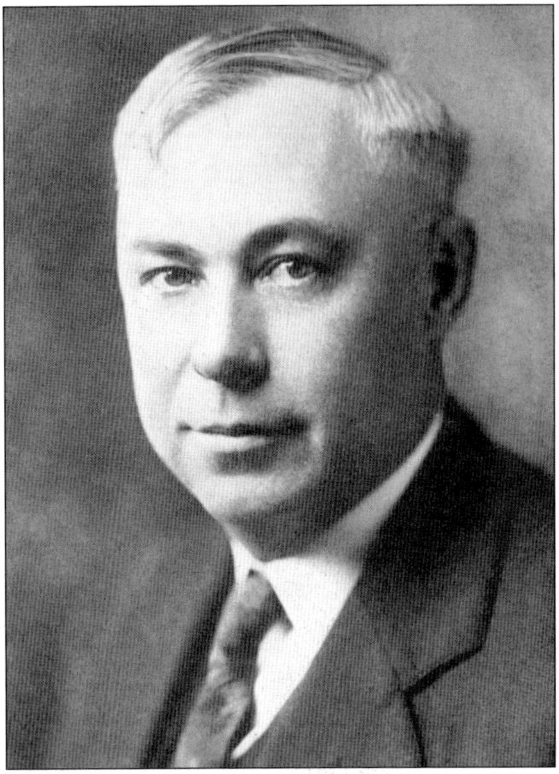

**Lawrence Peter Hollis.** Hollis came to Greenville in 1905 to serve as assistant director of the Monaghan YMCA at a salary of $40 per month. After being named director, Hollis spent summers at the national YMCA headquarters in New York, where he learned of Scouting and the newly formed game of basketball. In 1916, he became the head of elementary schools for the Victor-Monaghan Group and, in 1924, became superintendent of the new Parker School District, which included Parker High School. His vision for the school became a national model for vocational education. (Courtesy of the Greenville County Library System.)

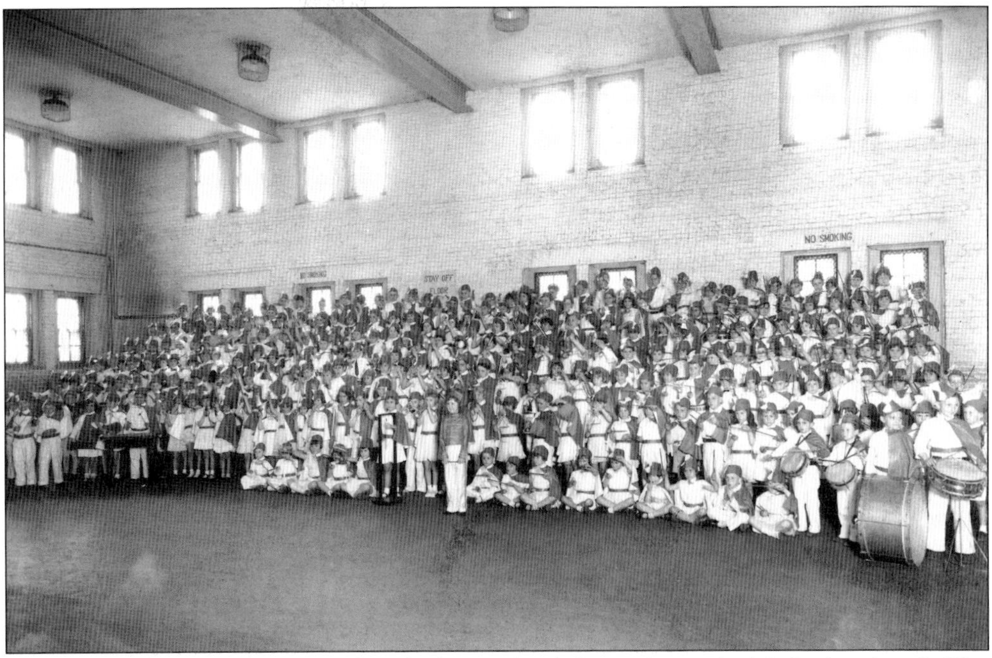


**Judson Mill Toy Orchestra.** Judson had two schools located near the Methodist church. The older two-story brick building housed first through fourth grades, and the former community center housed fifth through seventh grades, along with the village's medical and dental offices. (Courtesy of the Coxe Collection, Greenville County Historical Society.)

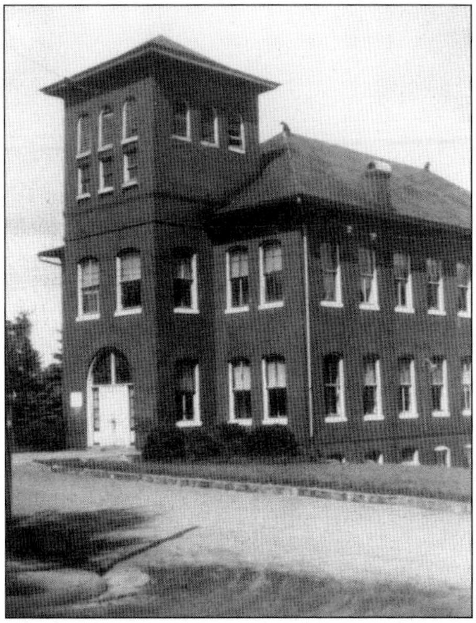

**AMERICAN SPINNING SCHOOL.** Located at the corner of Church and Hammett Streets, the three-story brick structure had a semicircular transom over the front doors. The school was directly across Hammett Street from the American Spinning Company office. (Courtesy of the Robert H. Duke Collection, Greenville County Library System.)

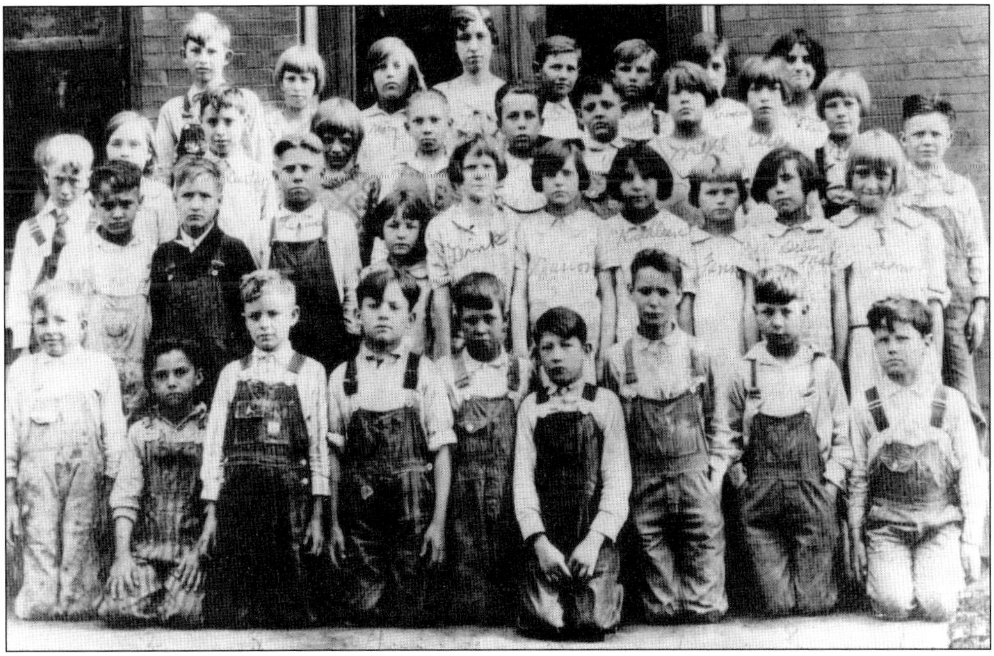

**AMERICAN SPINNING SCHOOL THIRD GRADE CLASS, 1929.** Pictured here are, from left to right, (first row) Alvin Land, James McCullough, Ray Miller, Talmadge Mayfield, Thomas Barton, Eugene Muarey, Dewey Gilreath, J.B. Hammond, and Leroy Greer; (second row) Alfred McDonald, Lewis Sanders, Leroy Sentill, Margaret Summey, Mary Moffett, Marion Wilbanks, Kathleen Belt, Fannie Mae Alexander, Della Mae Fox, and Juanita Freeman; (third row) Bill Morgan, Lila Bell Hall, Curtis Ferguson, Margaret Osborne, Charles Dodson, Frank Sammons, Boyce Bryant, Mildred Moon, Willie Wright, Geneva Pike, and Joe Carl Ammon; (fourth row) Gilbert Bagwell, Frances Owen, Mary Thomas, Inez Watts (teacher), Grady King, Willard Bagwell, Francis McClure, and Mamie Lee McDonald. (Courtesy of the Robert H. Duke Collection, Greenville County Library System.)

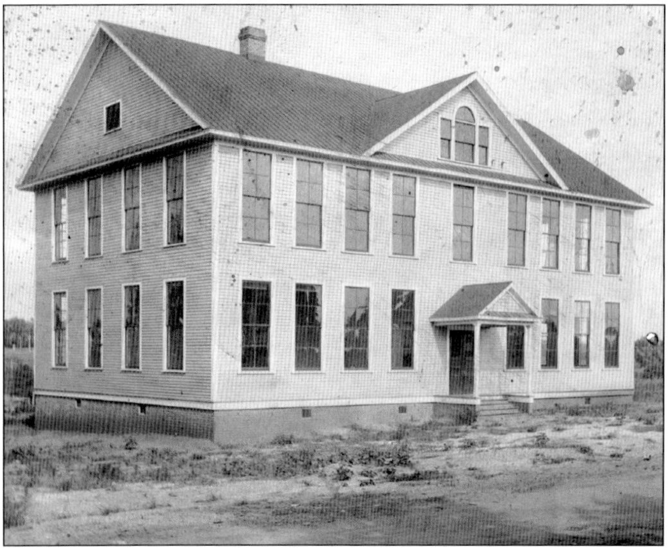

**Brandon Elementary School.** The first Brandon Elementary building was constructed by 1905; it was a two-story clapboard building with large almost floor-to-ceiling four-over-four windows. The building was later replaced with a new elementary school. The accessibility to schools was an attraction for families in rural areas to seek employment at the mills. (Courtesy of the Brandon Historical Society Collection, Greenville County Library System.)

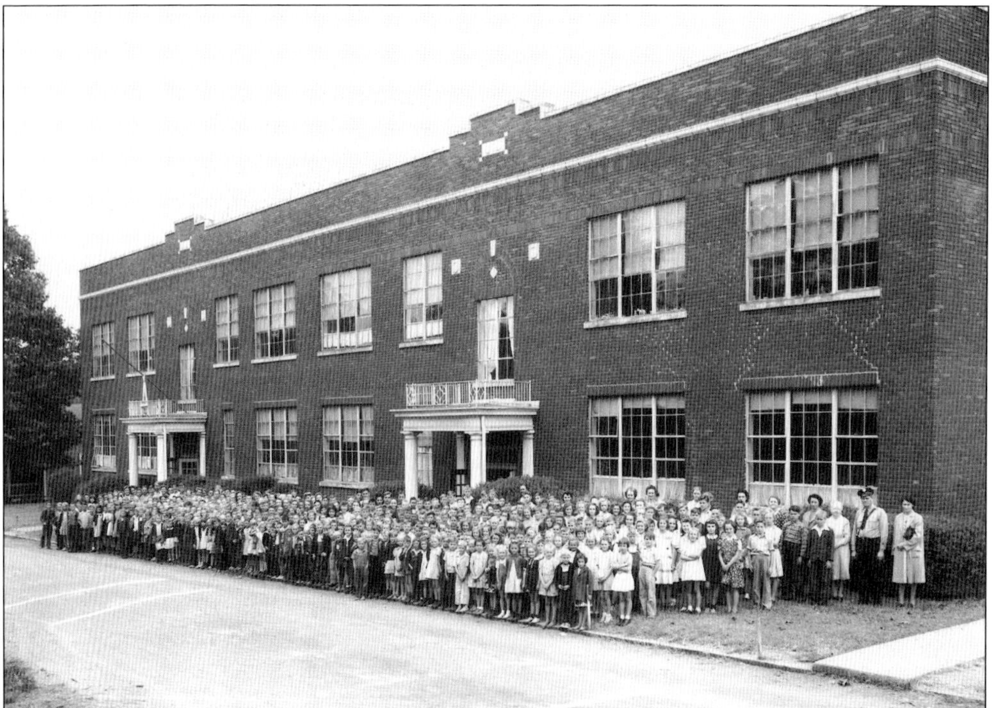

**Students of Brandon Elementary School.** With the formation of the Parker School District in 1922, schools were no longer operated by the mills. As a result, a new Brandon Elementary was built. The much-larger two-story brick building had two front entrances and larger classrooms. (Courtesy of the Coxe Collection, Greenville County Historical Society.)

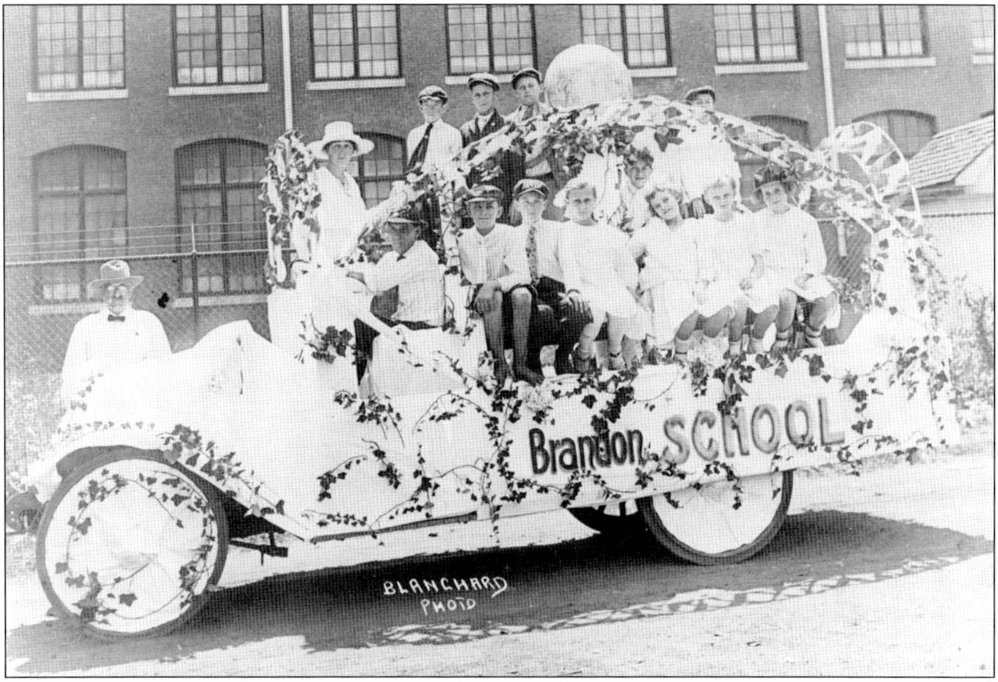


**BRANDON SCHOOL FLOAT.** This Blanchard Professional photograph shows the school's ivy-covered parade float. Pictured here are, from left to right, (first row) Dave Mahon, Earl Dill, unidentified, Hattie Taylor, Josie Carnes, Nonnie Watson, and Marcella Auston; (second row) James A. Taylor, Bessie Owens (principal), ? Mahon, Fred Young, Tom Long, and ? Doggett. (Courtesy of the Brandon Historical Society Collection, Greenville County Library System.)

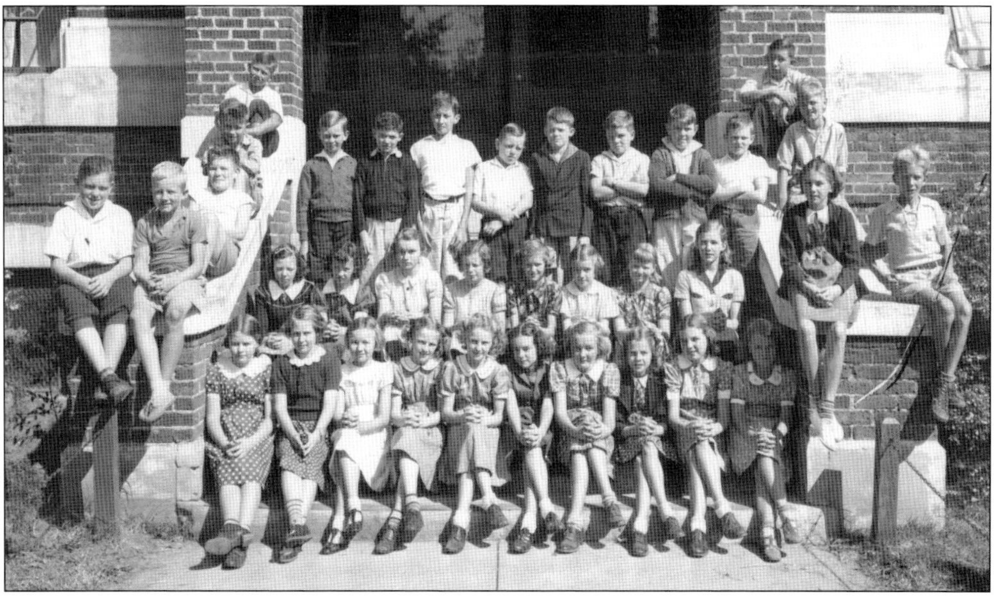

**POE MILL ELEMENTARY.** Located on Second Avenue, the school building was erected by the mill at a cost of $6,000. The mill also paid the salaries of four teachers. Principal Ellen Perry later became one of the most beloved librarians in the Greenville Library System. (Courtesy of the Coxe Collection, Greenville County Historical Society.)

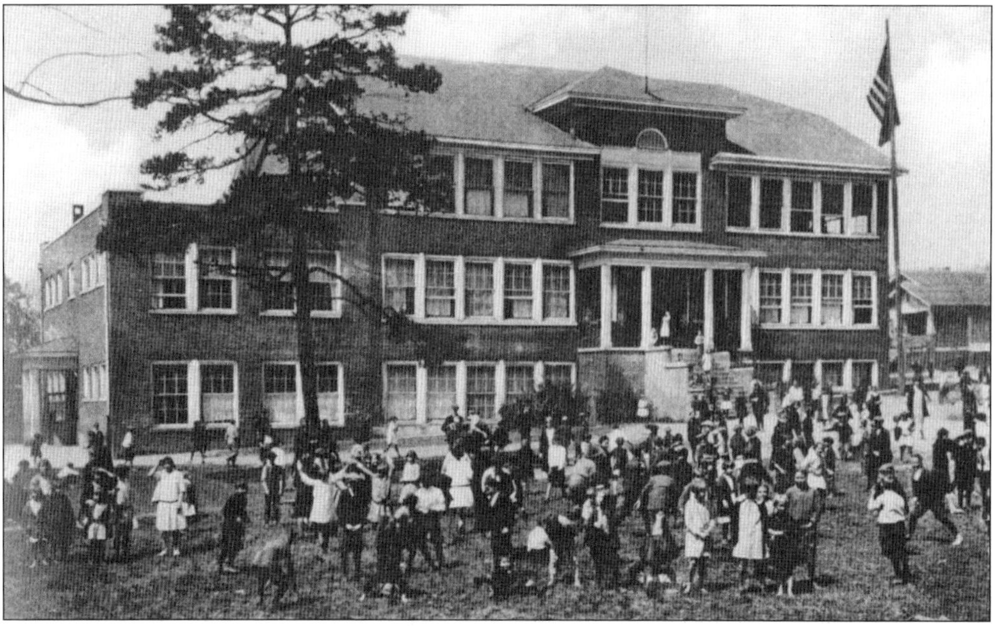

MONAGHAN GRAMMAR SCHOOL. The school building was built by Monaghan Mill, and the mill contributed $850 per year for operations. The school building burned to the ground in 1954. (Courtesy of the Monaghan Historical Society Collection, Greenville County Library System.)

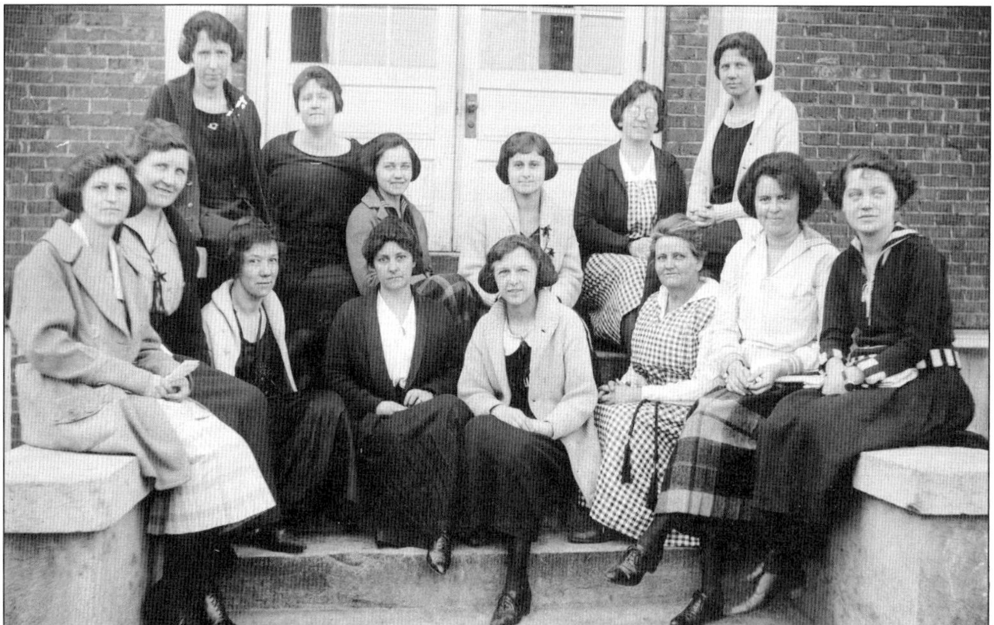

MONAGHAN SCHOOLTEACHERS. These educators gather for a photograph on the school steps. In 1917, the state superintendent cited the school as having a modern building erected at a cost of $17,000. The school had a domestic science room, library, gymnasium, auditorium, and nine classrooms. The staff included nine teachers and one special music teacher. Along with the state curriculum, the Monaghan School also taught gardening, singing, drawing, manual training, and domestic arts and sciences. (Courtesy of the Greenville County Library System.)

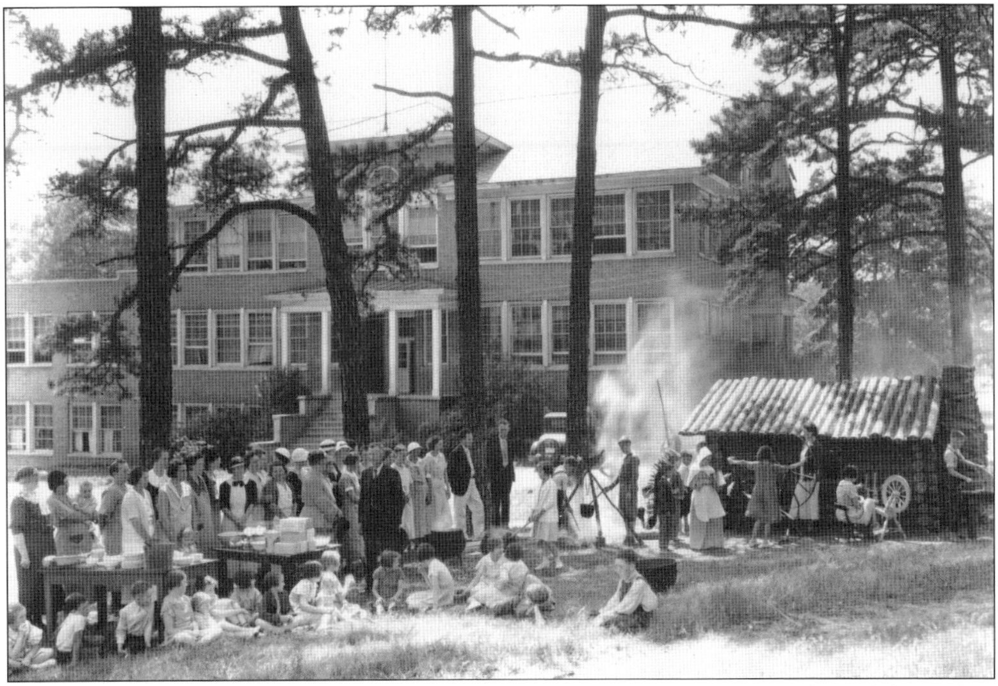

**Pioneer Day.** Parents and faculty at Monaghan Grammar School watch members of the student body put on a Pioneer Day show, complete with log cabin. Students dressed as pioneers and Indians reenact spinning thread, cooking over an open fire, and even shooting a musket and wild game. A meal was provided afterwards. (Courtesy of the Coxe Collection, Greenville County Historical Society.)

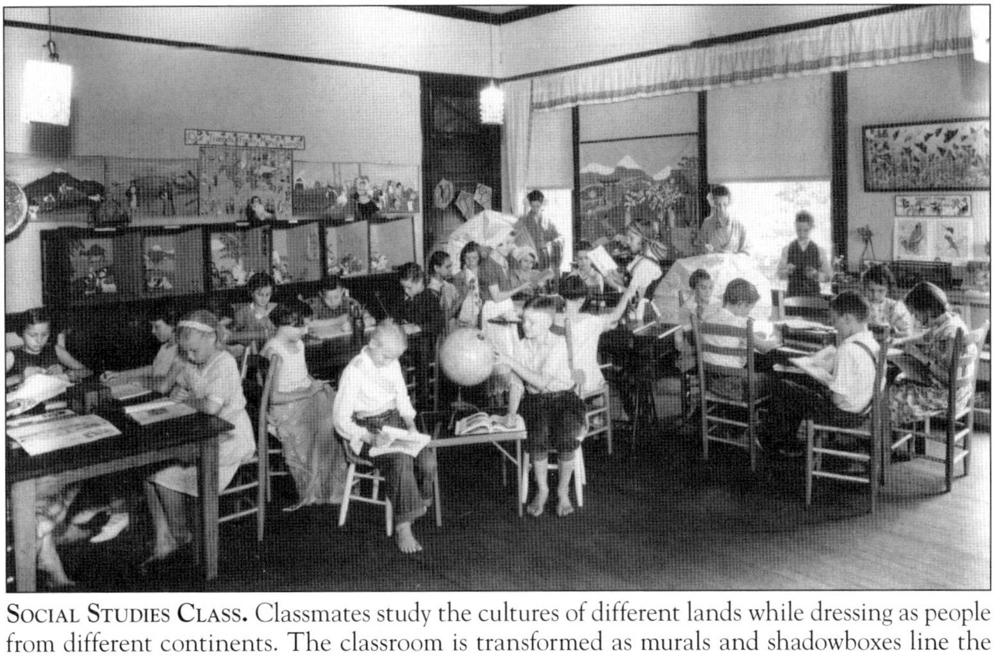

**Social Studies Class.** Classmates study the cultures of different lands while dressing as people from different continents. The classroom is transformed as murals and shadowboxes line the walls, depicting different ethnicities, and Japanese lanterns are hung over the lights. (Courtesy of the Coxe Collection, Greenville County Historical Society.)

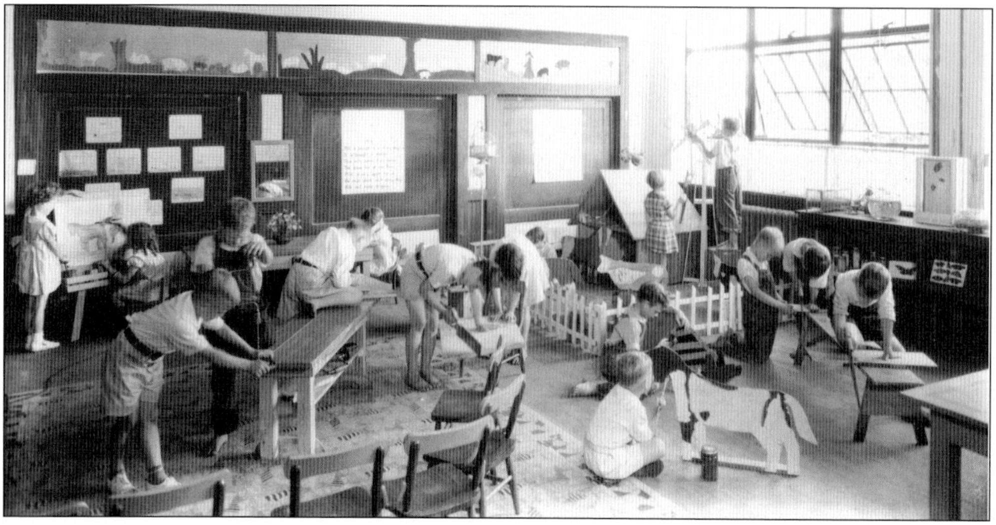

**West Greenville Elementary.** Students construct a farm in their classroom by sawing and painting livestock, a barn, fencing, and a windmill. Live fish and birds add to the learning experience. Prior to organizing the Parker School District, village schools only went through the sixth grade. The rationale was that children would then begin work in the mills. To continue their education, families would have to pay tuition at city or county high schools. With Parker, elementary schools went through the seventh grade, and mill youths could continue their education at no charge. (Courtesy of the Coxe Collection, Greenville County Historical Society.)

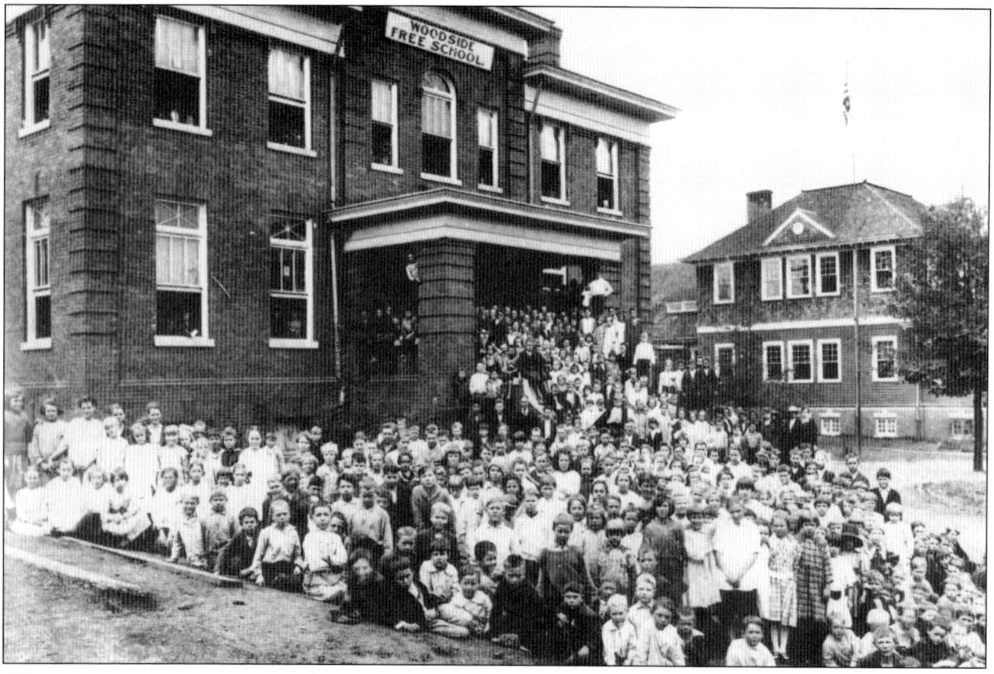


**Woodside Free School.** Woodside Cotton Mill Company built its first school in the village, which was a three-teacher schoolhouse attended by 150 of the village's 300 children. In 1910, the mill built the 7,200-square-foot two-story brick structure seen here. A three-story 13,200-square-foot building was added in 1926. The adjacent structure is the YMCA building, erected in 1910 at a cost of $10,000. (Courtesy of the John Hall Collection, Greenville County Library System.)

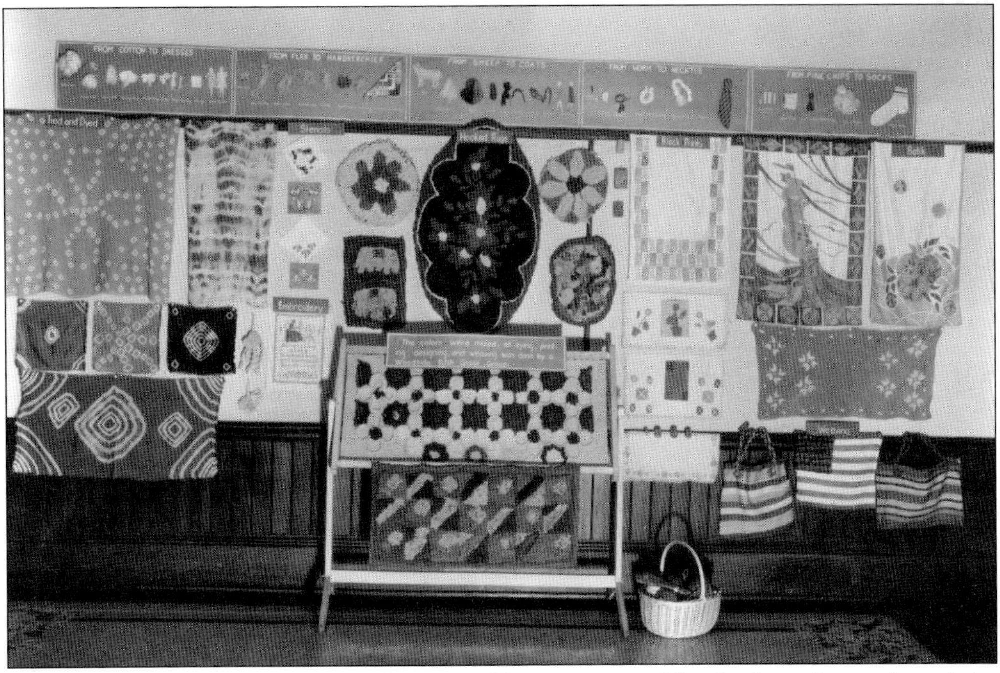


**WOODSIDE FIFTH GRADE TEXTILE DISPLAY.** Class projects of finished textile goods and the processes used to manufacture textiles are neatly on display. The chart on top shows how goods are made, starting with raw materials to finished products such as dresses, handkerchiefs, coats, neckties, and socks. Other goods that the students made include tied and dyed fabrics, stencils, hooked rugs, block prints, and batiks. (Courtesy of the Coxe Collection, Greenville County Historical Society.)

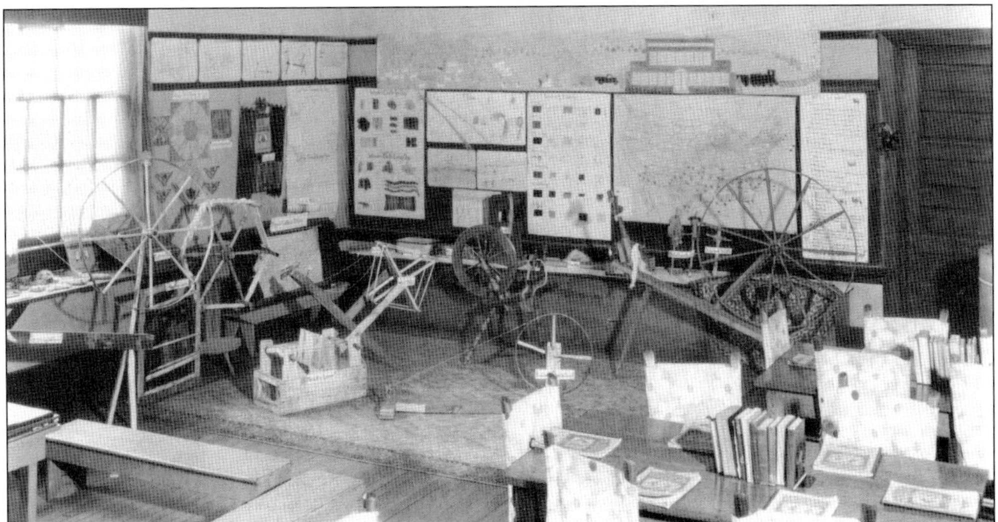

**CLASS PROJECTS.** A Parker School District elementary school classroom is filled with displays depicting various textile-manufacturing processes. A spinning wheel, Indian rug loom, cotton gin, heddle loom, and Russian flax wheel fill the floor, while charts showing the types of cotton, wool, fiber testing, and manufacturing cover the walls. (Courtesy of the Coxe Collection, Greenville County Historical Society.)

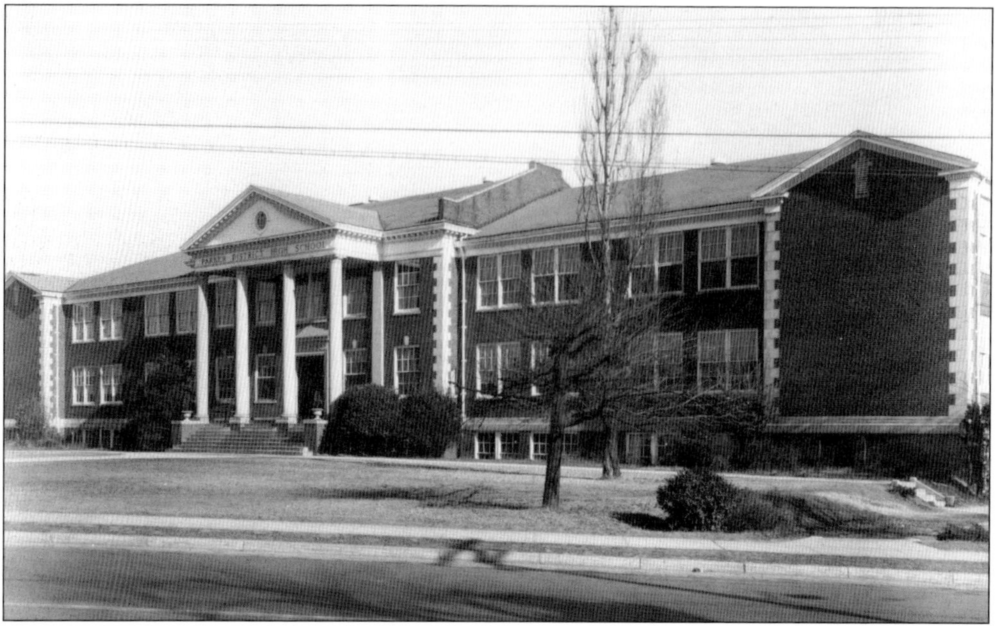

**Parker District High School.** In the early 1920s, textile manufacturing companies such as Brandon, Dunean, Judson, Monaghan, and others saw the need for a high school for mill youth the further their education. The mill owners, led by Monaghan president Thomas Parker, devised a plan to create a school district to meet these needs, and in 1922, the Parker School District was organized. (Courtesy of the Coxe Collection, Greenville County Historical Society.)

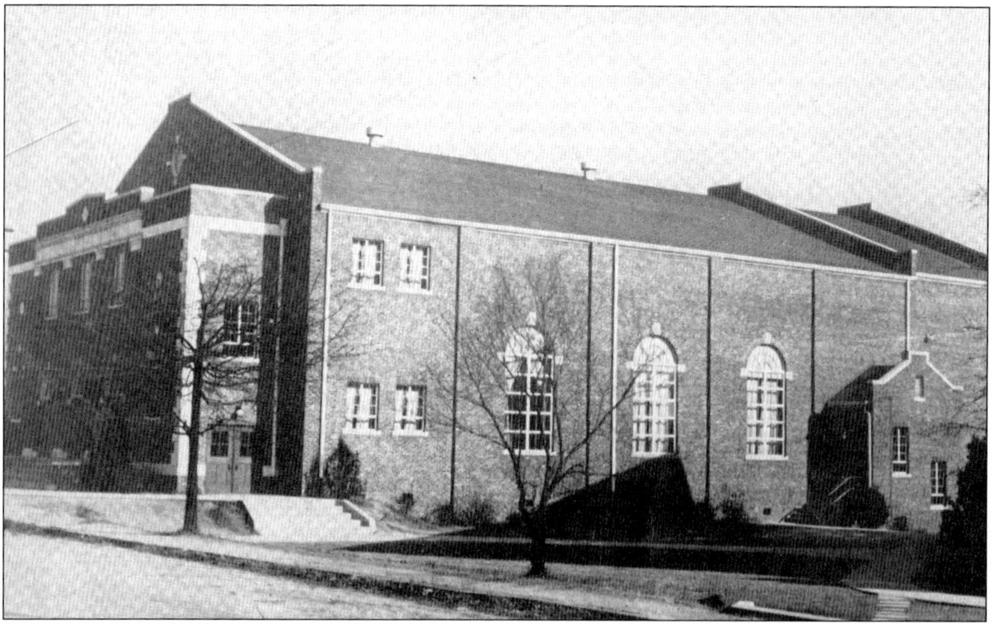

**Parker High Auditorium.** Built in 1938 with funding provided by the Works Progress Administration (WPA), the 7,500 square-foot brick rectangular building is a Classical Revival style with a gabled roof. It is the last remaining building from the largest WPA school project in the state of South Carolina. The auditorium was added to the National Register of Historic Places on February 26, 1996. (Courtesy of the Greenville County Library System.)

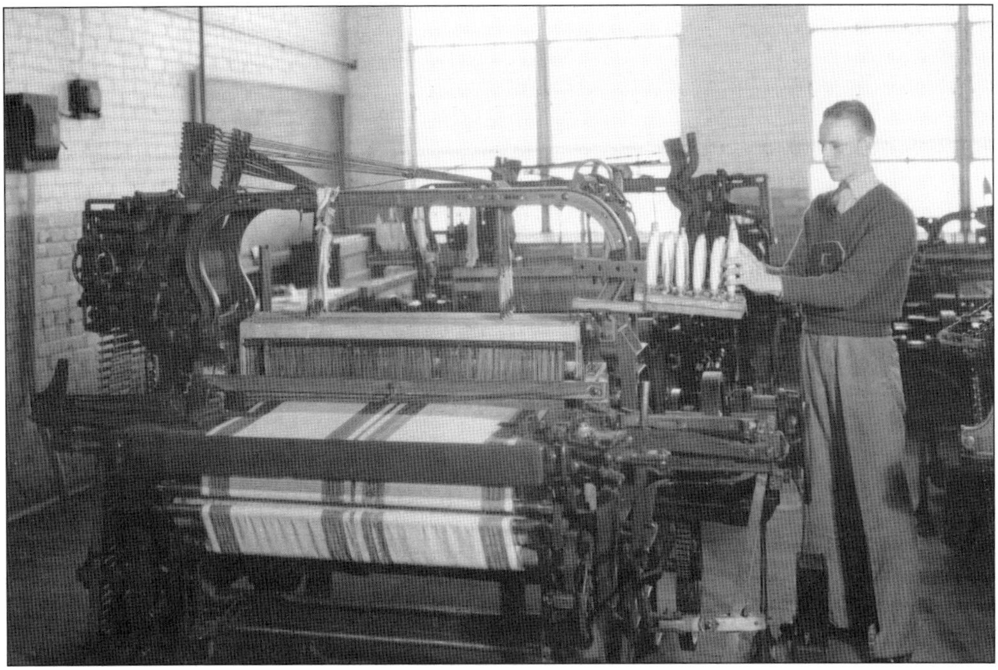

**Parker High Vocational Program.** A student in his letterman sweater observes a loom. The vocational department taught many different types of trades, including cosmetology, typing and shorthand, electronics, textiles, machine shop, arts and crafts, mechanical drawing, welding, and business mathematics. The first class to graduate Parker High School was in May 1924. (Courtesy of the Coxe Collection, Greenville County Historical Society.)

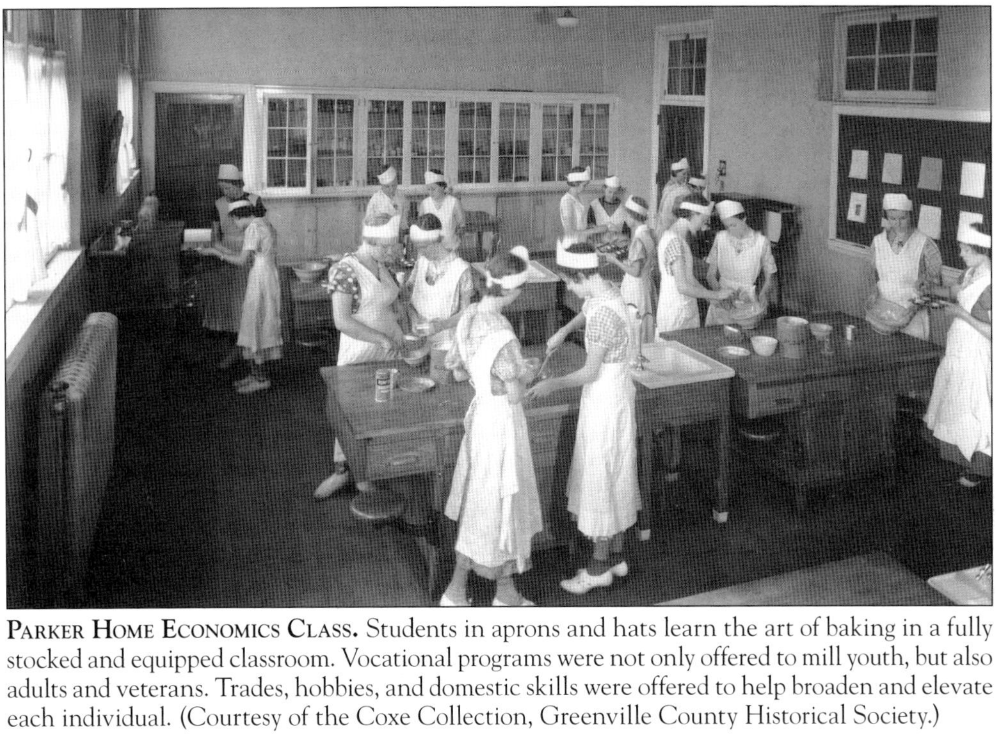

**Parker Home Economics Class.** Students in aprons and hats learn the art of baking in a fully stocked and equipped classroom. Vocational programs were not only offered to mill youth, but also adults and veterans. Trades, hobbies, and domestic skills were offered to help broaden and elevate each individual. (Courtesy of the Coxe Collection, Greenville County Historical Society.)

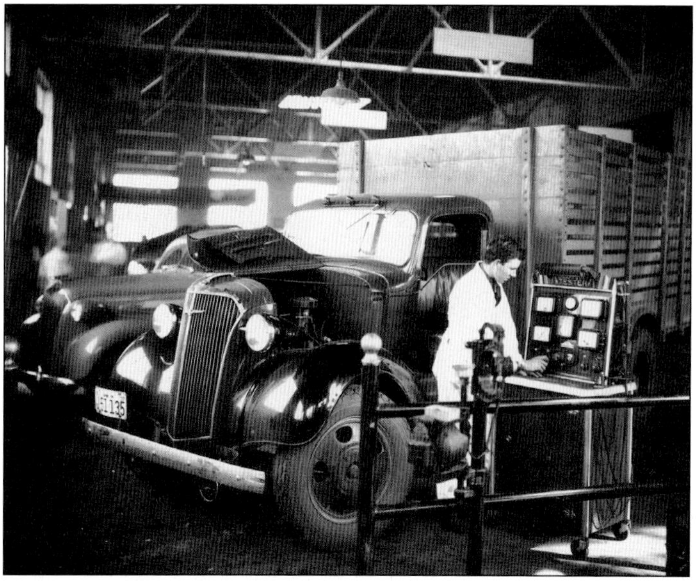

**Parker Vocational Engine Repair Shop.** A student reads the instruments of a diagnostics machine hooked up to a utility truck. Textiles was not the only vocational course offered. A well-equipped machine shop was located on the first floor. Body and fender, engine repair, and even automotive painting courses were available. (Courtesy of the Coxe Collection, Greenville County Historical Society.)

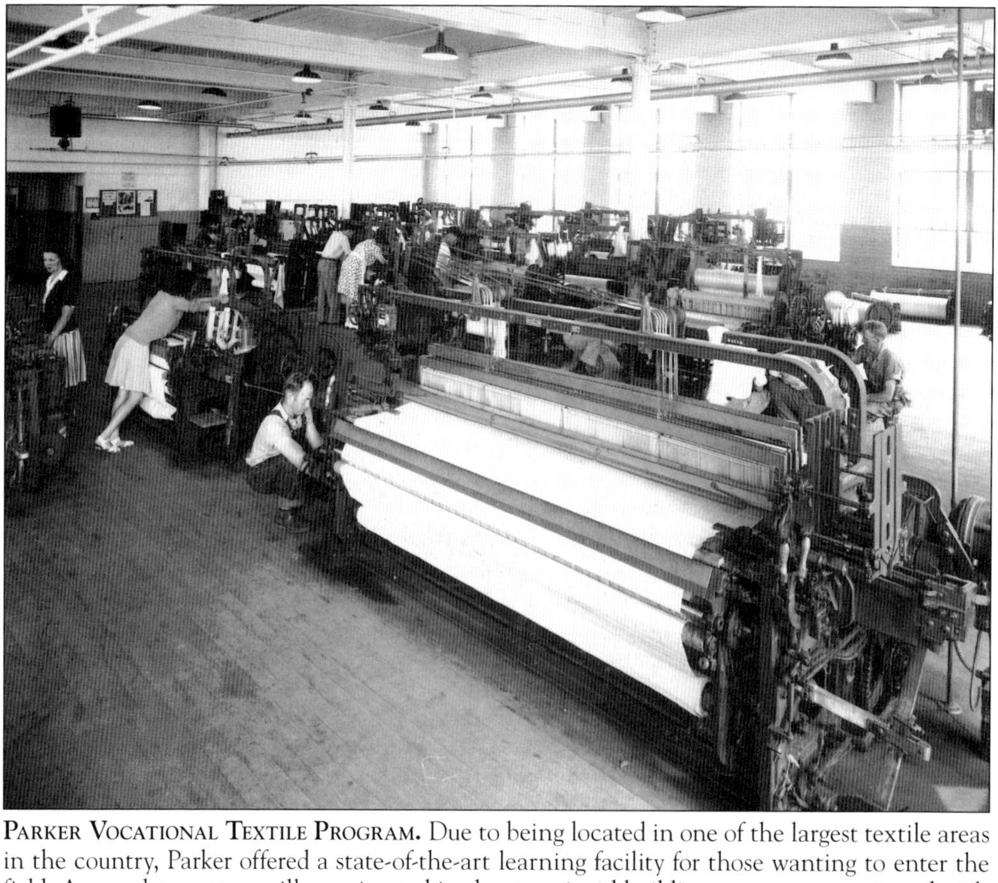

**Parker Vocational Textile Program.** Due to being located in one of the largest textile areas in the country, Parker offered a state-of-the-art learning facility for those wanting to enter the field. A complete cotton mill was situated in the vocational building on campus, equipped with machinery and materials donated by area textile executives. (Courtesy of the Coxe Collection, Greenville County Historical Society.)

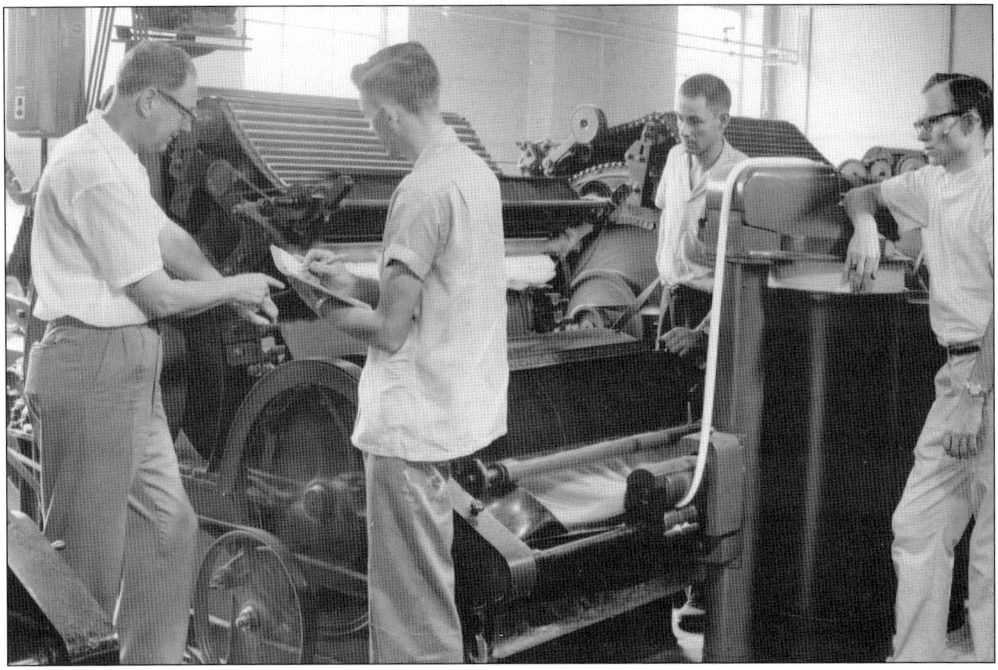

**PARKER TEXTILE CLASS.** An instructor teaches three students the carding process on a carding machine manufactured by Saco-Lowell Machine Shops of Upper Newton Falls, Massachusetts. Carding is the process when staple fibers are opened, cleaned, aligned, and formed into a continuous untwisted strand called sliver. (Courtesy of the Coxe Collection, Greenville County Historical Society.)

**PARKER TEXTILE CLASSROOM.** Dr. Hollis believed that the goals of education should be determined by the needs of the students, rather than mandating the students to conform to preconceived requirements. His vocational program brought national acclaim to the school. Instructors and educators from all over the United States and the world came to observe the curriculum at Parker High School. (Courtesy of the Coxe Collection, Greenville County Historical Society.)

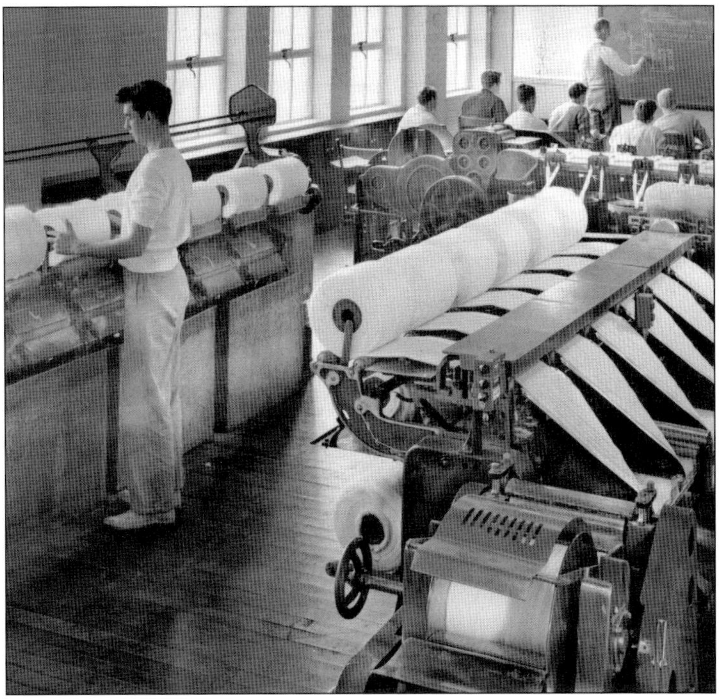

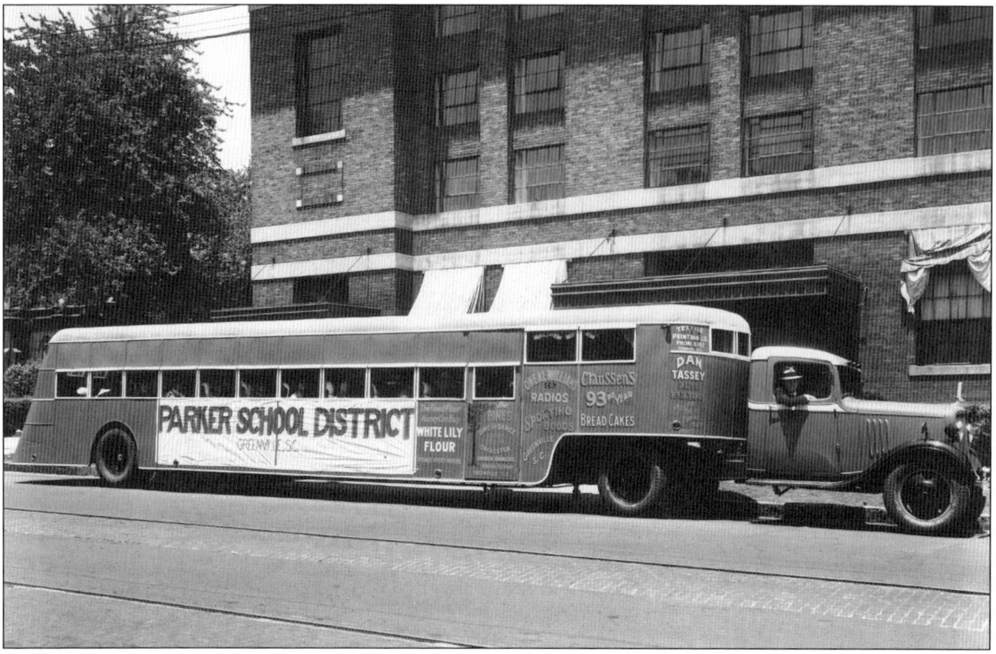


**Parker School District Bus.** Students take a field trip to see the exhibits at Textile Hall. The textile department brought many graduates to the textile plants in Greenville County. During Parker High's 64 years, more than 34,500 students graduated. (Courtesy of the Coxe Collection, Greenville County Historical Society.)

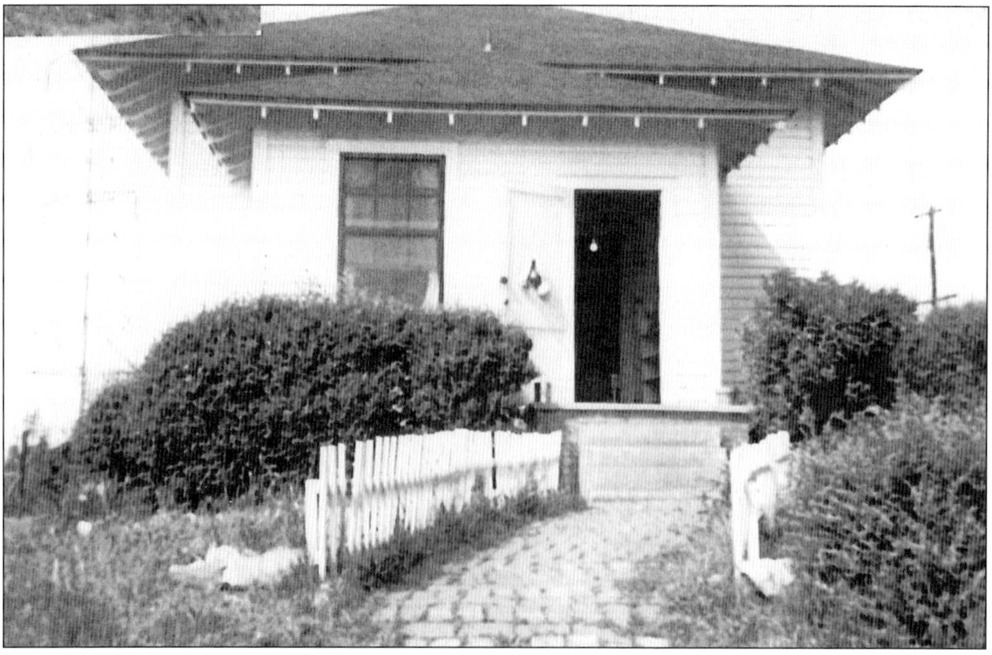

**Union Bleachery African American School.** Like many other mill villages, Union Bleachery had an African American area and school. The school seen here was located on Brooks Avenue near the 253 bypass. (Courtesy of the Union Bleachery Historical Society Collection, Greenville County Library System.)

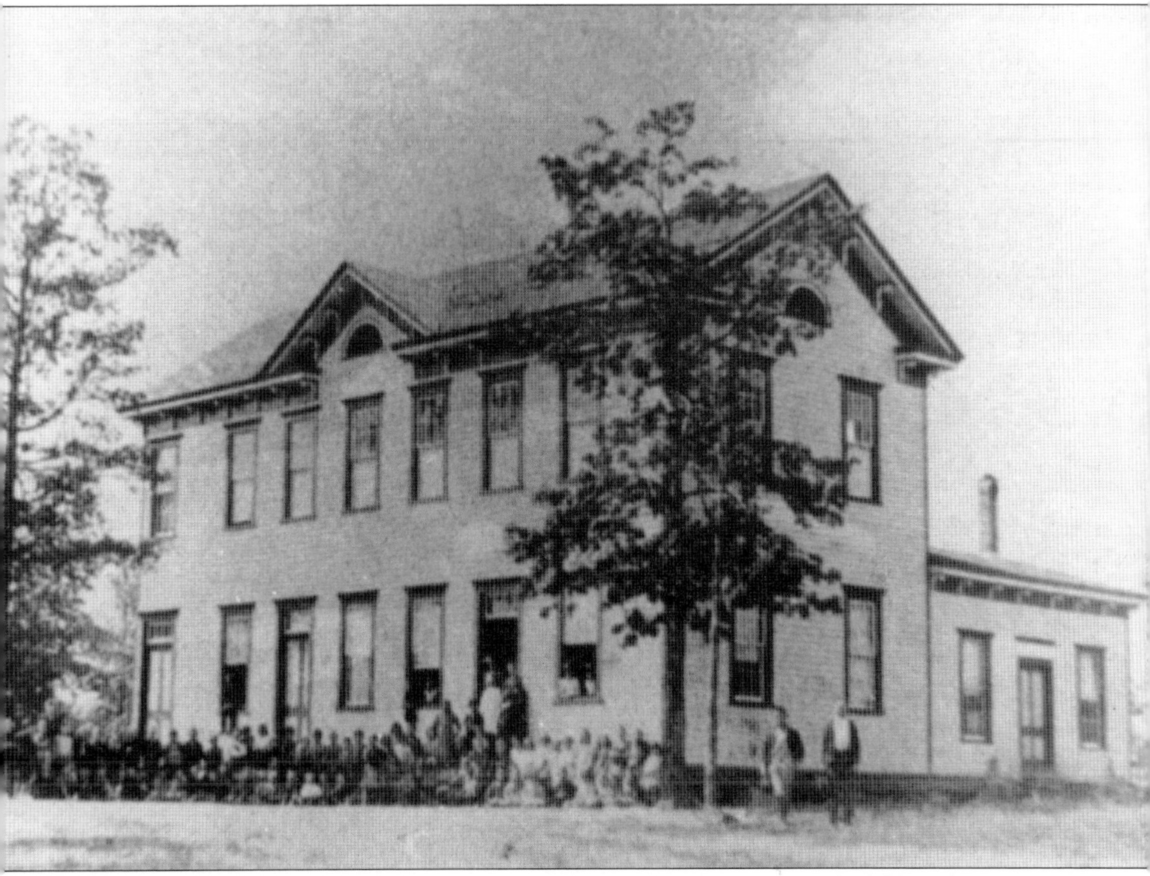

**Piedmont Union School.** Built in 1878, the two-story wooden structure had 80 students in its first year. The school closed in 1921 when the new Piedmont High School opened. (Courtesy of the Piedmont History Collection, Greenville County Library System.)

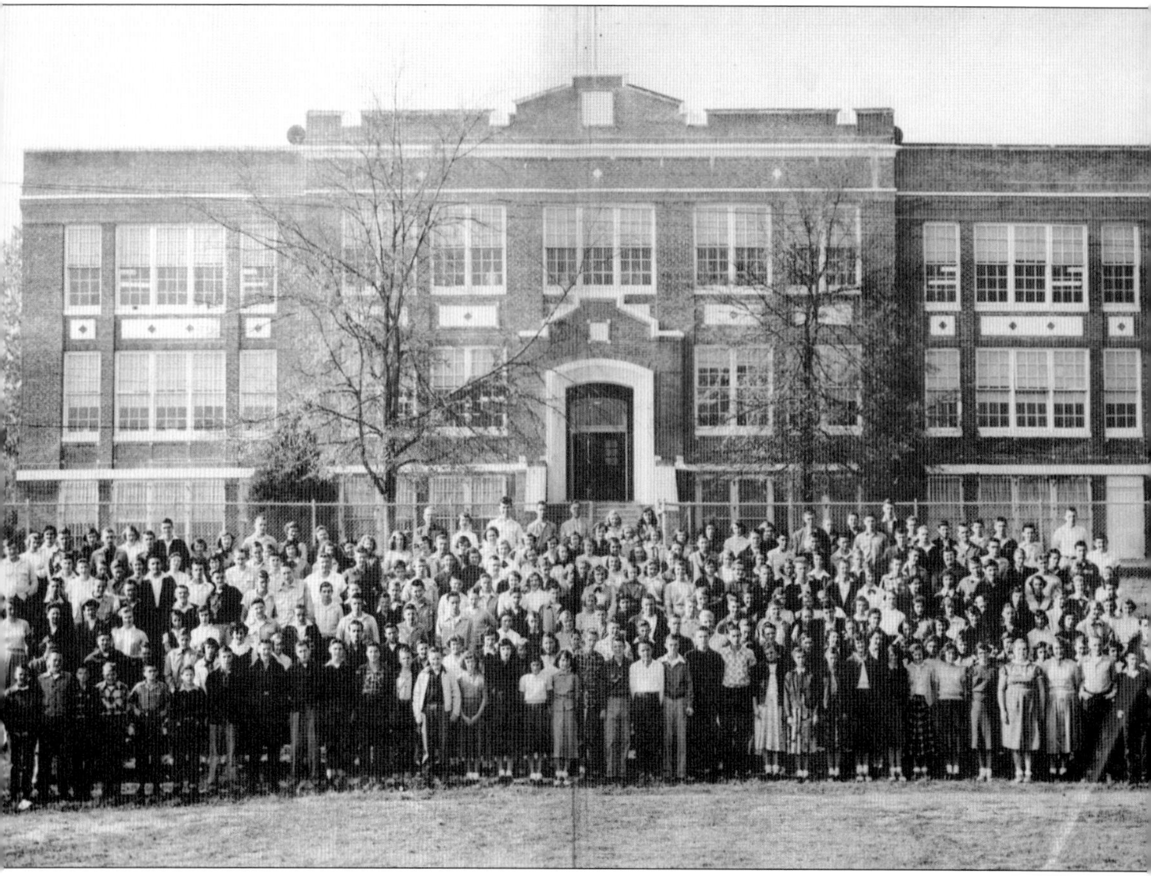

**Piedmont High School.** Originally built in 1920, the school was converted to a junior high school in 1962. Students were transferred to Carolina and Ellen Woodside when the school closed in 1965. (Courtesy of the Piedmont History Collection, Greenville County Library System.)

*Five*

# SPORTS

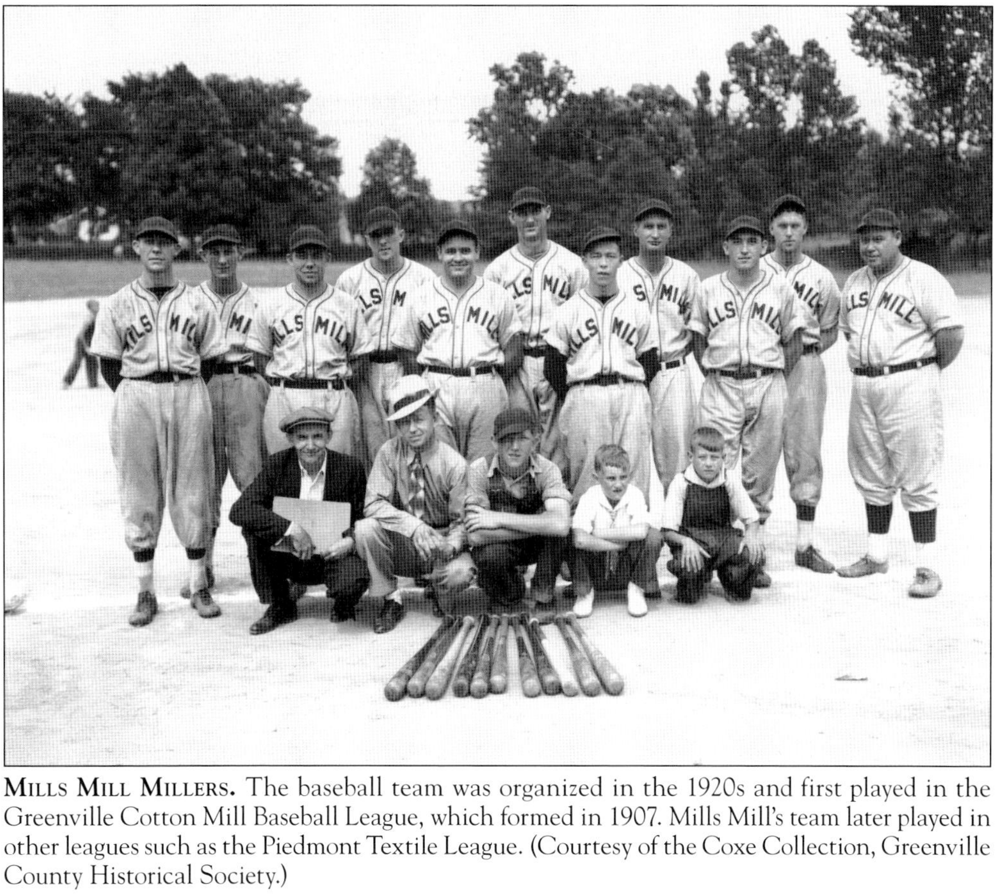

**MILLS MILL MILLERS.** The baseball team was organized in the 1920s and first played in the Greenville Cotton Mill Baseball League, which formed in 1907. Mills Mill's team later played in other leagues such as the Piedmont Textile League. (Courtesy of the Coxe Collection, Greenville County Historical Society.)

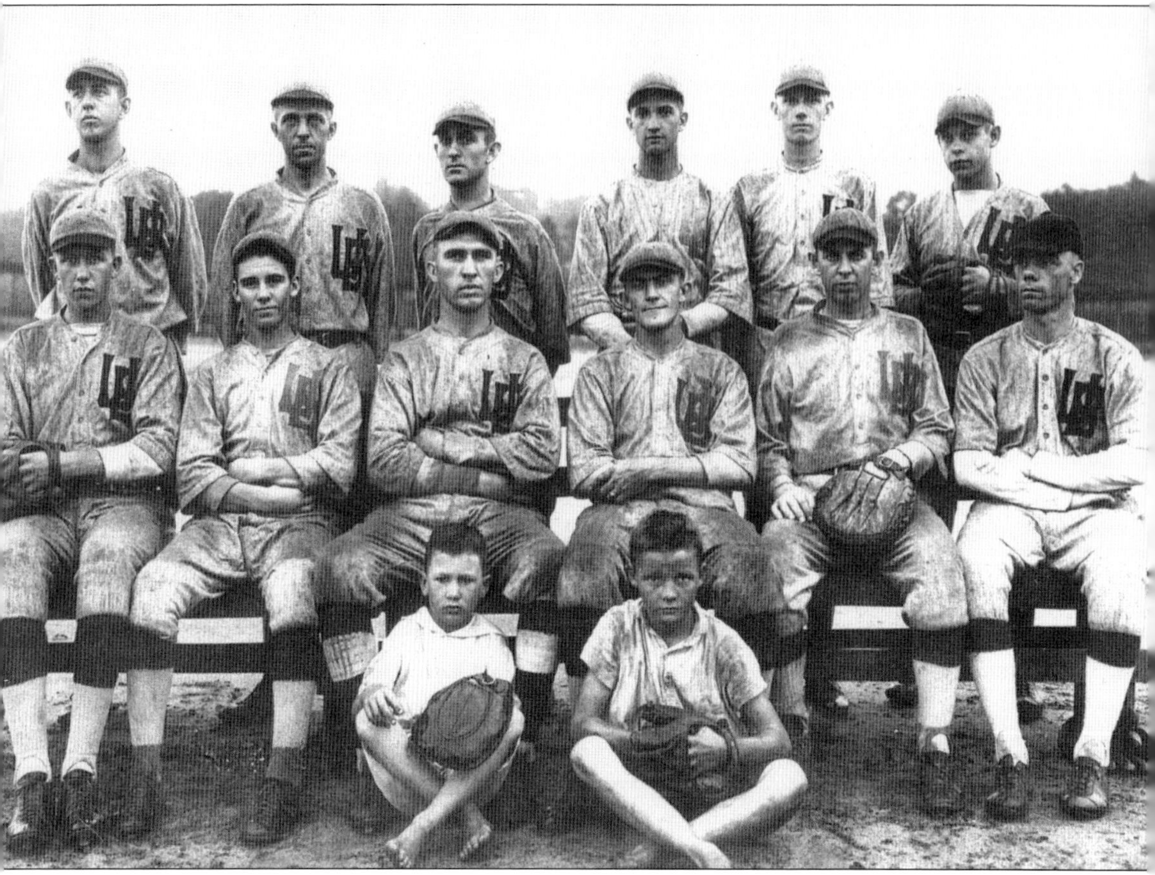

**UNION BLEACHERY BASEBALL TEAM, 1926 PIEDMONT TEXTILE LEAGUE CHAMPIONS.** Union Bleachery hired H. Clyde "Slick" Harrison as the community athletic director in charge of organizing the baseball and basketball teams for all age groups. In addition, he coached the baseball team to victory in the 1926 Piedmont Textile League Tournament. Pictured here are, from left to right, (first row) bat boys Bill Harrison and B.C. Barney Hawkins; (second row) Joe Revis, Ernest "Monk" Floyd, H. Clyde "Slick" Harrison (coach), Heyward Dobbins (mill general manager), "Gee" Turner, and Ralph Belcher; (third row) Paul Turner (pitcher), Tom Turner (mill supervisor), Toy Dalton, Joe Childress, George Belcher, and Raymond Hawkins. (Courtesy of the Elrod Collection, Greenville County Historical Society.)

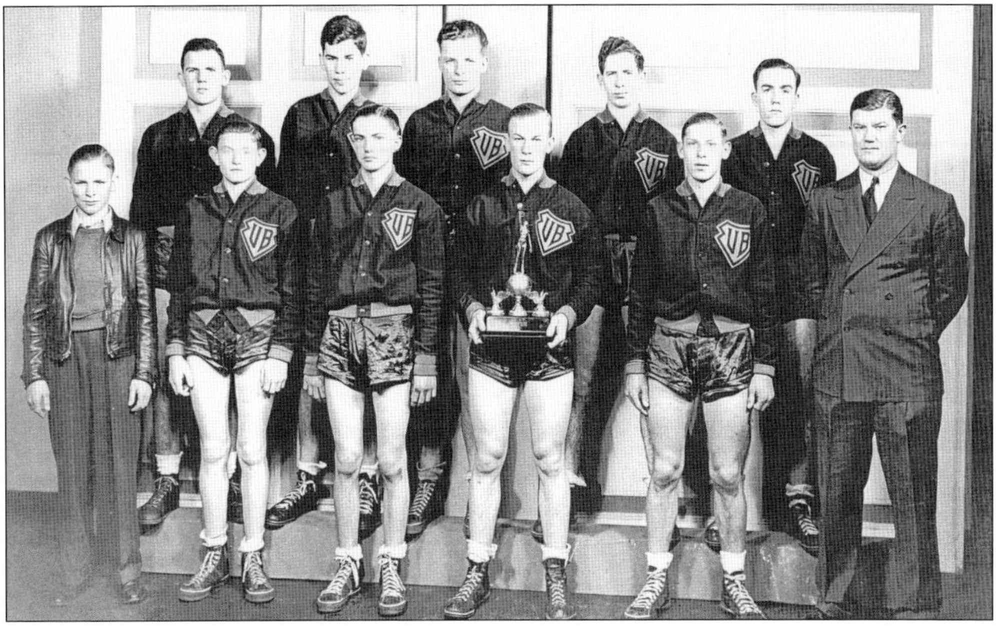

**Union Bleachery Basketball "B" Team, 1938 Southern Textile Basketball Tournament Champions.** Pictured here are, from left to right, (first row) Aromus Belcher, Beattie Eppes, Paul Turner Jr, Roy Brooks, Ansel Bridwell, and Charles Brooks; (second row) Harold Green, Bill Harrison, B.C. Hawkins, Walker Dillworth, and Booty Bishop. (Courtesy of the Union Bleachery Historical Society Collection, Greenville County Library System.)

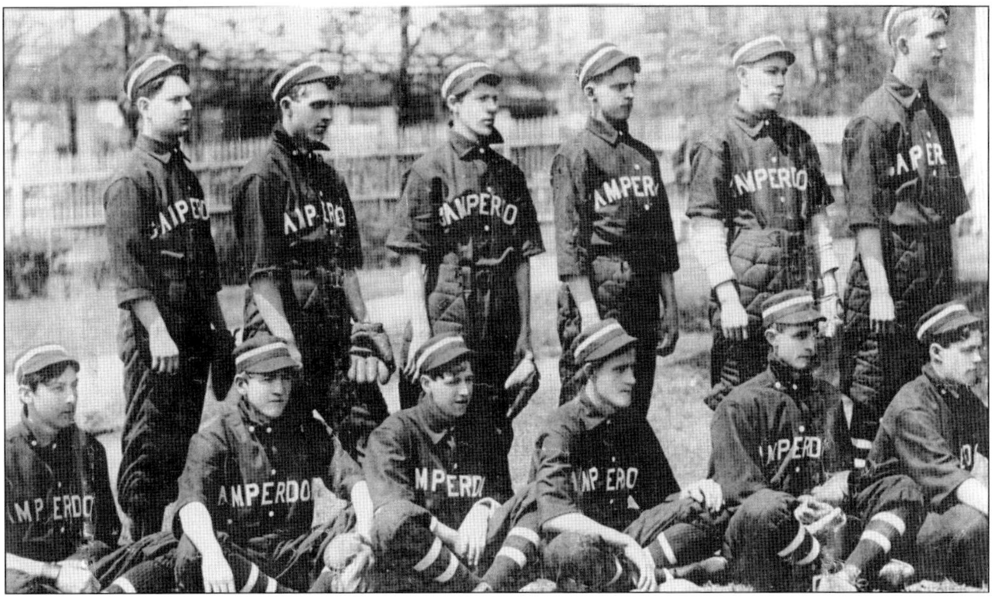

**Camperdown Baseball Team.** This 1906 team photograph was taken the same year Camperdown No. 1 was sold to Luther McBee as he started Vardry Cotton Mills. Members are, from left to right, (first row) Tom Melton, George Whitaker, Charlie Ross, Ford Marchbanks, and Boots Hatcher; (second row) ? Smith, Bob Jenkins, Charlie Hall, Charlie DeLong, Earl Steward, and Pink Barton. (Courtesy of the Camperdown Historical Society Collection, Greenville County Library System.)

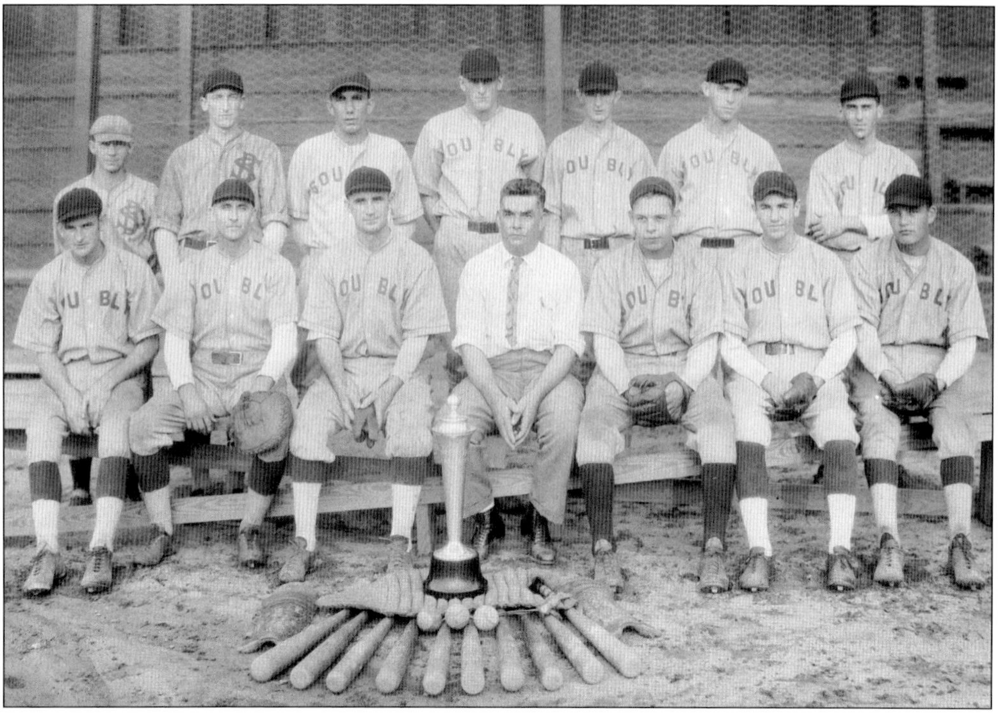

**SOUTHERN BLEACHERY BASEBALL TEAM, 1928 PIEDMONT TEXTILE LEAGUE STATE CHAMPIONS.** It is said that Southern Bleachery hired players away from the professional Greenville Spinners team in order to gain an advantage over teams such as the Dunean Dynamos. Southern Bleachery's baseball field had grandstands and was shared with Taylors High School. (Courtesy of the Elrod Collection, Greenville County Historical Society.)

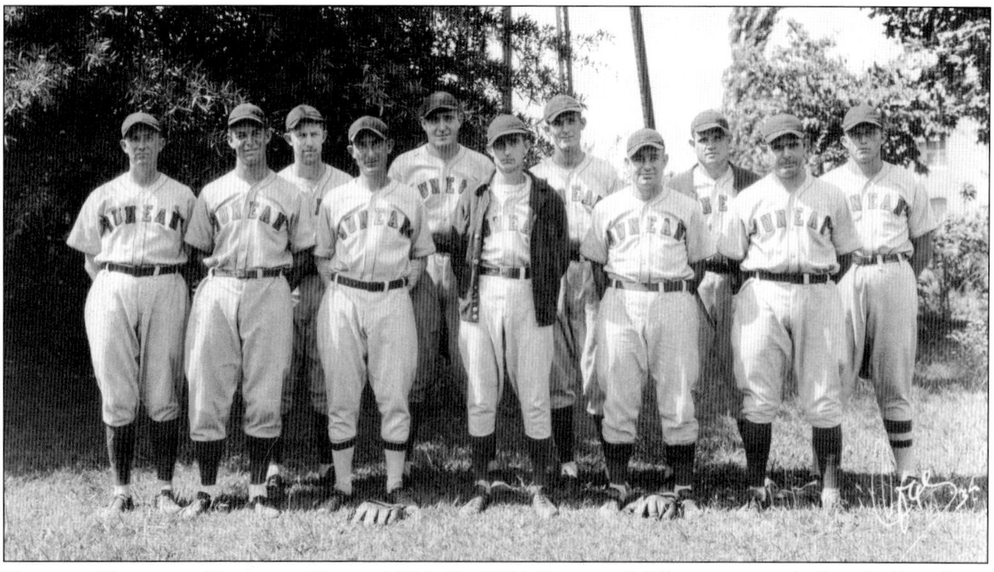

**DUNEAN DYNAMOS BASEBALL TEAM, 1934.** By 1924, Dunean Mill constructed a baseball park on the southern edge of the village. The mill team went on to win four consecutive Carolina Textile League pennants. Dunean Mill and its water tower can be seen in the background of this team photograph. (Courtesy of the Coxe Collection, Greenville County Historical Society.)

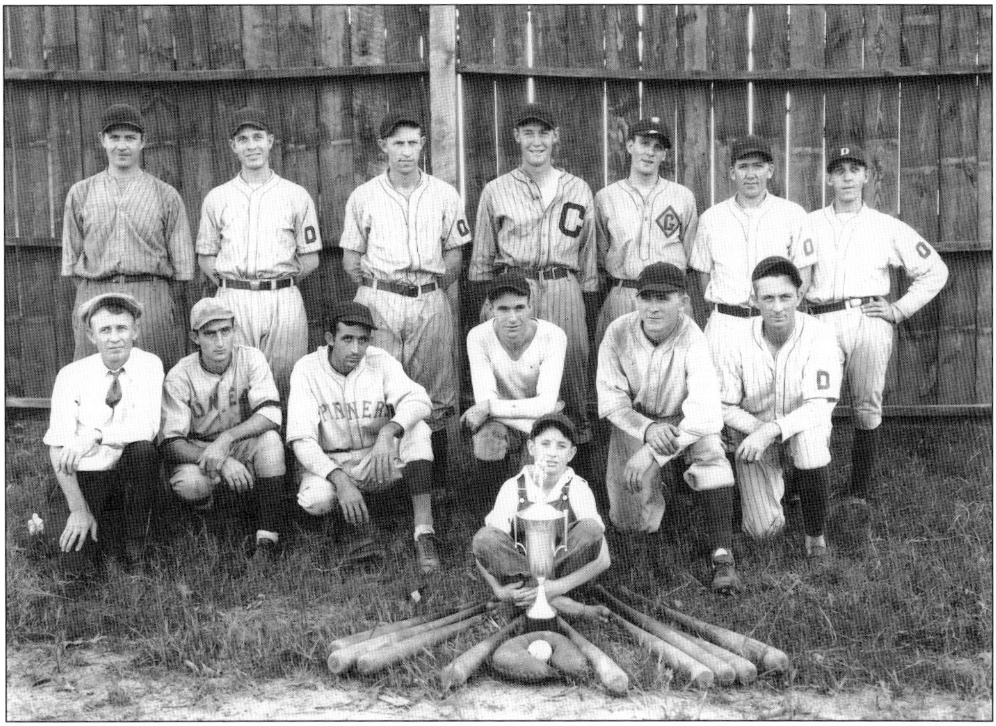

**DUNEAN BALL CLUB, 1930.** The 1930 team with a 16-6 record won the Piedmont Textile League Championship. Bat boy Bob Cooper kneels behind the championship trophy. Players pictured here are, from left to right, (first row) John Langston (team manager), Winfred Kelley, Julius Kelley, Gene Martin, Emerson Cashion, and Frank Floyd; (second row) Winslow Wood, Huldon Harvell, Fred Harvell, Jimmy Jones, Henry Huff, June Campbell, and Ralph Hudson. (Courtesy of the Coxe Collection, Greenville County Historical Society.)

**DUNEAN MILL LADIES' SOFTBALL TEAM.** This 1930s photograph taken outside Dunean Mill shows the team with manager C.H. "Doodle" Thomas. In 1940, the ladies' team beat Southern Weaving 10-9 to win the South Carolina Women's Softball Championship. (Courtesy of the Coxe Collection, Greenville County Historical Society.)

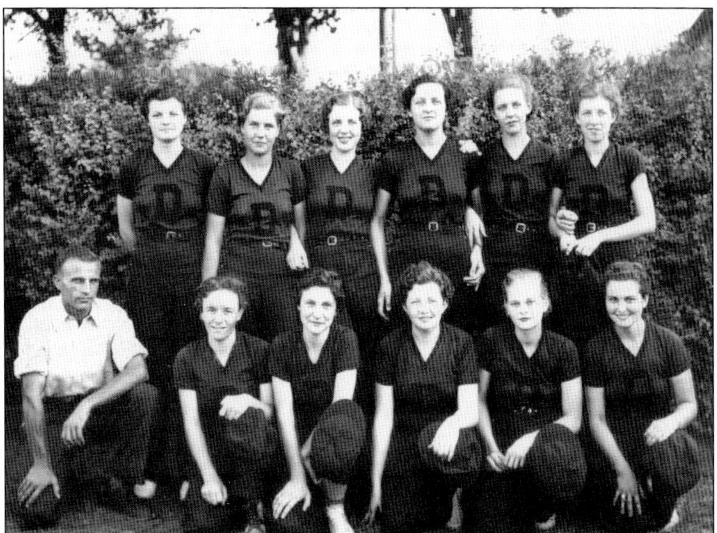

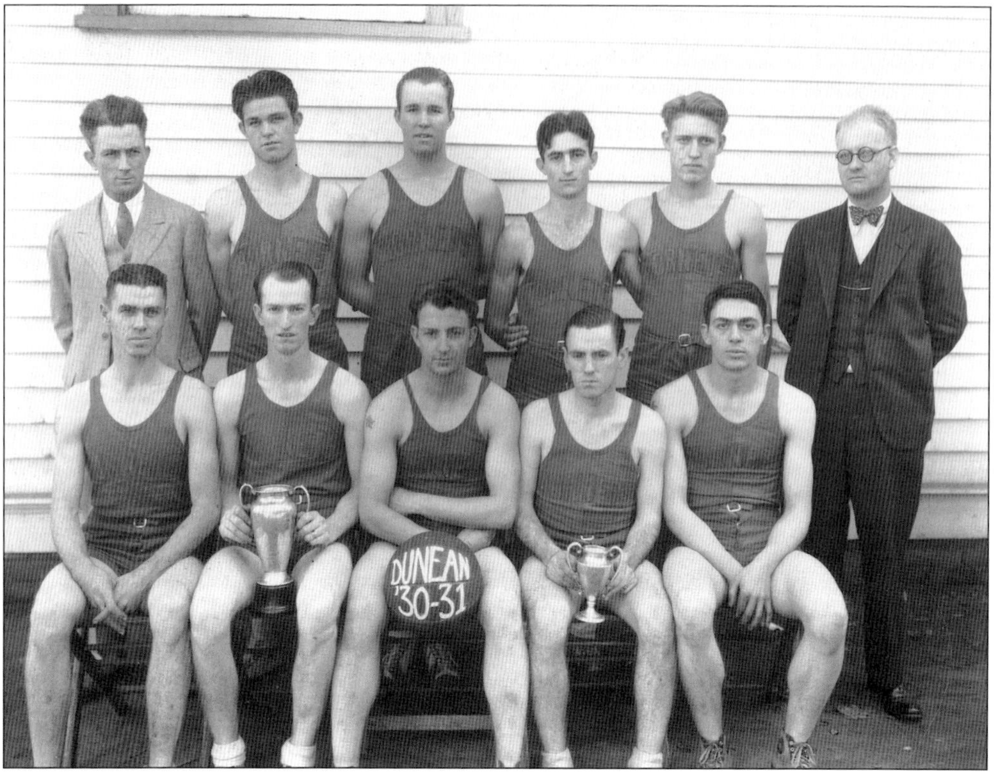


**Dunean Hornets Basketball Team, 1930–1931.** Seen here holding two trophies, the Class B boys team won the Southern Textile Basketball Tournament Championship title. From left to right are (first row) Willie Riddle, Grayson "Hap" Roddy, L.C. Davis, Emmery "Fuzz" Jones, and L.D. Davis; (second row) Frank Floyd, Homer Dendy, Carroll R. Owens, Winfred Kelley, Woodrow Barnes, and manager Leonard Howard. (Courtesy of the Coxe Collection, Greenville County Historical Society.)

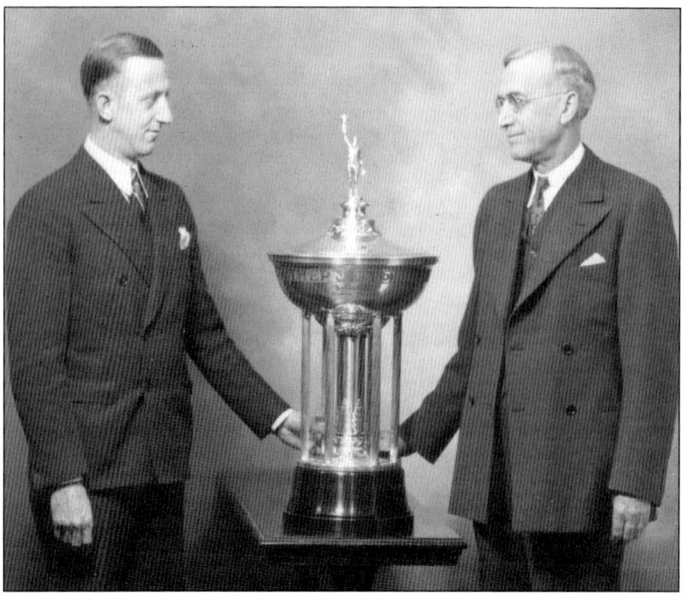

**Southern Textile Basketball Tournament Trophy with Mr. Lowe and Mr. Hall.** The league was started in 1921 with a meeting attended by Pete Hollis and other upstate mill community leaders. The first game was played on February 25, 1921, at Textile Hall, with Monaghan Mill playing against Schoolfield Mill. (Courtesy of the Coxe Collection, Greenville County Historical Society.)

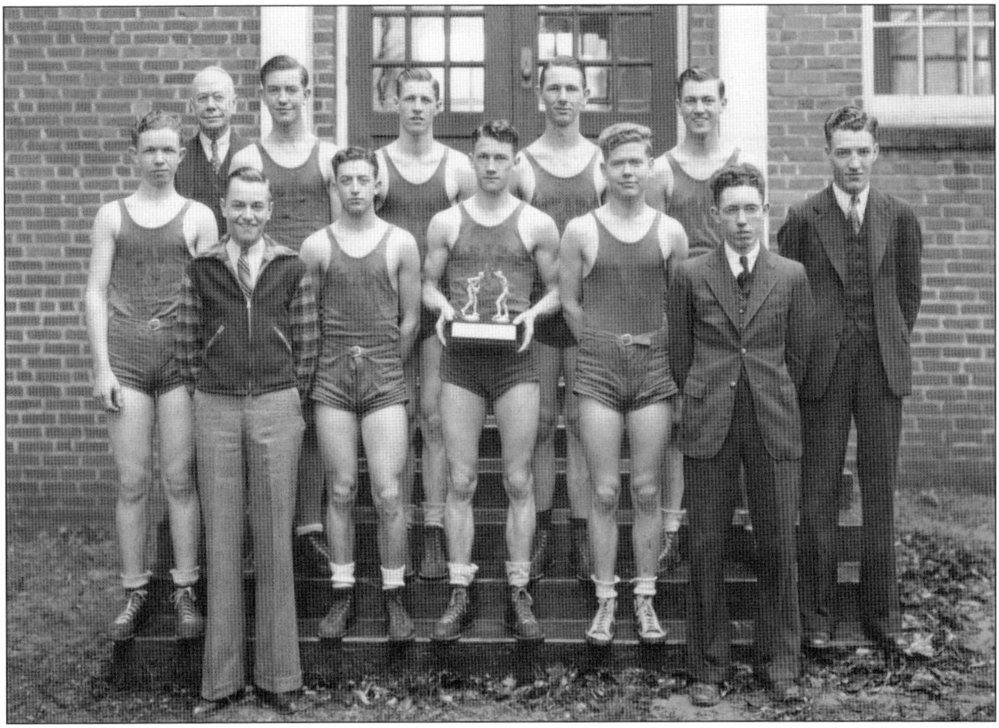

**WOODSIDE MILL BASKETBALL TEAM, 1937 TOURNAMENT CHAMPIONS.** Woodside was among the first mills in Greenville to have a basketball team, and it won the first Southern Textile Basketball Tournament, which was played at Textile Hall in 1921. Pictured in 1937 are, from left to right, (first row) Charlie Payne, Andrew Manley, "Peanut" Freeman, Monroe Ramsey, Joe Whitmire, Bud Hodge, and Dewey Bowen; (second row) W.C. Grier, Jack Harden, Ralph Harbin, "Spike" Bomar, and Harold McConnell. (Courtesy of the Coxe Collection, Greenville County Historical Society.)

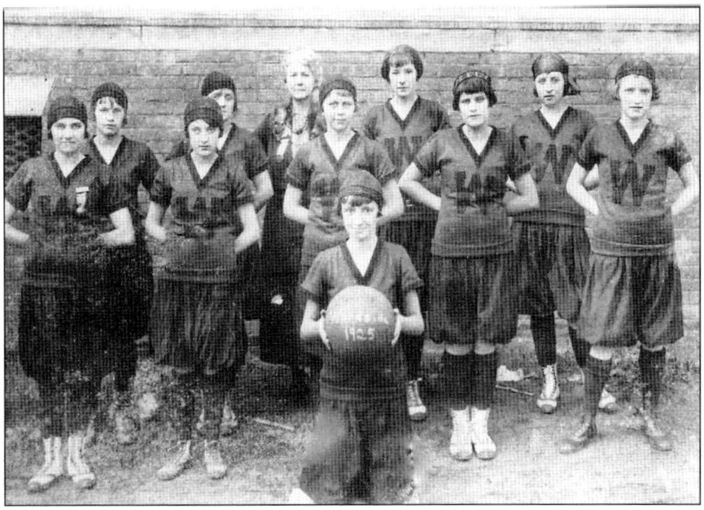

**WOODSIDE LADIES' BASKETBALL TEAM.** Included in this 1925 team photograph are Mrs. W.C. Grier, Ethel Blackwell, Sue Bowen, Mae "Lefty" Chandler, Evelyn "Lasso" Clippard, Marian "Speedy Barnett, Pauline "Frisky" Barnett, Elizabeth McCall, Emma Lee "Snowball" Johnson, Edith McCall, and Violet Turner. (Courtesy of the John Hall Collection, Greenville County Library System.)

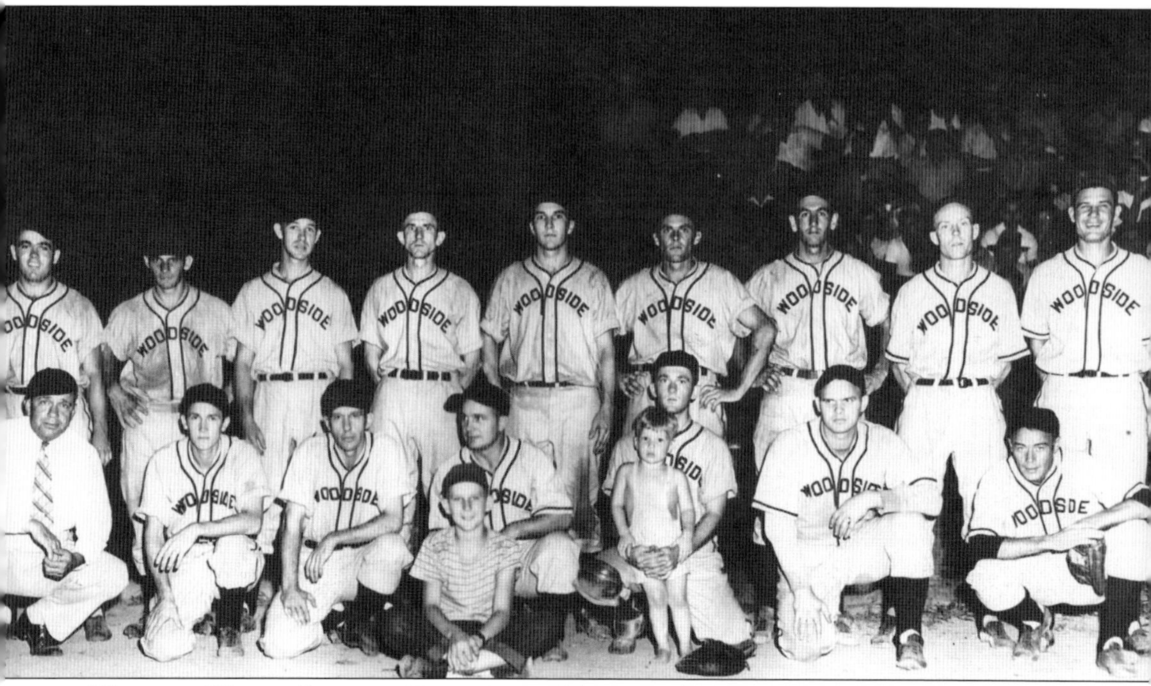


**Woodside Wolves Baseball Team.** Pictured here are the 1947 Textile Baseball Tournament champions; only identified by their last names, from left to right, are (first row) Bodie (team manager), Ramsey, Foster, Gillespie, Farrow, Limbaugh, and Lindstrom; (second row) Wakefield, Hines, Miller, Tucker, Tollison, Gaillard, Wilson, Hendrix, and Cox. The children are Reeves (bat boy) and McCall (team mascot). (Courtesy of the John Hall Collection, Greenville County Library System.)

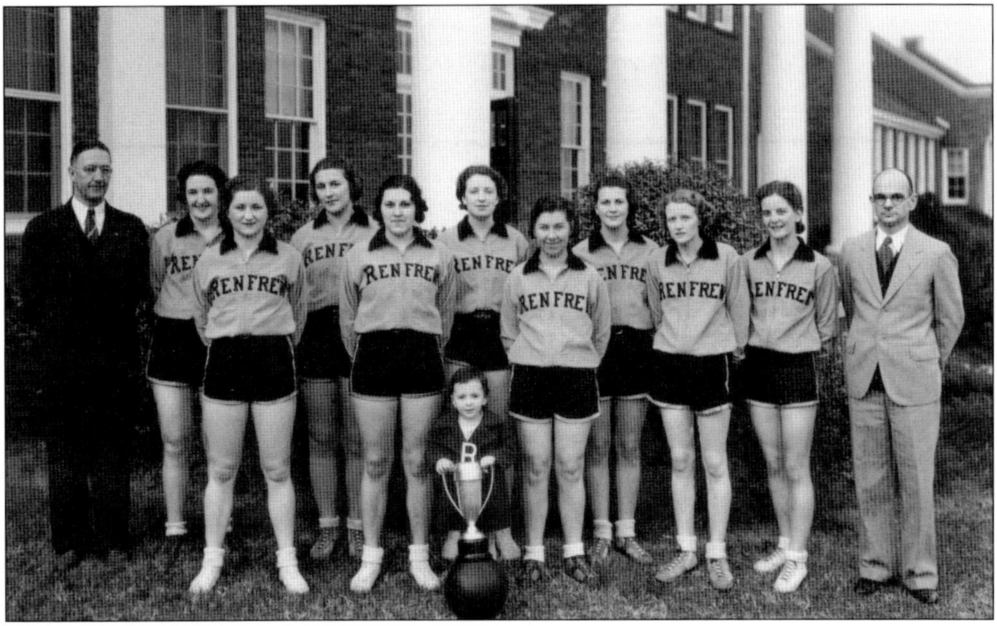

**Renfrew Women's Basketball Team, 1935 Champions.** The first women's basketball team at Renfrew Bleachery was organized around 1933. The team seen here played in the 1935 National AAU Tournament in Wichita, Kansas. Fay Sloan, third woman from the left, and Mrs. Roy Foster, third woman from the right, both continued to work for Renfrew for another 20 years. (Courtesy of the Coxe Collection, Greenville County Historical Society.)

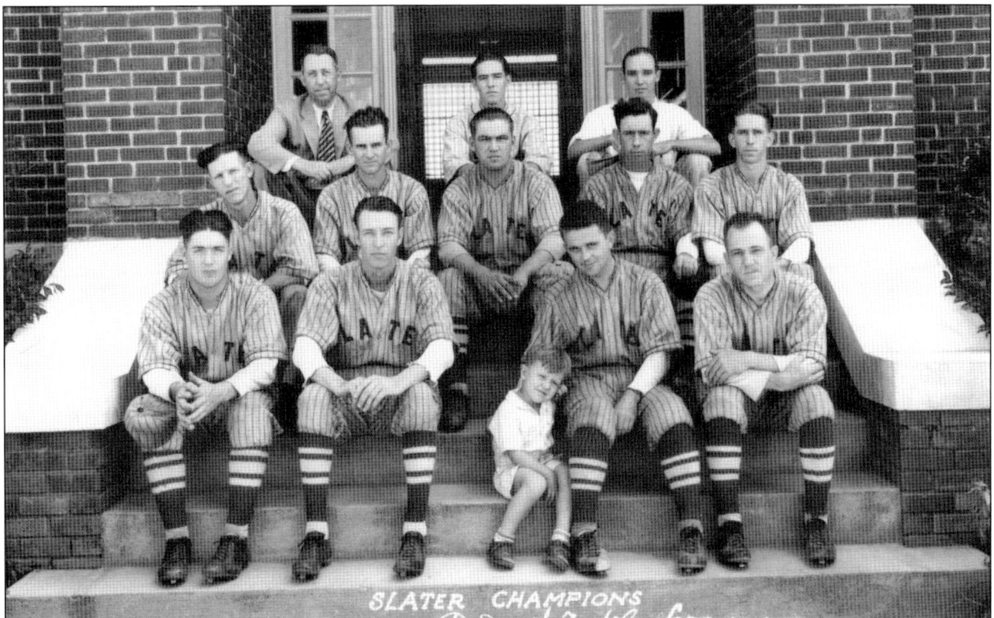


**Slater Sluggers Baseball Team.** The Slater Mill baseball team began playing in the summer of 1929, and in 1931, they won the Piedmont Textile League Championship against Renfrew Bleachery. The champions seen here are sitting in front of the Slater Mill office. (Courtesy of the Coxe Collection, Greenville County Historical Society.)

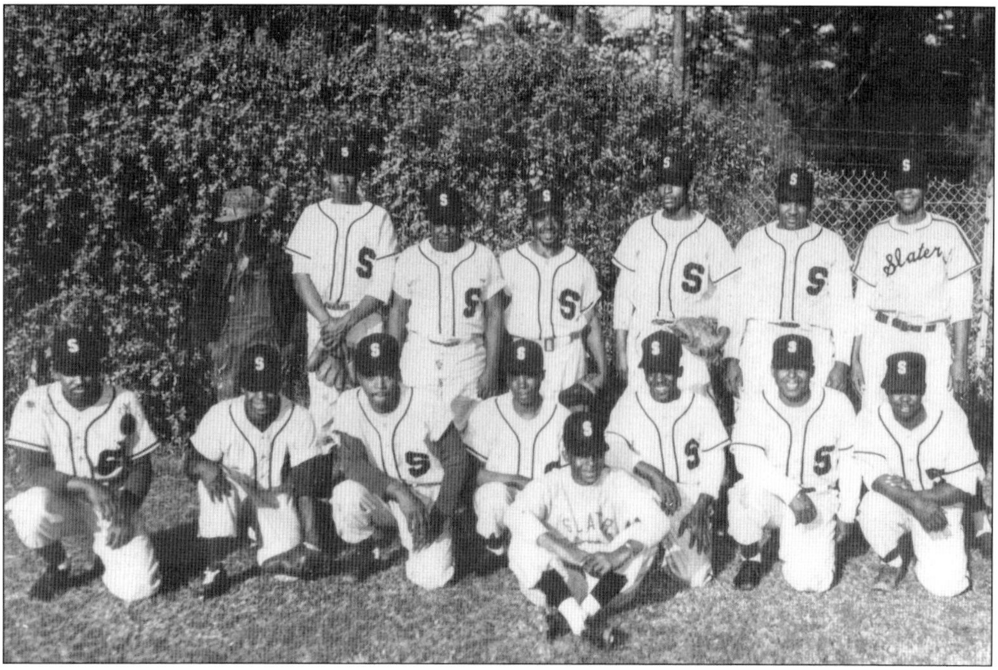

**Slater African American Baseball Team.** Slater's African American team competed in the Negro League in the 1950s and 1960s. Although the league was segregated, they used the same equipment as the other Slater teams and played against other local teams such as Renfrew and Southern Bleachery. Photographed at White Field seated is Thomas Cruell. From left to right are (first row) Landrum Cruell, Edward Cruell, Donald Young, Charlie Cruell, Spann Cruell Jr., Fred Workman, and D.J. Cruell; (second row) Eddie Young, Raymond Kirksey, Ray Cruell, William Cruell, Butch Butler, Paul Cruell, and J.C. Cruell. (Courtesy of Marion Cruell.)

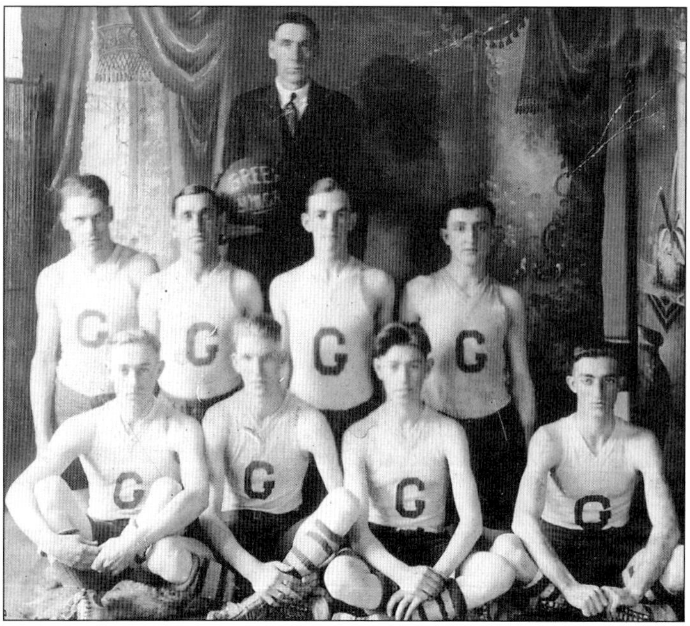

**Greer Mill YMCA Basketball Team, 1922.** L.P. Hollis introduced the game of basketball first at Monaghan Mill while acting as superintendent of its YMCA in 1905. He was taught the game by its inventor, Dr. James Naismith, at a YMCA training session held at Lake George, New York. Basketball quickly spread to the other YMCAs at area textile mills. (Courtesy of the Greer Heritage Museum Collection, Greenville County Library System.)

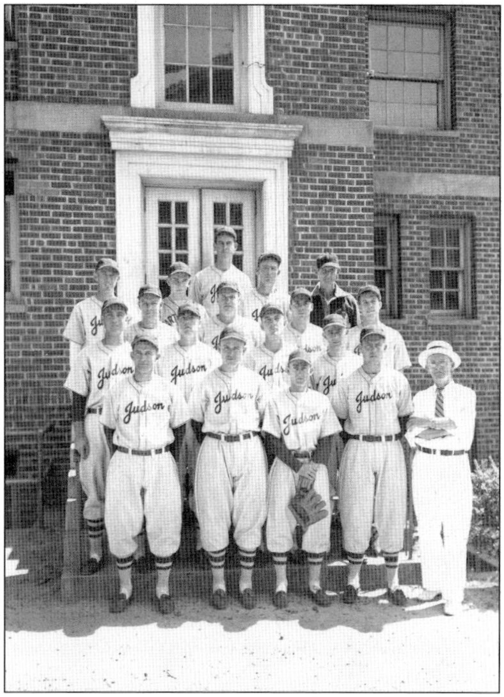

**Judson Mill Baseball Team, 1937.** By 1925, Judson was involved in the Piedmont Textile League and had a first, second, and third baseball teams. Baseball provided mill operatives and their families great entertainment and a diversion from the work in the mill. Having a team also created camaraderie in the village and pride in the mill. (Courtesy of the Coxe Collection, Greenville County Historical Society.)

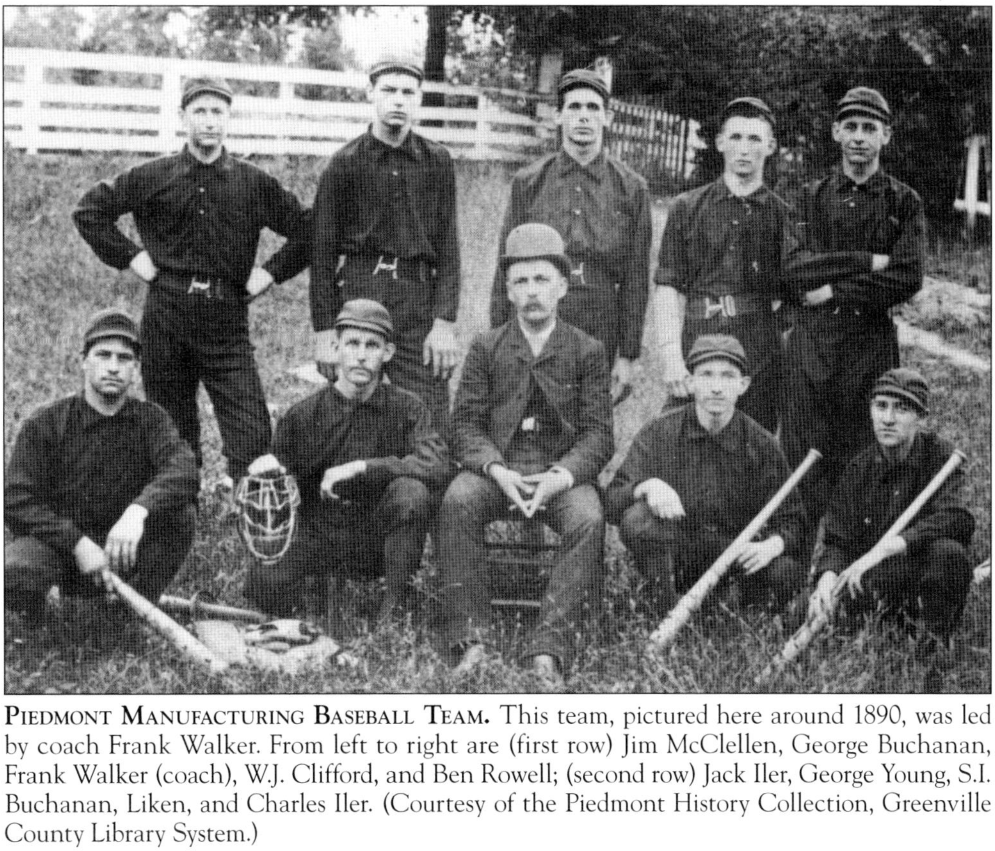

**Piedmont Manufacturing Baseball Team.** This team, pictured here around 1890, was led by coach Frank Walker. From left to right are (first row) Jim McClellen, George Buchanan, Frank Walker (coach), W.J. Clifford, and Ben Rowell; (second row) Jack Iler, George Young, S.I. Buchanan, Liken, and Charles Iler. (Courtesy of the Piedmont History Collection, Greenville County Library System.)

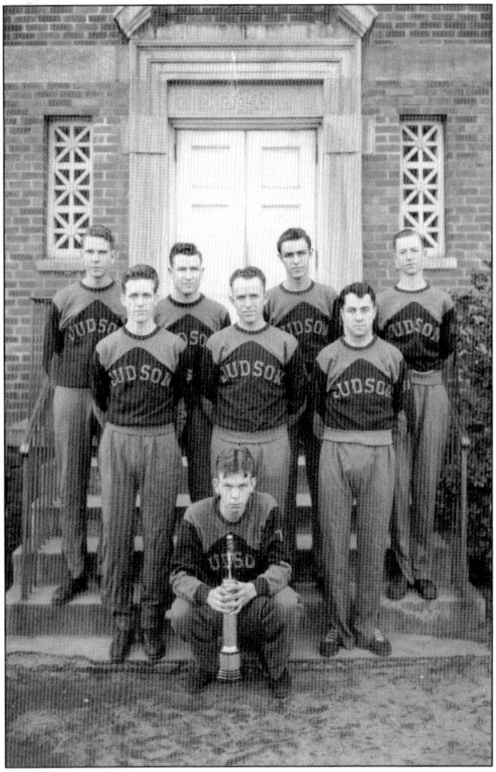


**JUDSON MILL BASKETBALL.** Judson became involved in the Southern Textile Basketball League in 1925. The mill fielded five teams: three boys' and two girls'. The team colors were green and white. Seen here are photographs of the Southern Textile Basketball League winning teams. (Both, courtesy of the Coxe Collection, Greenville County Historical Society.)

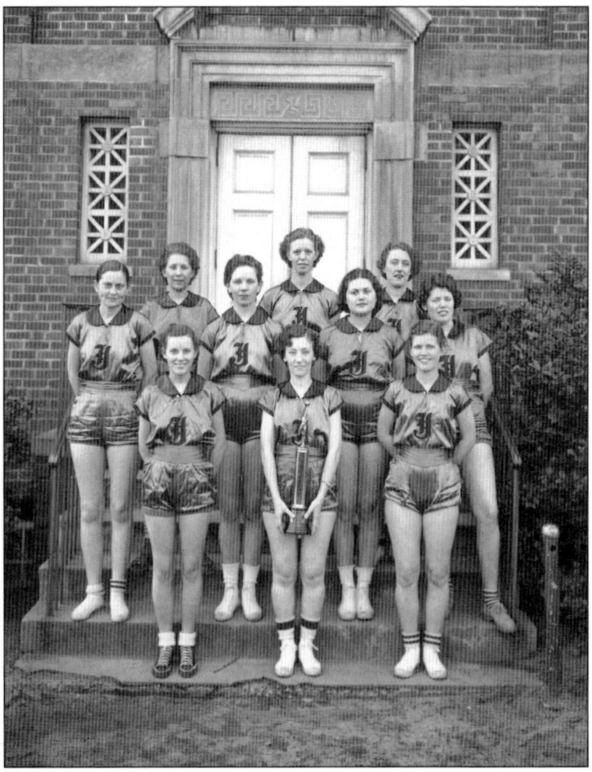

**JAMES "CHAMP" OSTEEN.** In 1883, at the age of six, James "Champ" Osteen's family moved from western North Carolina to Piedmont for employment at the mill. When he was 15, Champ had the opportunity to play baseball for Piedmont Mill after the first baseman sprained his ankle. He continued to play for the team, both as first baseman and shortstop. During his final year with the team in 1899, he helped Piedmont have a 19-6 record and win the textile league championship. After attending and playing for Erskine, he went on to play for major league teams such as the Washington Senators in 1903 and the New York Highlanders in 1904. (Courtesy of Out of the Park Baseball.)

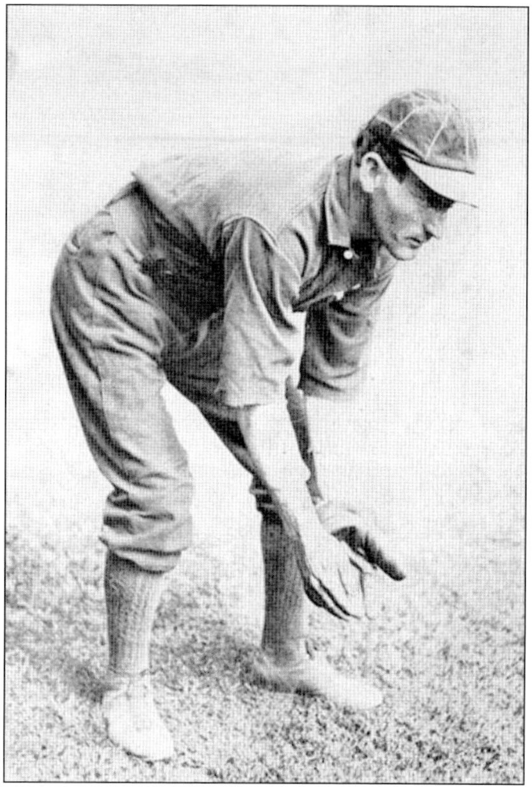

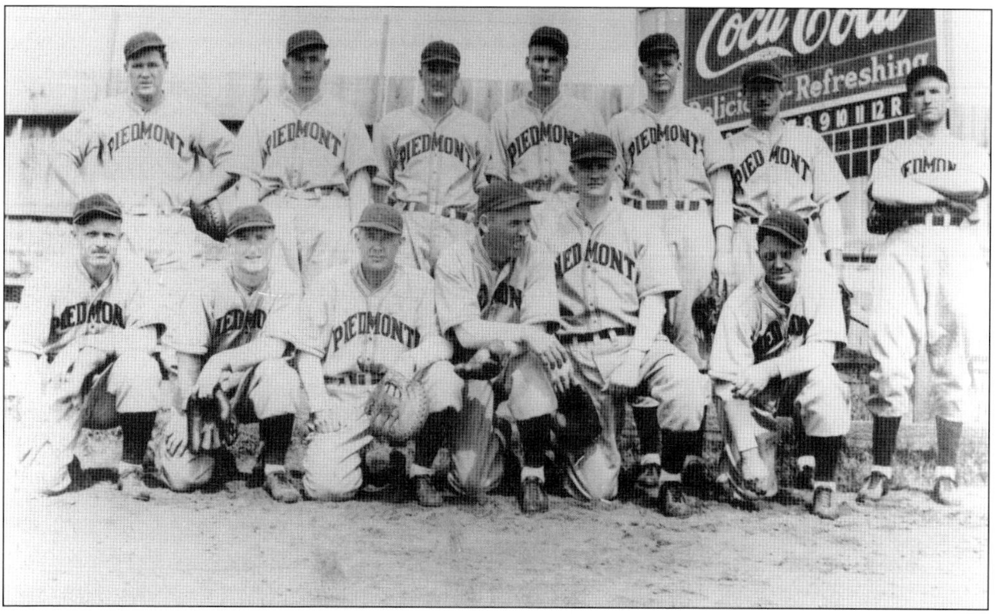


**PIEDMONT RANGERS BASEBALL TEAM.** The 1937 team pictured here were 13-11 in the King Cotton League. From left to right are (first row) J.W. Rampey, Sloan "Fussy" Terry, Joe Ed Fleming, Leroy Anderson, Ned Moore, and Earl Cooper; (second row) Tom Pack, John Emery, Jerry Underwood, "Coot" Henderson, Dave Galloway, Bennett Reeves, and Ray Darnell. (Courtesy of the Piedmont History Collection, Greenville County Library System.)

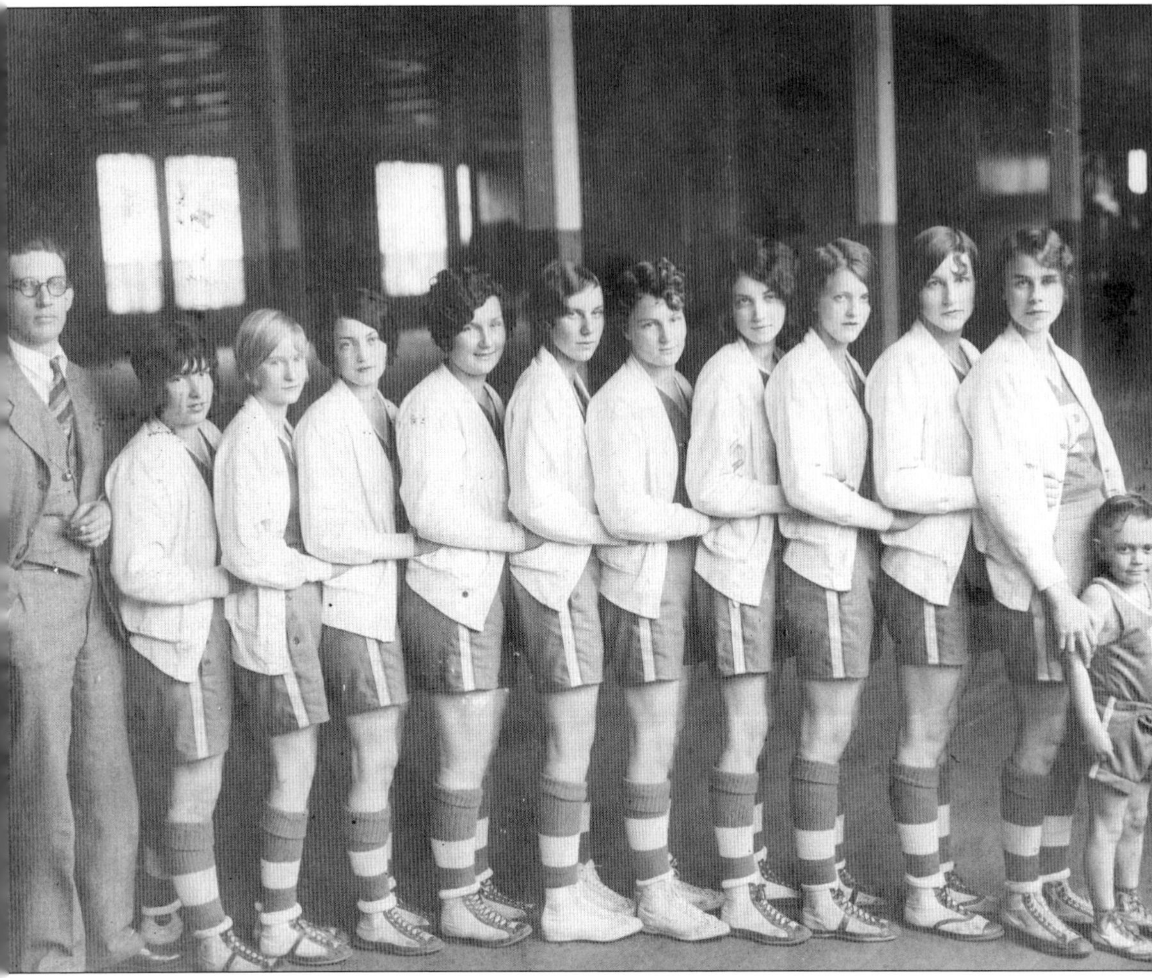

**PIEDMONT MANUFACTURING LADIES' BASKETBALL TEAM, 1928.** The team, along with coach Stuart Wilson (left) and mascot Wilton "Shorty" Smith, gather for a photograph in the Textile Hall basement before a tournament. (Courtesy of the Piedmont History Collection, Greenville County Library System.)

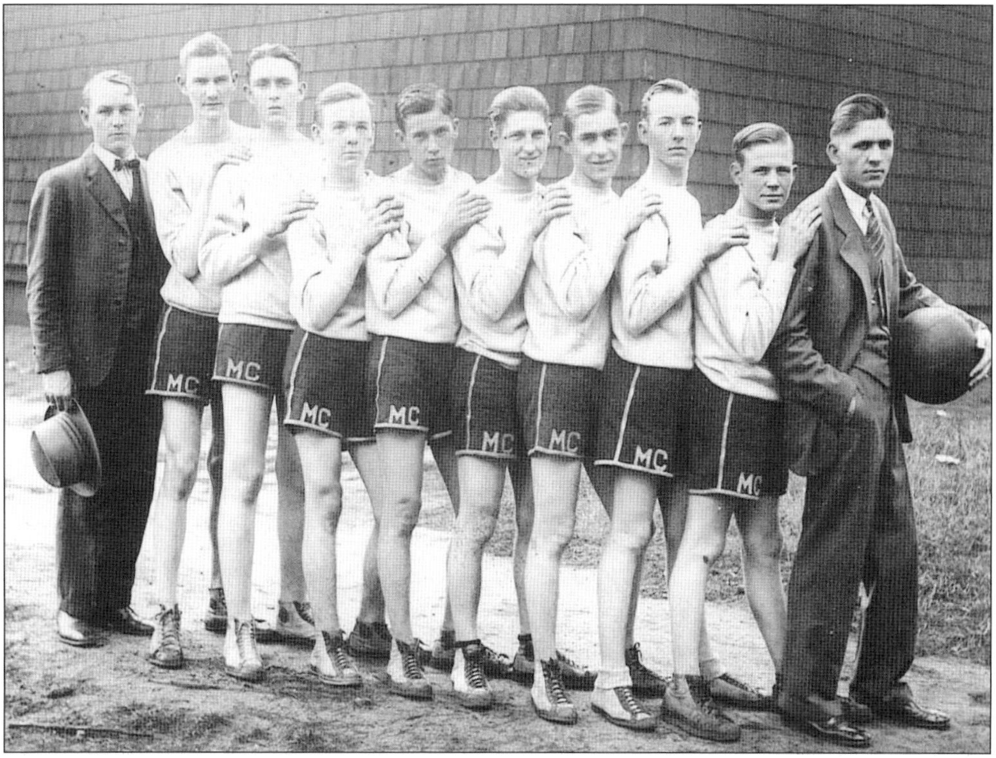


**MONAGHAN MILL BASKETBALL TEAM.** The team seen here is the Southern Textile Basketball Association's "C" champion of 1926. From left to right are YMCA director Jessie D. Brown, ? Reid, ? Ballenger, Buffy Henson, ? Mull, ? Stevens, ? King, ? Simmons, and Adger Campbell. (Courtesy of the Historical Society Collection, Greenville County Library System, Monaghan.)

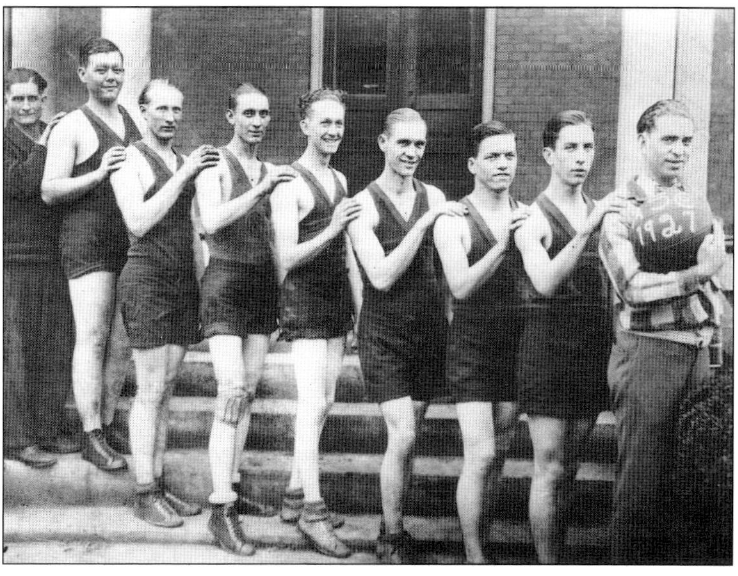


**AMERICAN SPINNING COMPANY BASKETBALL TEAM.** Lined up for the 1927 team photograph, from left to right, are J.D. Bridwell, "Fatty" McNeely, Lee Burns, Ed Duncan, Clay Porter, Dewey Quinn, "Hoot" Major, Bob Bridwell, and Velt Nix. (Courtesy of the Robert H. Duke Collection, Greenville County Library System.)

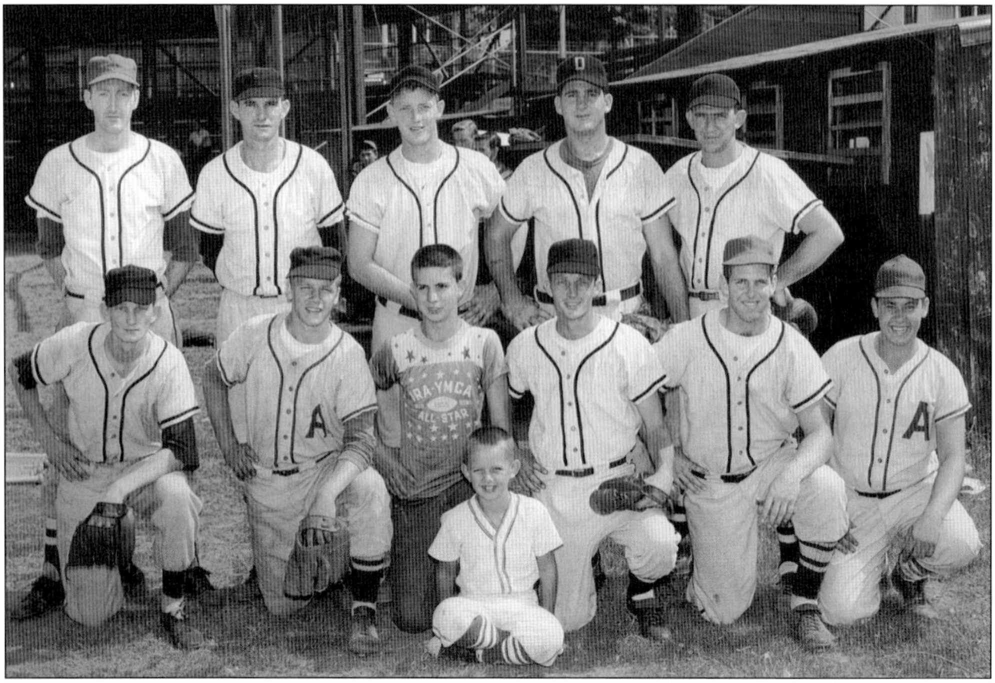

**American Spinning Company Spinners Baseball Team.** Seen here are the winners of the 1956 Piedmont Textile League Championship; from left to right are (first row) Danny Fowler, Leonard Owens, Marion McCall, Willard Fowler, Harold Morris, Allen Sprouse, and Wayne Nix (bat boy); (second row) Furman Burgess, Ed Harbin Jr., Bill Neely, Blackie Durham, and Firpo Finley. (Courtesy of the Robert H. Duke Collection, Greenville County Library System.)

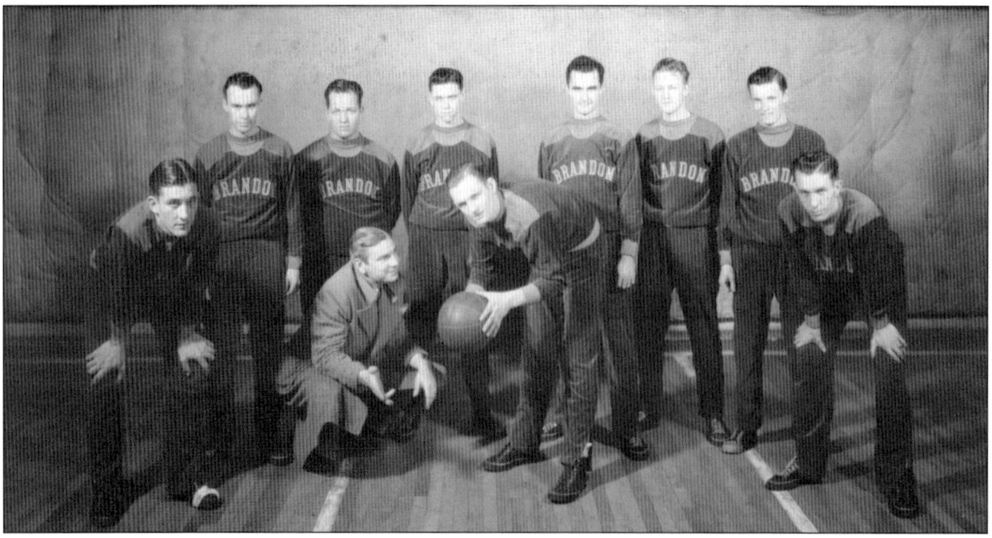


**Brandon Mill Basketball Team, 1936.** The 1936 Southern Textile Basketball Tournament was attended by 7,000 people, including South Carolina governor and textile employee advocate Olin D. Johnston. Abney Mills' merger with Brandon in 1949 resulted in the sale of mill housing and the release of financial responsibility for the village. This action included no longer supporting all sports programs, including basketball. (Courtesy of the Coxe Collection, Greenville County Historical Society.)

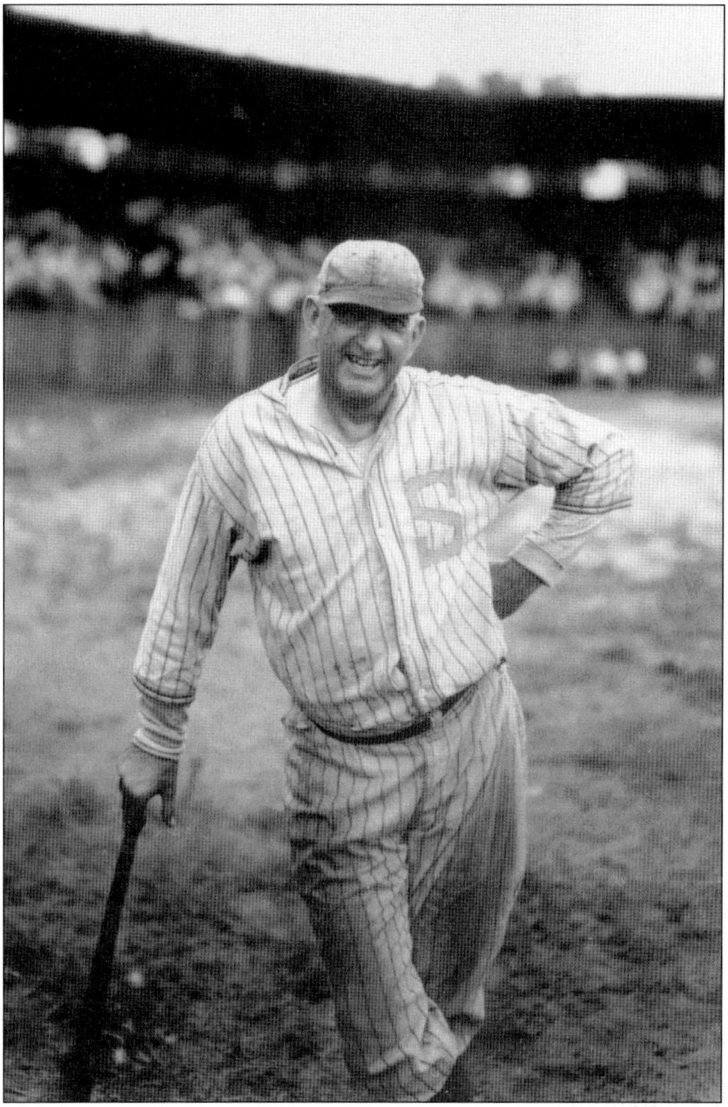

"SHOELESS JOE" JACKSON. Born in 1888, Joe Jackson and his family moved to Brandon from Pelzer Mill. At age 13, while working at Brandon, his throwing talents caught the eye of fellow workers, and he was asked to join the baseball team. When batting with "Black Betsy," his younger brothers would pass a hat among the spectators to collect tips. It was not until 1908, while playing for the Greenville Spinners, he earned the nickname "Shoeless Joe." After a new pair of spikes hurt his feet during a game, he took them off and went unnoticed until the seventh inning. From then on, the name stuck. Jackson went on to play for major league teams such as the Philadelphia Athletics, Cleveland Indians, and later, the Chicago White Socks. It was while playing for the White Socks when they lost the 1919 World Series to the Cincinnati Reds that he was accused of receiving $5,000 along with other players to throw the game. In 1921, Jackson was cleared by a grand jury of any involvement, but he was banished for life from baseball the following day by Commissioner Kennesaw Mountain Landis. He returned to Brandon in 1929 and was a proprietor of a dry cleaning business and a liquor store. Jackson passed away in 1951, and his funeral at Brandon Baptist Church was attended by hundreds of loyal fans. (Courtesy of the Coxe Collection, Greenville County Historical Society.)